THE MUSIC OF THE ARABS

٢٥٧
أمسك بيدك فأنت رئيس القوم وقد جعلتك
عليهم فجلس الحزب جميعهم يضربون بين يديه
وهذه صفتهم

An illustration from *Kashf al-ghumūm wal-kurab fī sharḥi ālāt aṭ-ṭarab* by an anonymous artist of the fifteenth century. Mss: 3465, Topkapi Saray, Istanbul, Turkey.

HABIB HASSAN TOUMA

The Music of the Arabs

New Expanded Edition

Translated by Laurie Schwartz

AMADEUS PRESS
Reinhard G. Pauly, General Editor
Portland, Oregon

Reprinted 1999

ISBN 0-931340-88-8
Designed by Carol Odlum
Printed in Singapore

AMADEUS PRESS
The Haseltine Building
133 S.W. Second Avenue, Suite 450
Portland, Oregon 97204, U.S.A.

Library of Congress Cataloging-in-Publication Data

Touma, Habib, 1934–
[Musik der Araber. English]
The music of the Arabs / Habib Hassan Touma ; translated by Laurie Schwartz. — New expanded ed.
p. cm.
Includes bibliographical references (p.) and index.
ISBN 0-931340-88-8
1. Music—Arab countries—History and criticism. 2. Music, Islamic—History and criticism. I. Title.
ML348.T6913 1995
780'.89'927—dc20 94–43650
CIP
MN

For my wife, Monika

Members of the Qādiriyah Brotherhood during a dhikr in Baghdad, Iraq. Photo: H. H. Touma.

Contents

Dancer of the Mawlawiyah Brotherhood of the Shaykh ʿAqīlī in Aleppo, Syria. Photo: J. Wenzel.

Illustrations

Transliteration and Pronunciation of the Arabic Alphabet

Arabic letter	Name	Transliteration	Pronunciation
ا	alif	ā	as in *fat*
ب	bā’	b	as in *baby*
ت	tā’	t	as in *table*
ث	thā’	th	as in *three*
ج	jīm	j	as in *job*
ح	ḥā’	ḥ	strongly aspirant *h* made in the throat
خ	khā’	kh	as the *ch* in German *Nacht*
د	dāl	d	as in *door*
ذ	dhāl	dh	as *th* in *this*

Arabic letter	Name	Transliteration	Pronunciation
ر	rā’	r	as in *row*
ز	zayn	z	as in *zero*
س	sīn	s	as in *sing*
ش	shīn	sh	as in *show*
ص	ṣād	ṣ	a darkening of the corresponding undotted letter made with a flat, broad tongue placement
ض	ḍād	ḍ	a darkening of the corresponding undotted letter made with a flat, broad tongue placement
ط	ṭā’	ṭ	a darkening of the corresponding undotted letter made with a flat, broad tongue placement
ظ	ẓā’	ẓ	a darkening of the corresponding undotted letter made with a flat, broad tongue placement
ع	‘ayn	c	a very strong guttural produced by the compression of the throat and expulsion of the breath
غ	ghayn	gh	a sound like gargling, pronounced between *g* and *r*
ف	fā’	f	as in *fish*
ق	qāf	a	a *k* sound produced far back in the throat
ك	kāf	k	as in *king*

Arabic letter	Name	Transliteration	Pronunciation
ل	lām	l	as in *little*
م	mīm	m	as in *main*
ن	nūn	n	as in *next*
ه	hā’	h	as in *hat*
و	waw	w or ū	as in *world* (the consonant form) as in *clue* (the long vowel)
ي	yā’	y or ī	as in *yet* (the consonant form) as in *feet* (the long vowel)
ء	hamzah	’	the glottal stop, as in the initial vowel of *absolutely*. A hamzah at the beginning of a word will not be transliterated

Diacritical signs for short vowels

َ	fatḥah	a	as in *bat*
ُ	ḍammah	u	as in *put*
ِ	kasrah	i	as in *pit*

Dipthongs

َ ي	yā’sukūn preceded by fatḥah	ay	as in *byte*
َ وْ	waw sukūn preceded by fatḥah	aw	as in *ouch*

Mijwiz and naqqārāt players from Iraq. Photo: H. H. Touma.

Foreword

The Music of the Arabs deals exclusively with the traditional secular and sacred art music of the Arab peoples and should serve, for the interested reader, as an introduction to Arabian music culture. The book presents an overview of the musical life of the Arabs throughout their cultural history and examines comprehensively the artistic production of musicians still actively involved in performing and nurturing Arabian art music today. Traditional music genres, musical instruments, the tone system, ensembles, and the performance practice of sacred and secular music are described in detail. Folk music, however, and contemporary popular music—the so-called new music—are not taken into account, for these fall outside of the scope and aim of the book, namely, to present the modal and rhythmic principles of traditional art music.

I would like to express my thanks to all the singers, instrumentalists, and scholars who stood by me in word and deed during my many stays in Arab lands. A very special thanks also goes out to Laurie Schwartz in Berlin, without whose untiring effort this English edition would not have been possible.

Khashshābah from Iraq. Photo: H. H. Touma

Preface

The music of the Arabs is an essential part of the music of the Near East and North Africa. It is based on a modal tone system—one of the few autonomous tone systems of our time—and is subject to the maqām phenomenon, a unique type of improvisation that is common to both secular and sacred Arabian art music. In fact, the art music of every culture native to the Near East and North Africa is characterized by musical structures based on modal improvisation and developed within the framework of the maqām phenomenon.

Despite differences in their musical and aesthetic forms, the peoples of the Near East and North Africa, conditioned by a common history spanning over two thousand years, can be said to have a homogeneous musical culture—one whose practice is clearly distinct from that of the Occidentals, the Africans (south of the Sahara), or the East and Southeast Asians. Although the music traditions belonging to this culture include the Armenian, Berber, Hebrew, Coptic, Kurdish, Syriac, and Caucasian, this book deals only with those created by the Arabs, the Persians, and the Turks. Having been embedded from their beginnings in permanent political systems, these three are clearly the most prominent musical cultures of the Near East, and they still boast an extensive repertoire, a well-founded theory, a documented history, and excellent musicians. Nevertheless, the music of other peoples native to this region, such as the Berbers, Maronites, Chaldeans, Nestorians, Jacobite-Syrians, and Jews, should not be overlooked. Even if these cultures are not always represented as political entities on the map of the Near East and North Africa, they have contributed and continue to contribute to the overall musical picture of the region.

The essence of Arabian culture is wrapped up in

- the Arabic language, which helps to express the intellectual and spiritual processes of the people and plays a decisive role in the development and transmission of cultural achievements;
- Islam, whose influence in the propagation and shaping of Arabian culture has been and remains so great that the social, spiritual, and material aspects of the culture cannot be understood without taking it into consideration;
- tradition, as manifest in the manners and customs that determine the conduct of the Arab in family and society.

An Arab, in the modern sense of the word, is one who is a national of an Arab state, has command of the Arabic language, and possesses a fundamental knowledge of Arabian tradition, that is, of the manners, customs, and political and social systems of the culture. Thus, those who may call themselves Arab include not only the inhabitants of the Arabian Peninsula or the Moslem community but anyone who satisfies these criteria.

It follows, therefore, that the term *Arabian* applies to the music of the Arab world in general and that treating this music as an expression of a unified music culture is justifable despite the large number of countries and traditions involved—despite the fact that styles, modes, and terminology in North Africa, for example, may differ somewhat from those in Iraq. Many aspects of music, such as the tone system, musical forms, rhythmic patterns, techniques of composition and improvisation, performance practice, the makeup of ensembles, the individual's perception of music, and the place of the musician in society, are essentially the same in all Arab countries. A singer is appreciated just as much in distant cities of the Arab world as in her home town. Umm Kulthūm, Fayrūz, and Wardah, for example, are admired with the same enthusiasm in Cairo, Beirut, Algiers, and Baghdad as in Mecca, Sanaa, Kuwait, Tripoli, or Rabat. Nonetheless, political, social, religious, revolutionary, and other movements in the unsettled Arab world of today exert their influence on musical life and threaten, time and again, to destroy the traditional music, notwithstanding the efforts of some forces to resist this trend.

The origins of the music of the Arabs lie in the distant past. The history of music in the Arabian world is closely linked to the political background of the people. During certain epochs, music was highly valued; during others, it was outlawed and condemned. But no matter how perspectives may have changed throughout history, music—specifically song—was and still is inseparably linked to the life of the Arab, assuming an indispensable function at many social events.

Arabian music emerged on the Arabian Peninsula during pre-Islamic times. It developed further during the Islamic era and crystalized in the schools of Mecca, Medina, Baghdad, and Córdoba. From the thirteenth century on, other centers of musical activity sprang up in Fez, Tetuan, Tlemcen, Algiers, Tunis, Tripoli, Cairo, Aleppo, Damascus, Beirut, Baghdad, Bahrain, Sanaa, and Aden.

Five components characterize the music of the Arabs:

1. A tone system with specific interval structures.
2. Rhythmic-temporal structures that produce a rich variety of rhythmic patterns, used to accompany the metered vocal and instrumental genres and give them form.
3. Musical instruments that are found throughout the Arabian world and that represent a standardized tone system, are played with standardized performance techniques, and exhibit similar details in construction and design.
4. Specific social contexts for the making of music, whereby musical genres can be classified as urban (music of the city inhabitants), rural (music of the country inhabitants), or Bedouin (music of the desert inhabitants). By way of example, consider the Bedouin who, by virtue of mass media, can listen to any kind of music in his desert tent but who would never make music himself outside of a specific context.
5. A musical mentality that is responsible for the aesthetic homogeneity of the tonal-spatial and rhythmic-temporal structures in Arabian music, whether composed or impro-

vised, instrumental or vocal, secular or sacred. The Arab's musical mentality is defined by

a. The maqām phenomenon, in which the performance of a single-voiced melody line is a largely improvised conceptualization of a particular modal structure. The fundamental characteristic of the maqām phenomenon is that the tonal-spatial component has a binding and previously fixed organization, whereas the rhythmic-temporal component is essentially free. Central to the maqām phenomenon is the tonal-spatial model, which varies from one maqām to another and can always be reduced to a nucleus of unique intervals. This nucleus determines the melodic line and helps create the characteristic emotional mood for the particular maqām. The modal structure of a maqām is named for the tone row of the Arabian tone system on which it is based.

b. The predominance of vocal music. Singer, vocal technique, song style, and text are all of essential importance in Arabian music.

c. The predilection for small instrumental ensembles, in which improvisation is far more practicable than it is in large orchestras.

d. The mosaiclike stringing together of musical form elements, that is, the arrangement in a sequence of small and smallest melodic elements, and their repetition, combination, and permutation within the framework of a tonal-spatial model.

e. The absence of polyphony, polyrhythm, and motivic development. Arabian music is, however, very familiar with the ostinato, as well as with a more instinctive heterophonic way of making music.

f. The alternation between a free rhythmic-temporal and fixed tonal-spatial organization on the one hand and a fixed rhythmic-temporal and free tonal-spatial structure on the other. This alternation, which occurs chiefly during the performance of longer maqāmāt such as the maqām al-ʿirāqī, the nūbah, and the waṣlah, results in exciting musical contrasts.

Although Arabian music culture never existed as an isolated phenomenon in the geocultural sphere of the Arab world, these five characteristics of Arabian music can be traced back to the earliest times of Arabian cultural history. They do not, however, exclusively identify Arabian music. As singular phenomena, they can also be detected to a greater or lesser extent in the music of the Assyrians, Turks, Turkmenians, Berbers, Armenians, Kurds, Copts, Azerbaijani, Tajikis, Usbekians, Iranians, Spaniards, and West Africans.

The musical connections between the Arabs and their various neighbors go back to pre-Islamic times. It is possible, however, on the basis of parallel musical events that have existed from time to time for over a thousand years, to demonstrate especially close musical relationships between the Arabs, the Turks, and the Persians.

Members of the Rifāʿiyah Brotherhood of the Shaykh Muḥammad Jalīlī during a dhikr in Aleppo, Syria. Photo: J. Wenzel.

1

Arab Musical Life Throughout History

The Pre-Islamic Period Until 632: The Qaynah School

The earliest information on the musical life of the Arabs originates from the sixth century A.D. More than one hundred years would pass before the Arabs attained world historical importance through Islam. Nevertheless, the period before the time referred to in these early documents encompasses more than one thousand years of Arab history, boasting a highly developed culture that to this day has not been fully researched. This pre-Islamic period is called the jāhiliyah because the life of the Arabs at the time was characterized by *jāhiliyah**—which translates roughly as "wrath," "pride," "impudence," and "fanaticism." The entire social organization of Arab society during this epoch was anchored in the tribal union, and tribal solidarity was the supreme law. Serving as a source for the musical life during the later period of the jāhiliyah was the traditional poetry. But while an examination of this poetry offers us insights into musical life on the Arabian Peninsula at that time, it does not substitute for detailed descriptions of the tone system and discussions of music theory.

* Throughout this book, Arabic terms defined in the glossary appear in italics on first use.

The musical life of the jāhiliyah was defined by the *qaynah*, a singer and servant in one, whose duties, besides singing and performing, also included pouring wine and providing other sensual pleasures. The qaynah and her activities made up a branch of the widespread slave trade that flourished then in the famous Arabian marketplaces like those of Medina, Ṭā'if, and ʿUkāẓ. Here is where the *qiyān* (plural of *qaynah*) established themselves, not least because of the many opportunities for contact with merchants and trading delegations. The task of the qaynah was to entertain the guest with song, wine, and eroticism. She poured wine while singing or while another qaynah made music. Her naked breasts were open to the glances of guests, and she was also receptive to the more direct advances of her customers.

As was similarly the case at the Eros houses during the jāhiliyah, the qaynah hoisted a flag over the door of her premises (*ḥānah*) in order to attract the attention of customers. These *ḥānāt* (plural of *ḥānah*) of the qiyān could be found everywhere on the Arabian Peninsula. In a second category were the qiyān who served only one owner, or master. A great number of them lived in the palaces of petty kings such as Ḥārith of Ghassān and Nuʿmān and Mundhir of Ḥīrah, or of lesser Arab nobles, and regularly entertained the owner and his family with singing and music. A qaynah would not only recite works by the great poets of the day—above all, those who glorified her own master (*sayyid*)—but she would also clothe these poems in song. She was expected to have an impeccable command of the Arabic language and a solid training in poetic arts.

Famous qiyān lived and worked in Medina, Mecca, Yamāmah, Yemen, and Ḥaḍramawt. Some of their names have been handed down—Jarādah of ʿĀd, Mulaykah, Bint ʿAfzar, Hurayrah, and others—yet a great many more have fallen into oblivion.

Two singing styles of the jāhiliyah are clearly distinguishable: that of the Bedouin nomads and that of the sedentary population (*ahl al-ḥaḍar*). The singing of the Bedouins, which is limited to the genres *ḥudā'* and *naṣb*, is generally described in the literature as simple and naive, while the singing of the sedentary population—precisely, the song tradition of the qiyān—is characterized as virtuosic and extraordinary. *Ḥudā*ʾ was the name given to the rousing song of the camel driver, its rhythm corresponding to that of the camel's steps. *Naṣb* was the general name given to the songs intoned by young Bedouins riding through the desert on their camels and to the dirges sung by the women.

The extraordinary, virtuosic singing of the qiyān and its poetic forms of expression fall into two categories with regard to form and content: *sinād* and *hazaj*. *Sinād* texts, which dealt with themes of seriousness, dignity, fame, pride, and arrogance, were composed in the long classical metrical feet of Arabian poetry. The *hazaj*, in contrast, were simple songs intended merely for the entertainment and amusement of the listener. Their texts were composed in short classical metrical feet, and they were accompanied by lute, flute, or hand-drum playing.

The musical instrument used by the qiyān that is most often mentioned in the poetry of the jāhiliyah is a stringed instrument, possibly resembling the present short-necked lute (*ʿūd*). It is called *mizhar*, *kirān*, *muwattar*, and *ṣanj*. Less often mentioned is a kind of flute, oboe, or clarinet (*quṣṣāb* or *mizmār*), as well as the hand drum (*duff*) and the rattle (*jalājil*). According to a poem by the poet al-Aʿshā, which describes a visit to the qiyān by Najrān, several instruments performed simultaneously as instrumental accompaniment to the song. Those mentioned were wind instruments (*quṣṣāb*/*mizmār*) and a lute (*ṣanj*).

Beauty and elegance were the distinguishing characteristics of the qiyān. The singers took care that they were tastefully dressed and richly adorned with jewelry. The pleasant fragrances of precious perfumes surrounded them. Besides that, the qaynah had a ravishing voice and a considerable fortune, which showed how much the society appreciated and rewarded her for her services. The artistic production of the qiyān led to the development of a special tradition and school that exerted its influence long after the appearance of Islam, specifically into the ninth century, the time of Isḥāq al-Mawṣilī. Among the hundred songs chosen for the Abbasid Caliph Hārūn ar-Rashīd in the eighth century, there was at least one attributed to the Jarādah sisters, qiyān who had lived during the jāhiliyah.

Without doubt, the qiyān and their masterful vocal performances depicted a purely Arabian musical life. It was Arabian in its origin, in its propagation within a certain social milieu, and in the language of the songs. A foreign influence can be detected only with difficulty, and venturing to define it more precisely would be fruitless. Too little is known about the influence over the centuries of cultural and economic relationships between early cultures. The slave class during the pre-Islamic period was composed of Persians, Byzantines, Egyptians, and Ethiopians. Thus, living side by side in this geographic area were Polytheists, Christians, Jews, and early Persian magicians, any of whom could certainly have influenced the qiyān musically through their liturgy, hymns, and other songs. Indeed, not to be underestimated is the possible influence of the Persians and Ethiopians, who could point to a highly organized musical life in their own lands. But however much the qiyān's artistic production may have been affected by foreign influences, their singing must have retained a characteristic Arabian element, for their audiences are known to have approved of not only of the texts of their songs, which were written by the great contemporary Arabian poets, but the music as well.

The Early Arabian Classical Music Tradition (632–850)

The song tradition of the qiyān endured unchanged through the first three decades of Islam, and the nomadic inhabitants of the Arabian Peninsula also continued unhindered in singing the dirges, love songs, and war songs that had been handed down from the jāhiliyah. For in the Koran, the holy book of Islam, singing and music are neither expressly forbidden nor expressly allowed. The differing theses of Islamic theologians, who later forbade music at one time and allowed it at another, were based on subjective commentaries to a few Koran verses. The authors of these commentaries detected in one verse or another references to music and singing even where none seem to exist. A second source to which the scholars referred in their opposing arguments was the *ḥadīth,* the handed-down body of conversations that the prophet Muhammad was said to have had with his companions during his lifetime, in which the Prophet appears to have approved music and singing at one time but forbidden it at another. Nevertheless, regardless of the official position taken by theologians and statesmen during the various periods following the emergence of Islam, music and song were cultivated without interruption in the Arabian empire, and it was often possible for the most pious among the faithful to live peacefully alongside the most high-spirited of the musicians and singers, as they did, for example, in Medina and Mecca during the reign of the third Caliph ʿUthmān and during the Umayyad empire.

The successful establishment of Islam was followed, into the middle of the seventh century, by the conquests of Libya, Egypt, Palestine, Phoenicia, Syria, Iraq, and Persia (almost all the cultures, except Asia Minor, that had ever played a role in the history of the Orient). Since the reign of the first Caliph Abu Bakr (A.D. 632–634), the booty from these conquered lands had been shared equally among the inhabitants of the captial city. Thus was Medina, where the standard of living had once been quite modest, transformed into one of the wealthiest cities of the Arabian empire. Not only treasures and monies flowed into the capital but also a host of prisoners and slaves, called *raqīq,* who radically changed life there by introducing new manners and customs, including new forms of artistic expression. Free to adopt anything from these other cultures that did not contradict Islamic teaching, the Arabs enthusiastically assimilated the aesthetic and spiritual legacies of the Greeks, Romans, Persians, Egyptians, Assyrians, and Babylonians, ultimately merging them into something new and unique.

The Arabs in Ḥijāz, and especially in the capital city Medina, were accustomed to an exuberant musical life. They considered singing a professional art and described it in terms that had previously been unknown in their language. In addition to the qiyān, male singers called *mukhannathūn* (plural of *mukhannath*) now appeared. They emulated the behavior and dress of women, and probably had homosexual tendencies. For the most part, these singers were *muwālī*, that is, converts to Islam who were disciples of a free-born Arab. But Arab singers came from all strata of society, and even women who were not qiyān could take pride in the art of singing and music making. One of the greatest female singers of this period was ʿAzzah al-Maylāʾ, who lived in Medina and had a superior command of the repertoire of the many qiyān active prior to Islam.

Most of the great male and female singers in the days of Islam were Persians, Ethiopians, or black Africans. Yet all of them had been born on the Arabian Peninsula, or at least had grown up there. An exception, of course, was the Persian Nashīṭ, who in fact was born and raised in Persia but who first became famous after he took lessons in the Arabian singing style from the Arab Sāʾib Khāthir.

For the first three centuries after the emergence of Islam, and for the time of the Umayyad reign until approximately A.D. 750, the Arabic language was used not only for the texts of songs but also for the names of musical instruments and for other musical terminology. The fact that singers heard Persian or Byzantine music and introduced it to the Arabian Peninsula meant neither a complete relinquishment nor a transformation of the song's Arabian character. To the contrary, the Arabs had most probably transformed the singing style they had borrowed mainly from the Persians and adapted it to their own, especially to that of the qaynah school. A new singing tradition characteristic of the Ḥijāz was thereby created, and because of its musical originality, it also lived on at the court of the Caliph, which had been transferred to Damascus in A.D. 661. During this time, the Ḥijāz, especially Medina, was looked upon as a musical center that could meet the demand throughout the Arabian empire for excellent male and female singers.

In Medina, Yūnus al-Kātib (d. A.D. 765), himself a singer of Persian extraction, wrote several treatises on the music and musical life of this city. He collected the songs of the time, as well as his own songs, into two books in which he documented the text of the song as well as the mode, the rhythm, and the names of the composer and poet. In two other treatises, Yūnus al-Kātib wrote about melody and the qiyān. His books later became the basis for two important historians of the ninth and tenth centuries, al-Mawṣilī and al-Iṣbahānī, in their studies on music in Ḥijāz and Medina. Although none of Yūnus al-Kātib's works have been passed down to us, there are more than enough quotations from them in al-Iṣbahānī's book to give us a clear picture of the highly organized musical life in Medina at that time.

The singers from Ḥijāz remained influential for several generations, until the beginnings of the Abbasid era (750–1258). The most famous singers from Ḥijāz, such as Ibn Surayj and Maʿbad, would meet at the impressive concerts that took place in the palace of the famous female singer Jamīlah (d. 720) in Medina, or during the pilgrimages that were staged almost like a music festival. Here guests danced and sang to the music that was performed by large choruses and instrumental ensembles. The ensembles comprised several lute, flute, and drum players. Besides the lute, there was the zither (*miʿzafah*), the flute (*qaṣṣābah*), the clarinet (*mizmār*), and a square hand drum (*duff*) that was played primarily by women.

Remarkable was the number of male and female singers who performed their own compositions in Medina and Damascus during the time of the first four Caliphs (632–661) and the time of the Umayyad dynasty (661–750). Detailed descriptions exist of their lives, their teachers, their students, and their performances. Yet not one single melody or rhythmic pattern has been handed down, so that we aren't able to form an exact idea of what the singing style of the time was like. Having attracted many students and instructed them in the artful singing style *al-ghināʾ al-mutqan*, "the perfect singing," the great singers of Mecca and Medina were able to establish an Arabian school of voice that would hold its own for more than a century against the Persian, Byzantine, and Ethiopian vocal traditions. Later singers and historians defined this school of singing as the Early Arabian Classical school. The classical music tradition dominated until the middle of the ninth century, handed down through an uninterrupted oral tradition. It was especially cultivated in Ḥijāz, where the first singers—actually also the founders of this school—lived and where several generations of singers were trained. From Ḥijāz came all the great singers who were active at the courts of the Umayyads and later also at the courts of the Abbasids.

The man considered to be the creator of al-ghinā' al-mutqan was Ṭuways (632–710), one of the early masters of Medina and the first effeminate singer (mukhannath) in the Ḥijāz. Al-ghinā' al-mutqan was characterized by a definite rhythmic pattern used as an accompaniment. This pattern did not, however, correspond to the organization of longs and shorts as represented in the metrical foot of the sung poem. Ṭuways was the teacher of the famous Ibn Surayj (634–726), who later instructed Algharīḍ (d. 720) in singing. Sā'ib Khāthir, a contemporary of Ṭuways, counted among his students Maʿbad (d. 743), famous for his seven *ḥuṣūn* songs. Yūnus al-Kātib (d. 765) was the most famous student of Sā'ib Khāthir. Al-Kātib composed the *Zayānib Songs*, which he had dedicated to his beloved, Zaynab. He in turn was the teacher of Siyāṭ (730–785) and Ibrāhīm al-Mawṣilī (742–804). The latter, together with Ibn Jāmiʿ and Ibn al-ʿAwrā', collected the hundred—in his opinion—most beautiful songs (*aṣwāt*) for the Abbasid Caliph Hārūn ar-Rashīd.

From the sources on classical Arabian song tradition, details can be gathered regarding the mode of a piece, which is determined by its beginning and second or third tones. Pitches were identified by the name of the finger used to stop that tone on the neck of the lute. For example, if the index finger was used for stopping the first tone, and the middle or ring finger for the next, this would imply a half- or a whole-tone step. In addition, these sources contain information about the accompanying rhythmic patterns, and they include the text, its metrical feet, and facts about the poet. Although each song (*ṣawt*) consisted of only a few lines of verse, several compositions with the same text could conceivably exist. The creator of the melody was its owner and could properly sell it. The purchaser would listen to the composer sing the piece time and again until the words and music had been committed to memory.

Despite all the information available to us on a ṣawt, we

still do not have an exact idea of its melody. Countless song texts, including modal and rhythmic information, have been handed down in the treatises of scholars from the ninth and tenth centuries. But while the authors give an account of the virtuosos of the time and their repertoire, nothing about melody is ever mentioned.

The Revival of the Early Arabian Music Tradition in Baghdad (820–1258) and Córdoba (822–1492)

The early Arabian classical tradition of the Ḥijāz experienced its culmination in the eighth and early ninth centuries, then lost its position of monopoly during the first half of the ninth century because of new musical developments in Baghdad that were actually of Persian origin. In Baghdad, singers began to free themselves from the classicism of the old tradition. They gathered around the highly talented singer and ʿūd player Ibrāhīm al-Mahdī (779–839) and practiced what he taught in terms of a relaxation and reformation of the early singing tradition. Ibrāhīm al-Mahdī, whose father and brother held the title of Caliph, was also the author of a book on song. An opponent of this new movement was Isḥāq al-Mawṣilī (767–850), one of the greatest musicians of his time. But although many musicians were, in fact, on al-Mawṣilī's side, he did not manage to stop the triumphant advance of Ibrāhīm al-Mahdī's musical innovations. The influences from Persia caused the classical singing of the Ḥijāz to be increasingly forced into the background, or enriched with new musical elements—elements that probably still set the tone of Arabian music today.

Although the music scholars developed their theories on the basis of musical practice and collected the music of their time, the tone systems fixed by exact numerical relationships and the pieces of music presented in anthologies can only convey a fraction of the total musical picture. Information about the essence of the sound cannot be gathered from the written evidence, and contemporary music that has been handed down to us through oral tradition has surely been transformed along the way, so that only a vague picture of the original sound can be obtained. This observation is not meant to downplay the work of the innumerable scholars. Of the many treatises that found their way into the bibliographies of the tenth century, only a few still exist. The most original and important of these come from the ninth, tenth, eleventh, and thirteenth centuries and are associated with names like al-Kindī (d. 874), al-Fārābī (d. 950), al-Iṣbahānī (d. 967), Ibn Sīnā (d. 1037) and Ṣafī ad-Dīn al-Urmawī (d. 1294). The latter lived to see the end of the Arabian Caliphate and the conquest of Baghdad (1258) by Hulago.

In his *Kitāb al-aghānī al-kabīr*, the "Great Book of Songs," al-Iṣbahānī does not provide musical examples per se. On the other hand, for every song, he gives information regarding the biographies of the poets, composers, singers, and instrumentalists, as well as the rhythm and mode of the song. His twenty-volume work covers a period of approximately four hundred years, from the seventh century to the tenth. Neither did al-Fārābī present any musical examples in his remarkable book *Kitāb al-mūsīqā al-kabīr*, the "Great Book of Music"; he did, however, employ rhythmic formulas and scales. He named the steps of the scales after the frets on the neck of the lute: "index finger fret," "middle finger fret," or "Zalzalian middle finger fret." The *Kitāb al-adwār*, the "Book of Modes" by Ṣafī ad-Dīn al-Urmawī (d. 1294), appeared in the thirteenth century. In this work, Ṣafī ad-Dīn al-Urmawī dealt in detail with tone (*nagham*), composition, mode, rhythm, and so on, and he also supplied the skeletal notation of a song with information about the rhythm and mode: above the text of the song he wrote the names of the tones of the melody and gave specifications for the accompanying rhythm. In another musical treatise, the author presented the division of the octave into seventeen tones (limmas and commas) and named them according to the letters of the Arabic alphabet as A, B, J, D, H, Ū, Z, Ḥ, Ṭ, Ī, etc. From his indications regarding the rhythmic accompaniment, it can be inferred that beats occur within a recurring rhythmic period.

At the beginning of the ninth century, a struggle had broken out between the followers and opponents of the early Arabian music tradition, with Ibrāhīm al-Mahdī on one side and

Isḥāq al-Mawṣilī on the other. Al-Mawṣilī, out of both envy and fear, found himself in a serious and vehement argument with his highly talented student Ziryāb. Since al-Mawṣilī believed that Ziryāb could become his most dangerous rival at the court of Hārūn ar-Rashīd, he let him know that this rivalry would not be permitted. He advised Ziryāb to leave the city of Baghdad immediately. To avoid having to fight a losing battle with his master, Ziryāb left for *al-andalus*, where the Umayyads had ruled ever since the downfall of their dynasty in Damascus (A.D. 750). In 822, Ziryāb arrived in Córdoba, where he was welcomed and warmly received by Sultan ʿAbd ar-Raḥmān II (822–852). In this way, the early Arabian music tradition, as conveyed to Ziryāb through Isḥāq al-Mawṣilī, was brought to Spain. But Ziryāb founded a music school in Córdoba that soon freed itself from the shackles of the traditional early Arabian school of the East and formed the nucleus of later *andalusī* music. In Córdoba, and soon, too, in Seville, Toledo, Valencia, and Granada, many generations of singers and musicians became familiar with the rules of the school of Ziryāb. The andalusī music that is still cultivated in North Africa today is the heir to this school, which became newly established in North Africa in the thirteenth, fifteenth, and seventeenth centuries, after the retreat of the Arabs from Spain. Only a few original music documents from al-andalus have been preserved; noteworthy are those of al-Majrīṭī (d. 1007), Abū Ṣalt Umayah (d. 1134), Ibn Quzmān (d. 1160), and al-Qurṭubī (d. 1258).

The Era of Decline: The Thirteenth Through Nineteenth Centuries

The innovations of al-Mahdī in the East and Ziryāb in the West took place in the ninth century, the golden age of the Arabs politically as well as culturally. Baghdad was the capital city of the Abbasids in the East and Córdoba the capital of the Umayyads in the Spanish West. This era is looked upon as a kind of *ars nova* in Arabian music history. Its characteristics would determine the musical practice of the Arabs well into the nineteenth century—regardless of whether the city was Baghdad, Aleppo, Cairo, or Istanbul.

Nevertheless, we should not overlook the influence of Turkish and Persian music on the music of the Arabs, especially after the downfalls of Córdoba in the eleventh century, Baghdad in the thirteenth, and Granada in the fifteenth. Nor should we disregard the constancy in many areas of the early Arabian music tradition from the Ḥijāz—a tradition, after all, that had determined the musical life and the musical culture of the Arabs for more than three centuries and whose origins were in the pre-Islamic qaynah school. Even under foreign rule, after the decline of the Arabian empire, Arabs continued to cultivate their own music and song. The influence in the thirteenth century of the Turks and Persians—representatives of a Near Eastern musical culture essentially identical with that of the Arabs—had a less disastrous effect on Arabian music than has the recent influx of European musical culture, with innovations like radio, film, and recordings. This European influence has been corrupting Arabian music since World War I.

Already at the beginning of the sixteenth century, the Islamic Near East experienced a fundamental change triggered by the Ottomans, who had put an end to the rule of the Mamlūks in Egypt and Syria and conquered the Ṣafawids in Persia. Through these double military victories, Egypt, Syria, and Iraq came under the sphere of influence of the Turks, and Istanbul became the hub of the Islamic world. For the Arab world, Turkish domination meant a time of general spiritual and cultural decline: a strong dwindling of national feeling could be registered, accompanied by a clear social downturn. Damascus, Baghdad, and Cairo, once the capital cities of the Arabian empire and centers of cultural and scientific life, were reduced in their importance to being the residences of Ottoman governors, who were sent from Istanbul to rule the land and collect taxes. A complete stagnation of Arabian literature, science, and art during this period of Arabian history was the result. The search for original and authentic creations of the Arabs from this period is futile. Ottoman rule in Mashriq (Egypt, Syria, Iraq, Ḥijāz, and Yemen) continued until the twentieth century.

In Maghrib (North Africa: Tunisia and Algeria), the Turks were replaced in the nineteenth century by a European colonial regime.

Cultural Awakening and Liberation from the Turks in the Nineteenth Century

In the nineteenth century, forces became manifest in Arabian society that were responsible for the first signs of a rebirth of a distinctively Arabian consciousness and thought. Men who worked in diverse areas launched the process of reorientation: politicians and leaders of the movement against imperialism, social and Islamic reformers, scientists and teachers, men of letters and artists—among them musicians such as ʿAbdū al-Ḥāmūlī, Muḥammad ʿUthmān, Salāmah Ḥijāzī, Mīkhāʾīl Mīshāqah, Raḥmallāh Shiltāgh, and Aḥmad Zaydān.

For the Arabs of the nineteenth century, too, music primarily meant song (*ghināʾ*)—combined with *ṭarab*, the joy that one feels when listening to music. The term *mūsīqā* is used by the Arabs for theoretical treatises on music, tone systems, musical instruments, music aesthetics, and similar subjects. Thus, ghināʾ and ṭarab have determined the musical life and practice of the Arabs from the first days of music history known to us up to the present.

Musical life and practice in the nineteenth century were also concentrated on the person of the singer and the instrumental ensemble accompanying him or her. Talented and popular singers used to perform with their instrumentalists in a local pub, where their music and song was presented on certain evenings of the month or the night before a celebration. Such a performance would sometimes last until the wee hours of the morning. The ensemble performed on a raised platform or, what was actually more often the case, on a staircase in the pub. The audience paid the musicians and singer according to its own discretion, for instance, by putting money in the cigarette package or tobacco box of one of the members of the ensemble. The only persons allowed to perform at weddings in front of women, besides female musicians, were blind musicians. If an ensemble was invited to perform for festivities celebrating a birth, circumcision, engagement, wedding, or Ramaḍān, the client was not only responsible for the fee, but also for the artists' board and lodging.

Belonging to public festivities since time immemorial are the many religious holidays that are celebrated with singing and music: the *ʿīd al-aḍḥā* (Feast of Sacrifice), the tenth day of *Muḥarram* (the first month of the Islamic year), the nights of *Ramaḍān* (the month of fasting)—especially the fourteenth and twenty-seventh nights—the *ʿīd al-fiṭr* (feast after the Ramaḍān fasting), the *dhikr* ceremonies of various religious brotherhoods, the birthday of the Prophet, pilgrim feasts, and so on. During the night before the holidays, the mosques are decorated and illuminated with lamps. A group of believers climbs the minaret and strikes up a song of praise to God and Muhammad.

In addition to the celebrations of the Moslem Arabs are those of the Christian Arabs who live predominantly in an area corresponding to that of former Syria, which once included Lebanon, Syria, Jordan, Iraq, and Palestine/Israel. Christmas, Easter, feasts of the Virgin, Pentecost, the Transfiguration of Christ, and so on, are also celebrated by the Arabian Christians with singing and instrumental performance and occasionally also with dance.

Musicians and singers of the nineteenth century had a repertoire consisting of traditional vocal and instrumental pieces learned from the old masters. Instruction and learning aids in the form of books and musical notation were not known: musical training was traditionally understood to be only the oral instruction of the student by the teacher. Relying upon a well-trained memory, the student would begin by only imitating the master but would ultimately attain freedom from the musical model and develop an individual style within the framework of musical tradition.

The nineteenth-century Arabian world encompassed five musical centers—Iraq, Syria, Egypt, the Arabian Peninsula, and North Africa—each representing a different musical style, as distinguished by variations in the manner of singing, the technique of plucking the lute instruments, the structure of the scales, the rhythmic patterns of the accompaniment, and the structure of the poems and their content. These kinds of distinctions can still be detected in the musical practice of the Arabs today.

During the nineteenth century, the Arabs maintained particularly close contacts with the Turkish and Persian musical cultures—contacts that had actually existed at least since the tenth century. In fact, from the beginnings of Arabian musical history, musical styles, forms, and song texts had been freely exchanged with neighboring cultures, including the ethnic and religious minorities inhabiting the same geographical area: the Armenians, the Druzes, the Jews, the Kurds, the Syrians, and the Oriental churches. It would therefore be wrong to assume that the Arabs developed a completely unique music, free from any semblance of foreign influence. Nevertheless, none of these contacts had serious consequences for the music of the Arabs during the nineteenth century. It was less a matter of any foreign culture exercising a one-sided influence on Arabian musical life than of similar musical cultures interacting with each other.

In the nineteenth century, the Turkish influence on the music of the Arabs manifested itself in formal structure and in song texts interspersed with Turkish words. Indeed, both the Turks and the Arabs of the nineteenth century continued to differentiate quite consciously between Turkish and Arabian elements in their music. The large dissemination in the Arabian domain of Turkish compositional forms like the *peshrev* and the *semai* also conclusively illustrates the influence of Turkish music traditions. Some works in these genres by Turkish composers were very popular among the Arabs: for example, a peshrev of the rāst genre (see page 29) by the Turkish composer Asim Bey (1851–1929) was performed with great dedication almost everywhere throughout the Arabian world. And the propagation of musical instruments of Persian and Turkish origin, such as the *sanṭūr* (struck box zither) and the *ṭanbūr* (long-necked lute), demonstrates another aspect of Persian and Turkish influence.

At the end of a period of stagnation that had lasted since the thirteenth century, Arabian music theory experienced a genuine revival through the work of Mīkhā'īl Mīshāqah (1800–1889), who was the first to propose the division of the octave into twenty-four roughly equal quarter-tone steps. Despite their political dependency on the Ottomans and immediate proximity to them, the Arabs had thus ensured a steady continuation of their own music tradition—a music tradition that is also perceived by Turks and Persians, now as then, to be Arabian.

The Twentieth Century: Alienation from the Authentic Musical Language

Until the downfall of the Ottoman empire in the year 1918, the music of the Arabs essentially remained a part of the musical culture of the Near East. Not until coming into contact with European music, especially during the colonial rule of the British, Spanish, Italians, and French after World War I, did Arabian musical life change fundamentally in its content and in its formal and sociological aspects. Then a kind of cultural catastrophe took place. The responsibility for this transition lay with a group of leading Arabian intellectuals who believed (and still believe today) that European culture is superior to Arabian. As a result, they regarded their own musical culture with disdain. It is because of these intellectuals that one must search very long and hard in the Arab world today before encountering the authentic music of the Arabs.

Nonetheless, despite the irresponsible behavior of many of these Arabs, the traditional music has been able to maintain its ground in certain areas. Those who have contributed to its preservation are the musicians of the *maqām al-ʿirāqī* in Iraq, the singer Umm Kulthūm in Cairo, the singers of the *muwashshaḥāt* in Aleppo, the musicians of the *ma'lūf* in North Africa, and the artists of andalusī music. Most Arabs today, however, whatever their level of education might be, no longer know true Arabian music.

2

Music Theory and the Arabian Tone System

Throughout the course of Arabian music history—especially between the ninth and thirteenth centuries—innumerable treatises on the tone system have appeared. Two tone systems were recognized, a Greek and an Arabian, whose main difference was in the way tetrachords were divided. Thus the Arabs must have either used a source different from the Greeks' for their music theory or developed the Greek tetrachord divisions further. But since the Arabs illustrated their music theory, and in particular their tone system, by means of the lute—an instrument that has enjoyed enormous popularity among Arabian musicians and singers since pre-Islamic times and is still considered the definitive instrument for Arabian music—it is certainly possible that their theory was derived directly from musical practice, which would inevitably have led to divergence from Greek theory and its tetrachord divisions.

Both tone systems set forth in the numerous musical treatises from the Arabian-Islamic Middle Ages are still valid for present-day music theory. Today's Turkish and Persian tone systems are based on the calculations of Ṣafī ad-Dīn al-Urmawī (d. 1294), who further developed the Pythagorean system. In contrast to al-Urmawī's system is a purely Arabian tone system that was first propagated by al-Fārābī (d. 950).

On the basis of al-Fārābī's system, modern Arabian music theorists undertook the division of the octave into twenty-four equivalent intervals. From this point on, each tone in Arabian music possessed its own name, which was not repeated in either the upper or the lower octaves. The function of a tone depended not upon its absolute pitch but upon its position within the scale and its distance from its neighboring tone. The lowest tone of the scale corresponds to the lowest tone of the singer's register and is called *yakāh*, the corresponding next higher octave is called *nawā*, and the second higher octave *ramal tūtī*. The modes are, as a rule, named after a particularly characteristic tone of the scale, which only in rare cases is the first tone of the scale.

It wasn't until the second half of the nineteenth and the beginning of the twentieth century that some Arabian musicians attempted to notate their music. Referring to Western musical notation, they gave the tones corresponding names, even though the Western method of notation is in many respects inaccurate and inappropriate for the transcription of Arabian music. The musicians had to reach an understanding about which tone of the Arabian system should correspond to which note in the European system. To begin with, the lowest tone of the system, yakāh, was fixed as the tone D. During the time following Ottoman rule, the D was changed to G throughout the Arabian world. But the pitch of yakāh had nothing in common with the absolute pitch G, for Arabian music has never been notated in absolute pitches like those we are accustomed to in European music. Actual pitches can deviate from notated pitches by as much as a fourth in either direction. The extent of this deviation depends upon the vocal range of the singer, to which the instrument is also tuned.

The Arabian tone system that is valid today includes all tones that appear in the more than seventy modes, or *maqām* rows, which are based on heptatonic scales that can be put together from augmented, major, medium, and minor second intervals. The exact sizes of these intervals were calculated by music theorists on a purely abstract basis. Although there are perhaps as many different specifications for interval structures as there are theorists who devised them, the calculations vary only negligibly from one another. The interval sizes within the Arabian scale have not yet been comprehensively investigated by means of electronic measuring instruments.

Not until the nineteenth century—half a millenium after al-Urmawī divided the octave into seventeen parts (limmas and commas)—did an original theoretical work on music that reinvigorated the field of Arabian music theory once again appear. In this work, the Lebanese author Mīkhā'īl Mīshāqāh (1800–1889) presented the division of the octave into twenty-four equal parts. He illustrated the spacing of the twenty-four frets on the neck of the lute with the aid of a geometric drawing (see page 20) that was intended to serve as a model for instrument builders. He defined the value of the quarter tone mathematically as $\sqrt[24]{2} = 50$ cents, where a cent is a logarithmic measurement equal to $1/100$ of the semitone in the well-tempered scale.

Passionate discussions and arguments among musicians and music scholars about the following two questions supplied the impetus for new calculations: (1) how far apart should the frets on the neck of the long-necked lute be—in other words, how large should the intervals of both octaves be—in order to allow for a transposition of the maqām row? and (2) are the intervals of the lower octave equivalent to those of the higher octave—that is, can a melody be played in parallel octaves on two different instruments simultaneously? The fact that such questions were raised indicates that musicians at this time were already familiar with the idea of twenty-four steps to the octave, even if only in relation to their practical experiences.

As early as the tenth century, al-Fārābī had theoretically divided the octave into twenty-five intervals, which he demonstrated by means of the lute as well as the flute. For the division of the tetrachord, he calculated ten possible intervals:

Fraction	1/1	256/243	18/17	162/149	54/49	9/8	32/27	81/68	27/22	81/64	4/3
	c					d				e	f
Cents	0	90	98	145	168	204	294	303	355	408	498

Thus the octave, which comprises two tetrachords and a whole tone, contained twenty-five different tones, from which al-Fārābī extracted the following intervals: octave, fifth, fourth, seventh, whole-tone, half-tone, and quarter-tone. He defined the distance on the lute string between the two frets of the first quarter-tone as $35/36$ of the total length of the string.

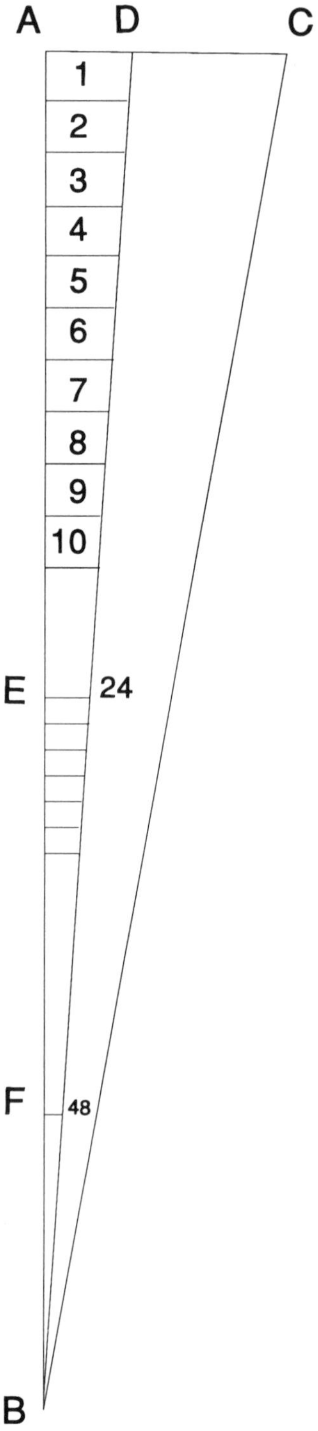

AB = string length
AC = $\frac{1}{9}$ AB
AE = EB = $\frac{1}{2}$ AB
EF = FB = $\frac{1}{2}$ BE
AD = $\frac{1}{4}$ AC = $\frac{1}{36}$ AB
BAC = 90 degrees

Divide AE into 24 equal parts.
Divide EF into 24 equal parts.
Connect DB.

AD 1, AD 2, AD 3, AD 4, . . . , AD 48 represent the distance between frets on the neck of the lute, whereby AD 1 is the first quarter-tone; AD 2, the second; AD 3, the third; . . . ; AD 48, the forty-eighth.

Al-Fārābī chose only combinations of seven tones from the twenty-five tones of the octave. He recommended this heptatonic scale as the basis for melodic structure. One of the tone rows he defined includes the octave specified below. The first tetrachord is identical to the modern rāst row:

tone	oscillation ratio	relative cents	cumulative cents
c	1/1	0	0
d	9/8	204	204
e	27/22	151	355
f	4/3	143	498
g	3/2	204	702
a	18/11	151	853
b	19/9	143	996
c	2/1	204	1200

By way of comparison, the following table presents al-Urmawī's division of the tetrachord, in which natural fifths and fourths are added and subtracted to arrive at seventeen tones per octave. According to al-Urmawī, this apportionment has the so-called Arabian tone system as its basis. Because fifth and fourth relationships are consistently created, all interval relationships can be reduced to $3^x/2^y$ or $2^x/3^y$. For example, e𝄫 is 65536/59049, which equals $2^{16}/3^{10}$.

tone	oscillation ratio	relative cents	cumulative cents
c	1/1	0	0
d-flat	253/243	90 (limma)	90
e-flat-flat	65536/59049	90 (limma)	180
d	9/8	24 (comma)	204
e-flat	32/22	90 (limma)	294
f-flat	8192/6561	90 (limma)	384

tone	oscillation ratio	relative cents	cumulative cents
e	81/64	24 (comma)	408
f	4/3	90 (limma)	498

Whereas al-Fārābī assigns the so-called *wusṭā-zalzal* tone (a third that is larger than a tempered minor third and smaller than a tempered major third) a value of 27/22 (355 cents), al-Urmawī defines it as $8192/6561 = 2^{13}/3^{8}$ (384 cents).

Like al-Fārābī, al-Urmawī also selected combinations of seven tones from among the supply he calculated for the octave. Altogether, al-Urmawī succeeded in creating twelve maqām rows that he recommended for melody building, one of which is presented in the following table:

tone	oscillation ratio	relative cents	cumulative cents
c	1/1	0	0
d	9/8	204	204
f-flat	8192/6561	180	384
f	4/3	114	498
g	3/2	204	702
a	27/16	204	906
c-flat	59049/32768	180	1086
c	2/1	114	1200

Here, again, the first tetrachord is identical to that of the rāst row used in contemporary Arabian music.

Some Arabian theorists, of course, attempted to define the Arabian tone system, with reference to the circle of fifths (which was also used by Turkish theorists), on the basis of the unit of measure known as the comma. The Syrians, in particular, subdivided the octave into fifty-three equivalent steps, from which they also selected seven at a time to construct a heptatonic maqām row. Their calculations were based neither on the Pythagorean comma (23.46 cents) nor on the syntonic comma

(21.306 cents) but on the so-called Arabian comma, also known as the Holdrian comma, whose value is $\sqrt[53]{2}$, or 22.6415 cents. The term *Arabian comma* is indeed found only in the European treatises of the Middle Ages, not in the Arabian. The absence of written documentation in the Arabian world may possibly be explained by the fact that the comma was handed down from master to student as a kind of trade secret.

Indeed, as early as 45 B.C., the Chinese Ching-Fang had calculated the value of this comma. He discovered that the highest tone in a row of fifty-three natural fifths built one on top of the other is almost identical to the lowest tone of the row, if the fifty-third fifth is transposed down by thirty-one octaves. Thus the ratio of the lowest tone of the row to the transposed highest tone (that is, $(3/2)^{53}$ minus 2^{31}) is $176777/177147$, which corresponds to the value of the Arabian comma.

Some music theorists describe the maqām row of the rāst, for example, on the basis of comma units as follows:

	c		d		e		f		g		a		b		c'
Comma		9		8		5		9		9		8		5	

The maqām row of the nahawand (see page 32) is determined as follows:

	c		d		e♭		f		g		a♭		b♭		c'
Comma		9		4		9		9		4		9		9	

In all of these subdivisions, the intervals d–e, e–f, g–a, a–b, and b–c' are neither minor nor major seconds. Rather they are medium seconds—approximately the size of a three-quarter-tone (150 cents)—and they have given Arabian music its unique quality since as early as the tenth century. Because the quarter-tone is not to be found in any maqām scale and exists only in theory, it should not be considered the characteristic interval size in Arabian music; on the contrary, it is the three-quarter-tone that merits this significance.

Theorists argue about the exact size of the quarter-tone, and in practice, the three-quarter-tone does not have a fixed size that holds for all maqām rows. In fact, the breadth of deviation of this musical step is a crucial ingredient in the peculiar flavor of Arabian music. To temper the scale by dividing the octave into twenty-four quarter-tones of equal size would be to surrender one of the most characteristic elements of this musical culture. In practice, singers and musicians ultimately avail themselves of a number of pitches that can be empirically reduced to twenty-four unequal steps within the octave. Moreover, many fewer tones are generally used during a performance than would be offered by the tempered system—even when additional sound material is included through transposition.

For transcribing the twenty-four tones into Western notation, the Arabs use European accidental marks in original and modified forms:

- 𝄳 lowers a tone by a quarter-tone
- ♭ lowers a tone by a half-tone
- 𝄳♭ lowers a tone by a three-quarter-tone
- 𝄲 raises a tone by a quarter-tone
- ♯ raises a tone by a half-tone
- 𝄲♯ raises a tone by a three-quarter-tone

A two-octave range is fully adequate for traditional Arabian music; hence, the Arabs have only given individual names to the forty-eight tones of two octaves. The names were, for the most part, adopted by the Turks and Persians, but the intervals of the Arabs differ in their details from those of the Persians and Turks. A tone that lies outside the two-octave range is defined as the second (or third) upper (or lower) octave of the tone *x*. The tones of the first octave begin with yakāh (G).

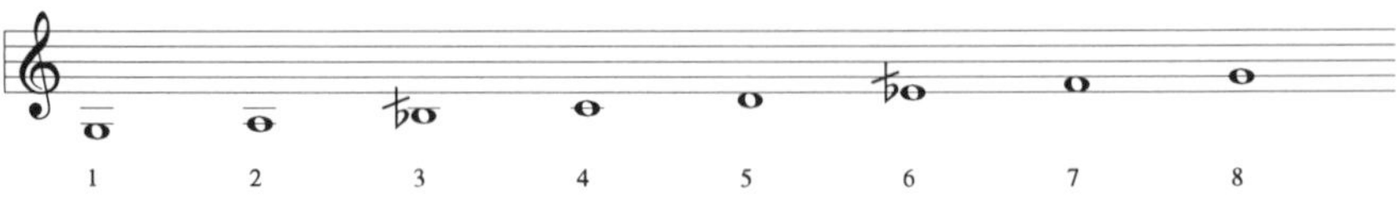

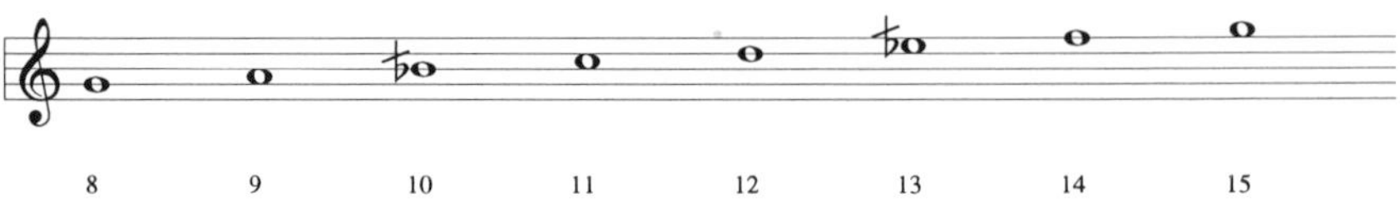

The Arabian musician understands the twenty-four tones within the octave as individual pitches, differentiated according to their importance. The most important (frequently occurring) tones support the tone system, as the pillars of a building support its roof. These tones are considered particularly important because they occur more frequently in traditional music and because most maqām rows begin with them. Scattered among the pillars are other pitches that are differentiated as either important (less frequently occurring) or less important (seldom occurring).

The Tones of the First and Second Octave

frequently occurring	less frequently occurring	seldom occurring
1. yakāh G		
		2. qarār[*] nīm[†] ḥiṣār G𝄲/A𝄳♭
	3. qarār ḥiṣār A♭/G♯	
		4. qarār tīk[‡] ḥiṣār A𝄳/G𝄲♯
5. ʿushayrān A		
		6. qarār nīm ʿajam A𝄲/B𝄳♭
7. qarār ʿajam B♭		
8. ʿirāq B𝄳		
9. qawasht B		
		10. tīk qawasht B𝄲
11. rāst C		
		12. nīm zīrkūlah C𝄲/D𝄳♭
13. zīrkūlah D♭/C♯		
		14. tīk zīrkūlah C𝄲♯/D𝄳
15. dūkāh D		

* *qarār* = lower octave
† *nīm* = slightly lowered
‡ *tīk* = slightly raised

The Tones of the First and Second Octave

frequently occurring	less frequently occurring	seldom occurring
		16. nīm kurdī E𝄳♭/D𝄲
17. kurdī E♭		
18. sīkāh E𝄳		
	19. būsalīk E	
		20. tīk būsalīk E𝄲/F𝄳♭
21. jahārkāh F		
		22. nīm ḥijāz (ʿarbāʾ) F𝄲/g𝄳♭
	23. ḥijāz F♯/g♭	
		24. tīk ḥijāz g𝄳/F𝄲♯
25. nawā g		
		26. nīm ḥiṣār g𝄲/a𝄳♭
	27. ḥiṣār g♯/a♭	
		28. tīk ḥiṣār g𝄲♯/a𝄳
29. ḥusaynī a		
		30. nīm ʿajam a𝄲/b𝄳♭
31. ʿajam b♭		
32. awj b𝄳		
33. nihūft b		
		34. tīk nihūft b𝄲
35. kurdān c		
		36. nīm shāhnāz c𝄲/d𝄳♭
	37. shāhnāz c♯/d♭	
		38. tīk shāhnāz c𝄲♯/d𝄳
39. muḥayyar d		
		40. nīm sunbulah e𝄳♭/d𝄲
	41. sunbulah e♭	

The Tones of the First and Second Octave

frequently occurring	less frequently occurring	seldom occurring
42. buzurk e𝄳		
	43. ḥusaynī shadd e	
		44. tīk ḥusaynī shadd e𝄲/f𝄳♭
45. māhūrān f		
		46. jawāb ʿarbāʾ f𝄲/g'𝄳♭
	47. jawāb ḥijāz f♯/g'♭	
		48. jawāb tīk ḥijāz g'𝄳/f𝄲♯
49. ramal tūtī (saham) g'		

In accordance with the structure of the tone system, three tones lie between yakāh and ʿushayrān—qarār nīm ḥiṣār, qarār ḥiṣār, and qarār tīk ḥiṣār. Qarār ḥiṣār is the most important of these. *Qarār* means lower octave, *nīm* indicates a slightly lowered pitch, and *tīk*, a slightly raised pitch. Qarār nim ḥiṣār thus indicates a slightly lowered pitch—in this case, ḥiṣār—in the lower octave. However, in the perception of the native musician, ḥiṣār is less an abstract sound than one of three possible fret positions of the index finger on the neck of the lute. The designation and notation of the tone as g♯/a♭ is actually done only to describe this tone for European understanding through a musical translation. "Modern" Arabs, however, believe that Arabian music can be at least fairly exactly notated with a musical transcription.

If we examine the tones ʿirāq, sīkāh, awj, and buzurk (B𝄳, E𝄳, b𝄳, e𝄳), which make up the principal tones of the Arabian musical scale, we can observe that each of the intervals ʿushayrān–ʿirāq, ʿirāq–rāst, dūkāh–sīkāh, sīkāh–jahārkāh, ḥusyanī–awj, awj–kurdān, muḥayyar–buzurk,. and buzurk–māhūrān (A–B𝄳, B𝄳–C, D–E𝄳, E𝄳–F, a–b𝄳, b𝄳–c, d–e𝄳, and e𝄳–f) forms a second that is neither major nor minor but rather constitutes a medium second approximately the size of a three-quarter-tone. By transposing the three-quarter-tone that appears here in the second, third, fifth, and sixth steps of the scale to the first, fourth, and seventh steps, one arrives at the twenty-four intervals of Mīkhā'īl Mīshāqah—the first and most original of a great many theorists who dealt with the question of how to divide the octave into twenty-four steps.

As previously mentioned, the maqām row includes merely a selection from the supply of available tones and is made up of a characteristic combination of minor, medium, major, and augmented seconds. Consequently one maqām row might be made up exclusively of medium and major seconds, while another might consist of only minor and major seconds. As a rule, the tones of the first lower octave function as beginning tones: yakāh, ʿushayrān, ʿirāq, rāst, dūkāh, sīkāh, jahārkāh, and nawā (G, A, B𝄳, C, D, E𝄳, F, and g). Approximately forty maqām rows begin with dūkāh (D), about twenty begin with rāst (C), and approximately ten with sīkāh (E𝄳). Yakāh, ʿushayrān, ʿirāq, ʿajam, and nawā (G, A, B𝄳, B♭, g) are each represented approximately five times as beginning tones, with būsālīk (E) once and jahārkāh (F) twice. Still, the classification of a maqām row is determined not only by its beginning or final tone but also by the character of its consecutive seconds. In particular, the structure of the descending cadential sequence of seconds leading to the final tone is the criterion by which the genre of a maqām row is determined.

I. The *rāst* genre

Characteristic for the modes of this genre is the descending sequence of seconds—medium-medium-major—leading to the final tone. The maqām row of the rāst constitutes the main mode of this genre:

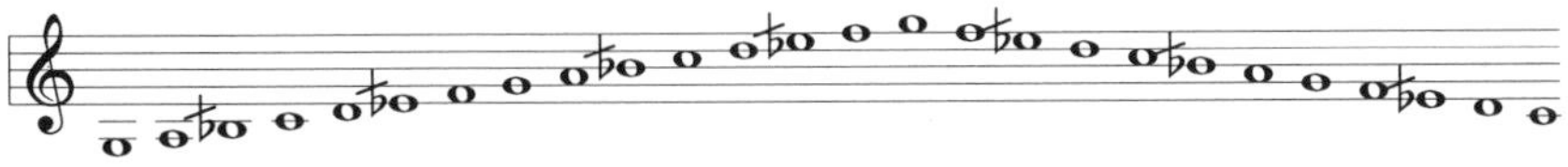

Belonging to the rāst genre are approximately twenty other modes, of which the following four should be presented:

1. rahāwī

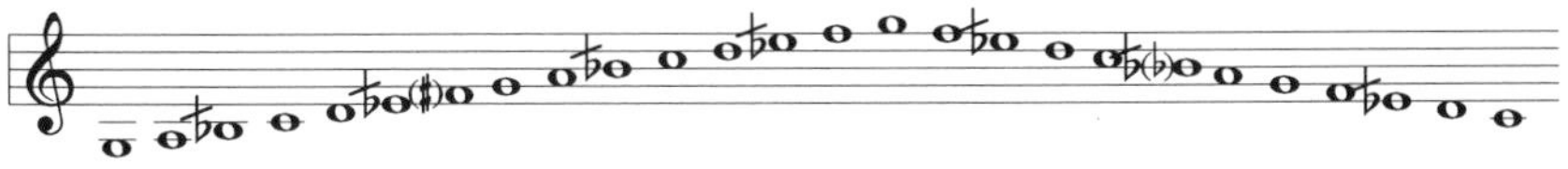

2. māhūr

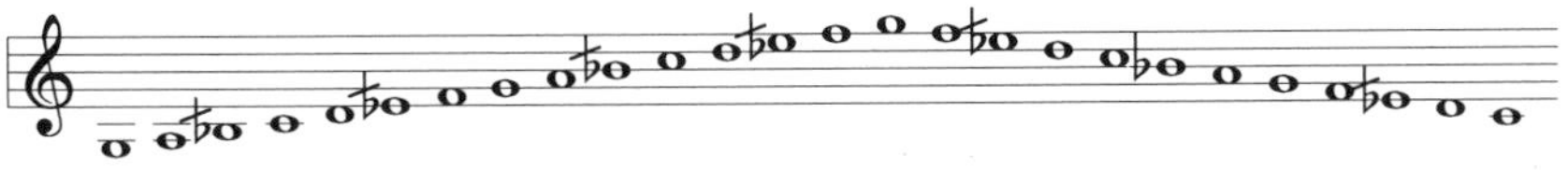

3. yakāh

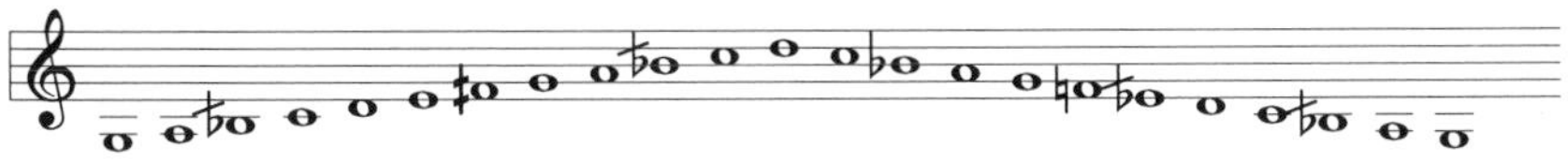

4. dilnishīn

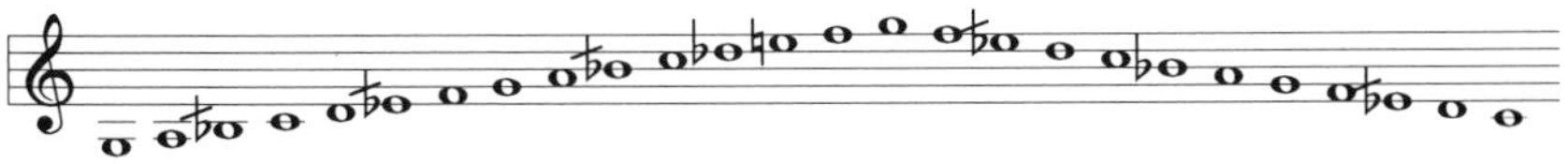

II. The *bayātī* genre

Characteristic for the modes of this genre is the descending sequence of seconds—major-medium-medium—leading to the final tone. The maqām row of the bayātī constitutes the main mode of this genre:

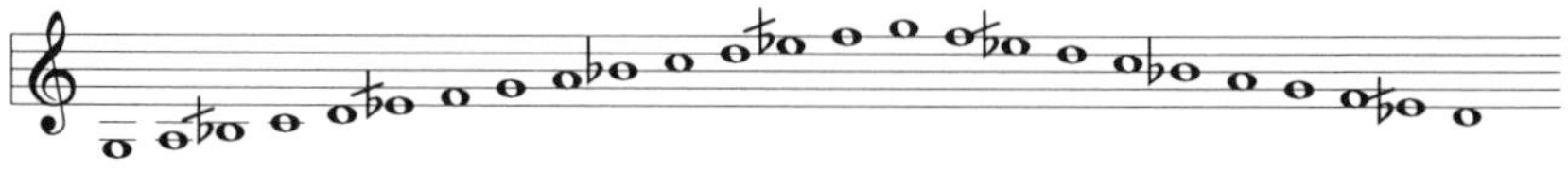

Approximately twenty other modes are ascribed to the bayātī genre, among which are the following four:

1. ḥusyanī

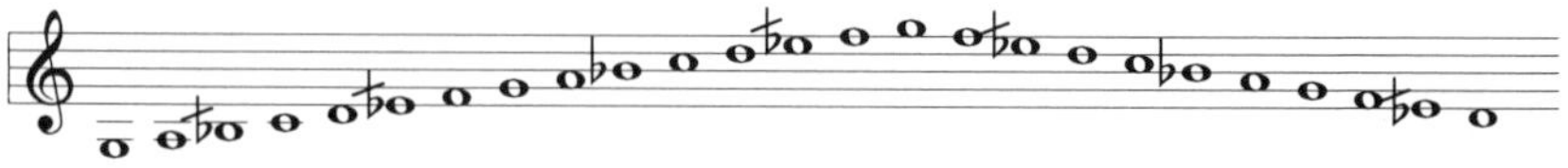

2. muḥayyar

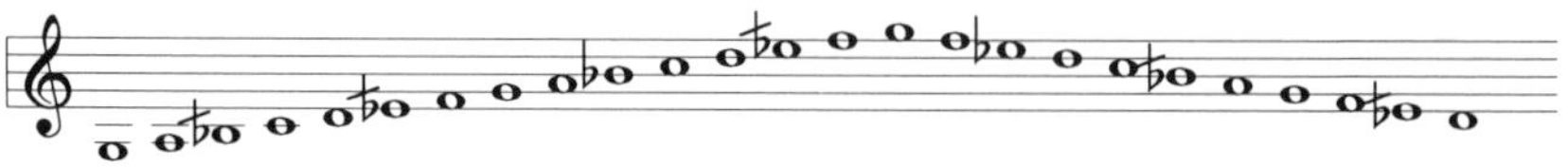

3. ṣabā

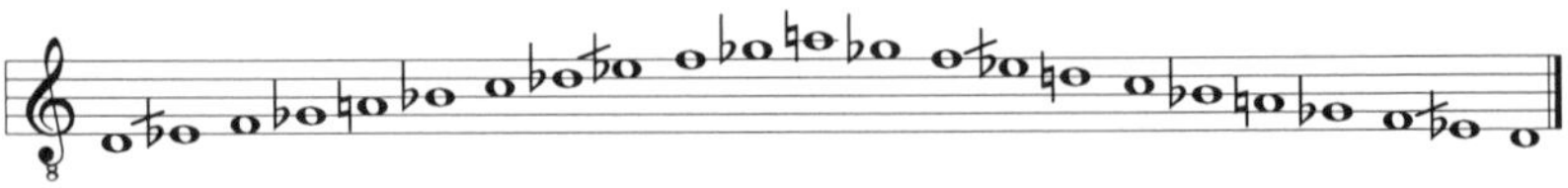

4. qārjighār

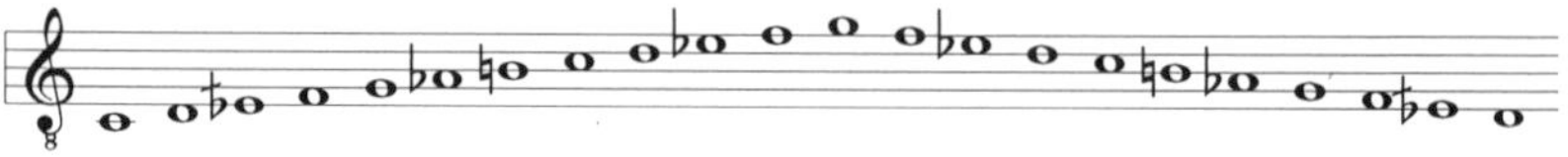

III. The *sīkāh* genre

Characteristic for the modes of this genre is the descending sequence of seconds—major-major-medium—leading to the final tone. The maqām row of the sīkāh constitutes the main mode of this genre:

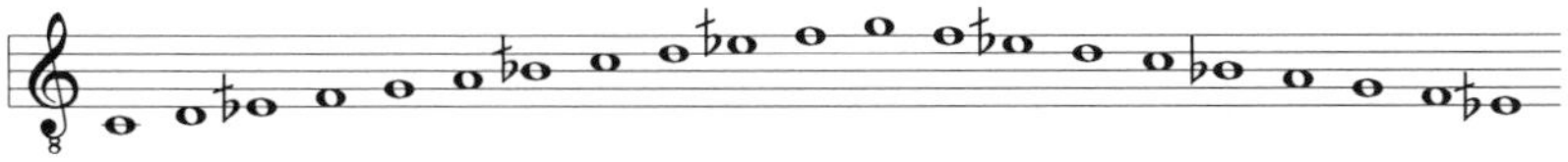

Approximately ten other modes belong to the sīkāh genre, of which the following four should be presented:

1. huzām

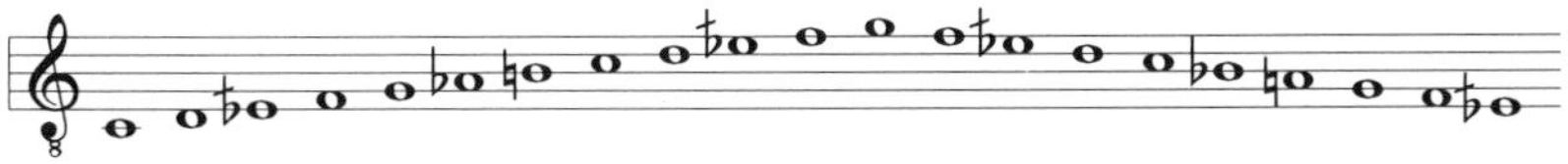

2. musta'ār

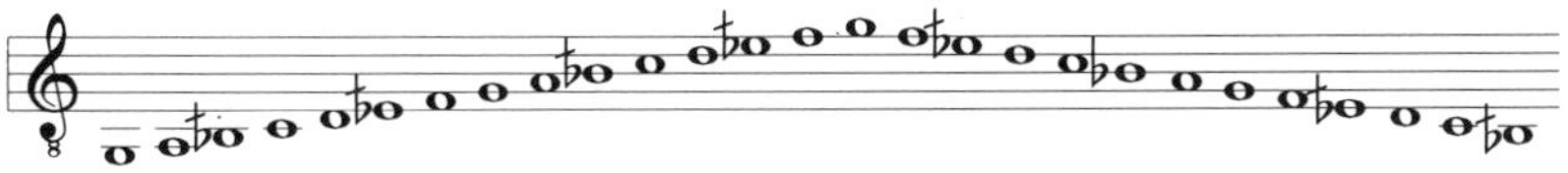

3. 'irāq

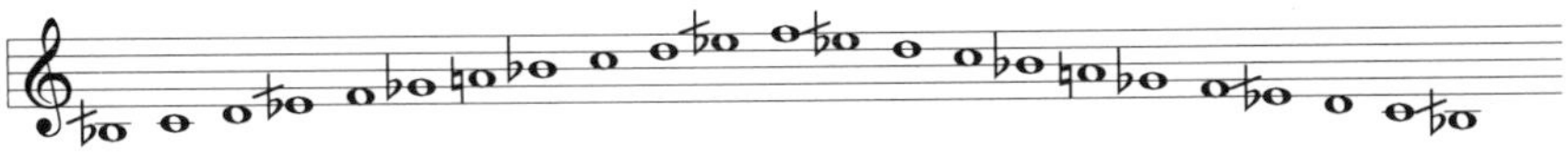

4. bastanikār

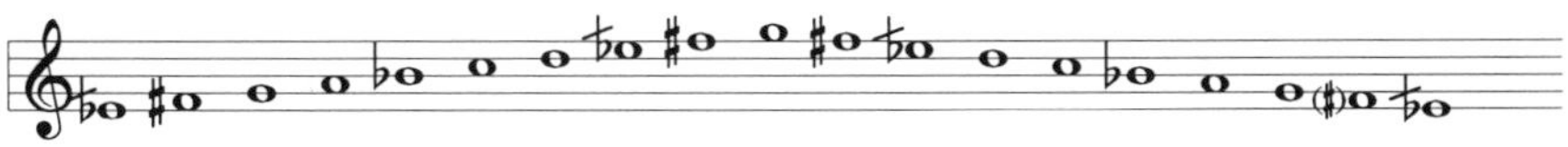

IV. The *nahawand* genre

Characteristic for the modes of this genre is the descending sequence of seconds—major-minor-major—leading to the final tone. The maqām row of the nahawand constitutes the main mode of this genre:

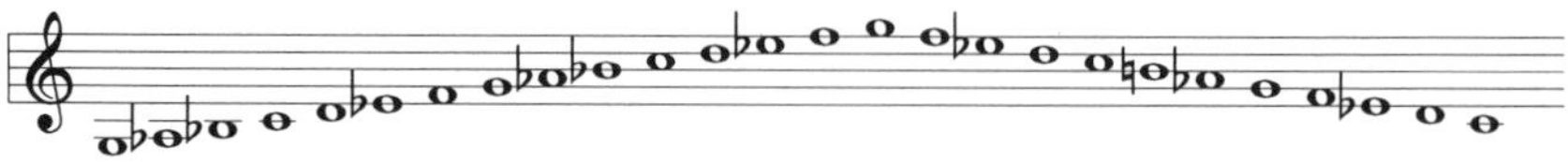

Belonging to the nahawand genre are approximately ten other modes, which include the following four:

1. būsālīk

2. rāḥat fazā

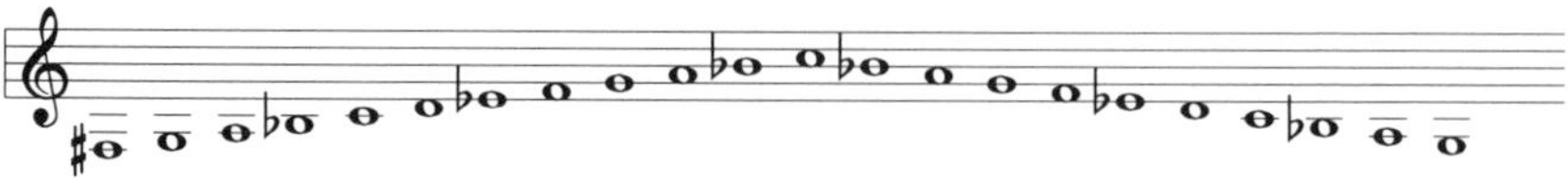

3. faraḥ fazā

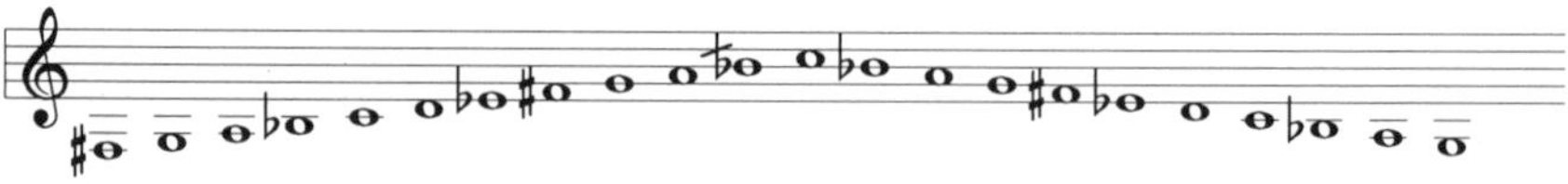

4. dilkashīdah

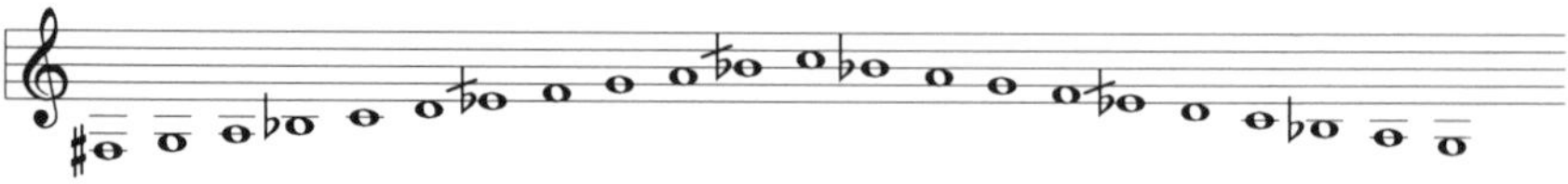

V. The *ḥijāz* genre

Characteristic for the modes of this genre is the descending sequence of seconds—minor-augmented-minor—leading to the final tone. The maqām row of the ḥijāz constitutes the main mode of this genre:

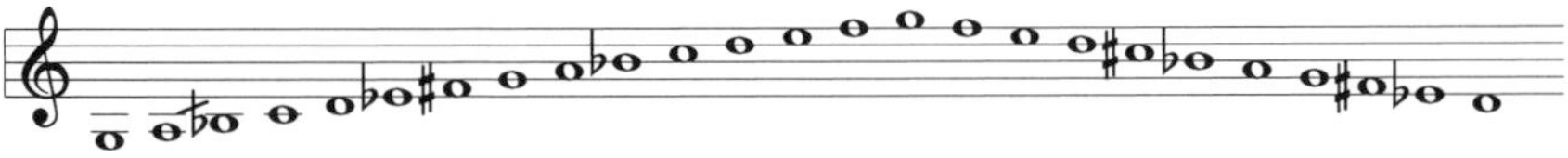

Approximately seven other modes belong to the ḥijāz genre, including the following four:

1. shāhnāz

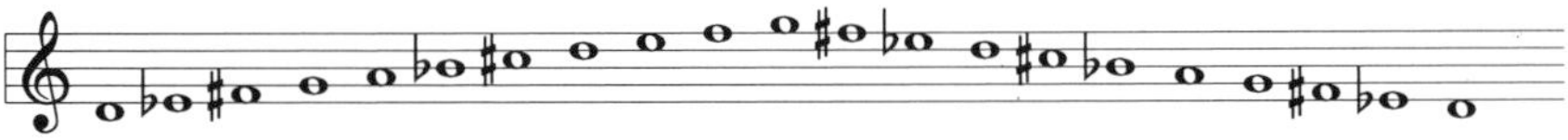

2. shadd ʿarabān

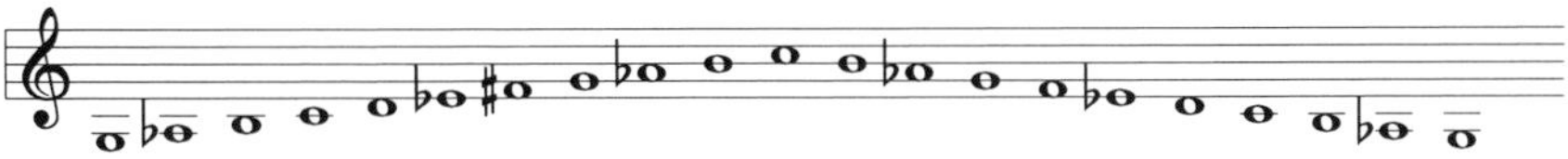

3. hijāzkār

4. sūzdil

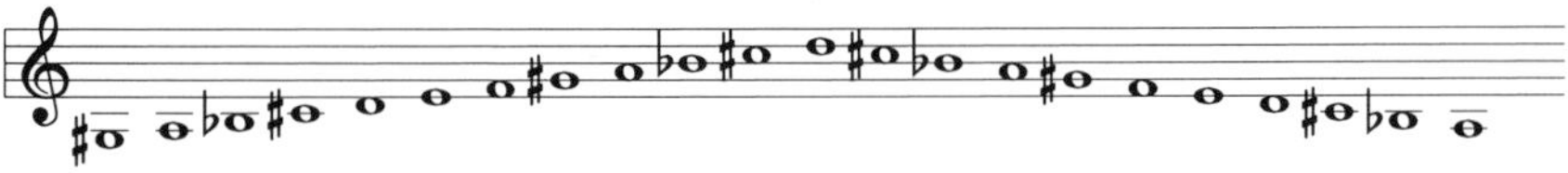

VI. The *nakrīz* genre

Characteristic for the modes of this genre is the descending sequence of seconds—minor-augmented-minor-major—leading to the final tone. The maqām row of the nakrīz constitutes the main mode of this genre:

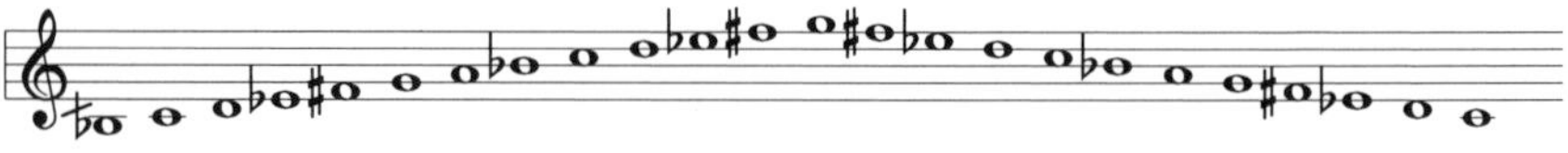

Approximately five other modes belong to the nakrīz genre, including the following four:

1. nawā athar

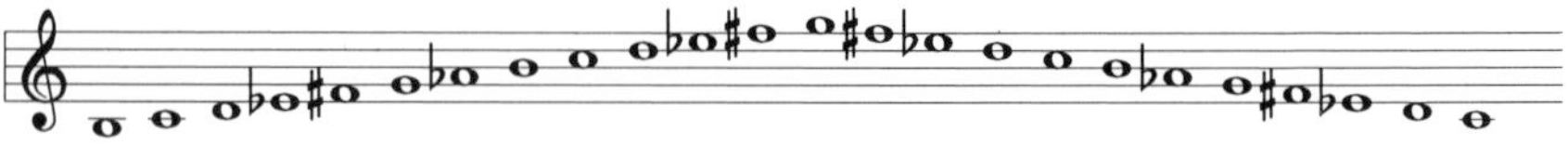

2. ḥayyān

3. ḥiṣār

4. basandīda

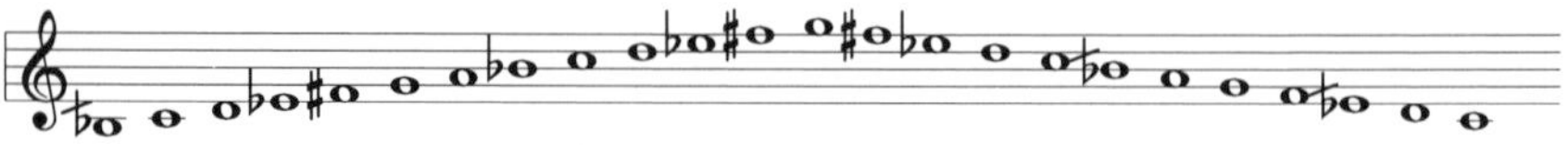

VII. The ʿ*ajam* genre

Characteristic for the modes of this genre is the descending sequence of seconds—minor-major-major—leading to the final tone. The maqām row of the ʿajam ʿushayrān constitutes the main mode of this genre:

Approximately six other modes belong to the ʿajam genre, including the following four:

1. shawq afzā

2. shawq awīr

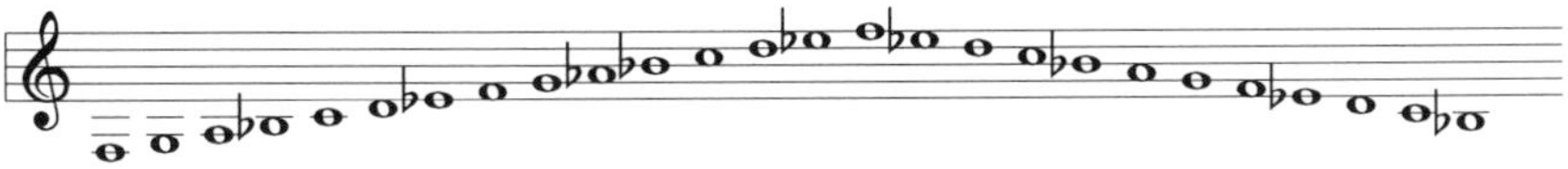

3. shāh wār

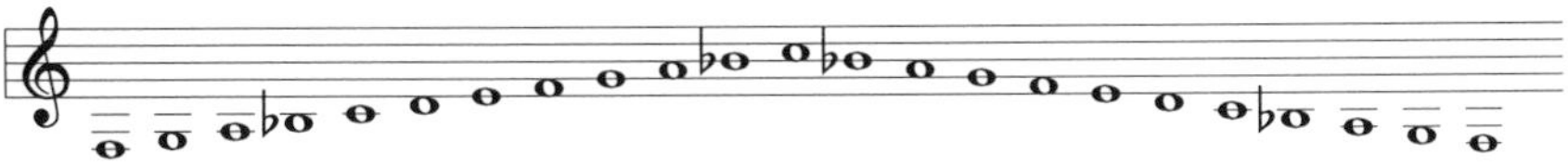

4. jahārkāh/mazmūm

VIII. The *kurd* genre

Characteristic for the modes of this genre is the descending sequence of seconds—major-major-minor—leading to the final tone. The maqām row of the kurd constitutes the main mode of this genre:

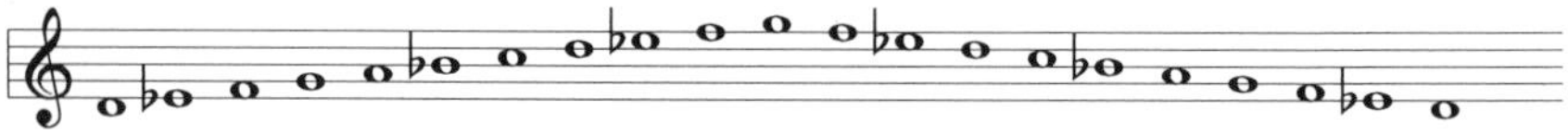

Belonging to the kurd genre are approximately five other modes, which are structured like the following four:

1. shāhnāz kurdī

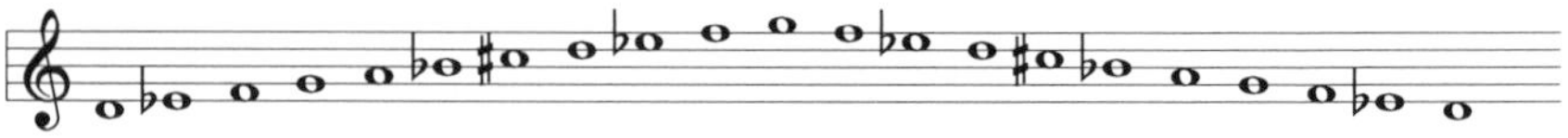

2. ṭarznawin

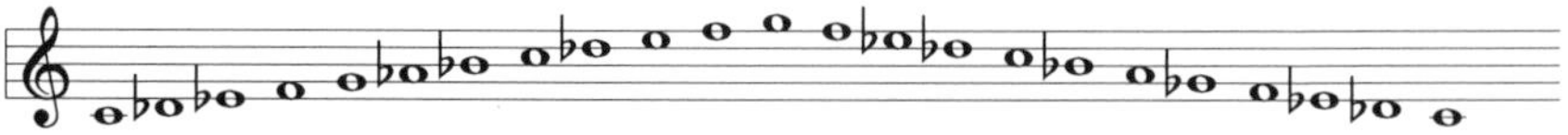

3. hijāzkār kurdī

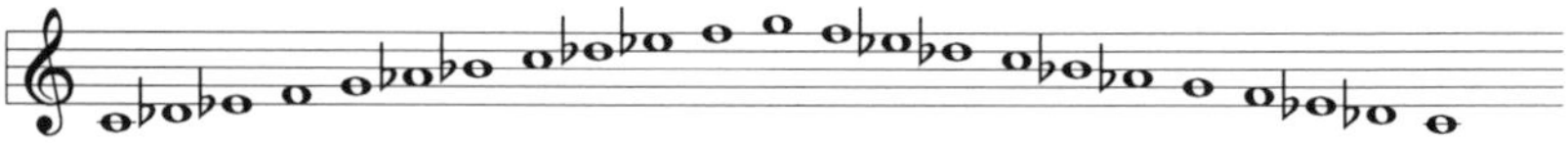

4. shawq ṭarab

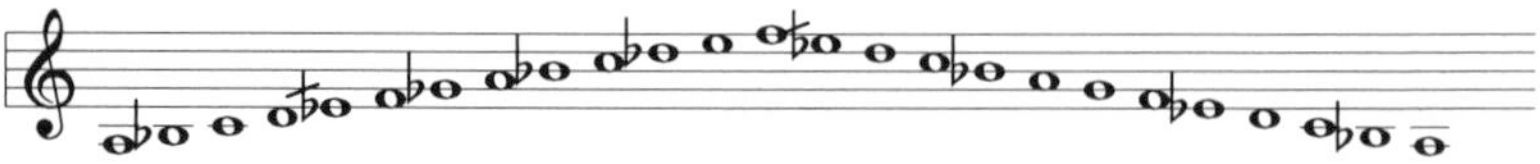

The following is a final review of the cadential sequence of seconds that characterize the eight maqām genres:

m2 = minor	m = medium
M2 = major	a = augmented

1. rāst

2. bayātī

3. sīkāh

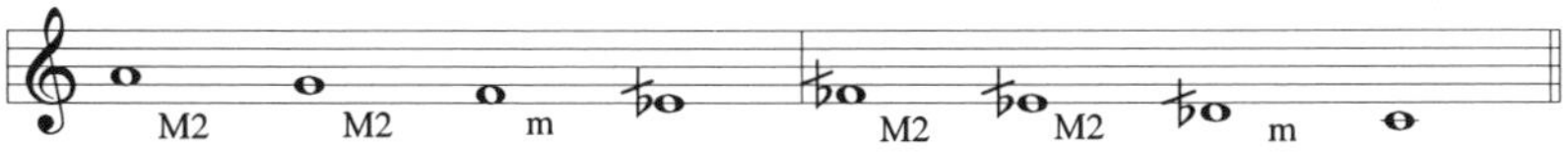

4. nahawand

5. ḥijāz

6. nakrīz

7. ʿajam

8. kurd

3

The Maqām Phenomenon

The maqām phenomenon, a technique of improvisation unique to Arabian art music, is at the root of all genres of improvised vocal and instrumental music of the Arabs. This technique of improvisation is found throughout the entire Arabian world, in secular as well as in sacred music.

Every musical structure is determined by two factors: space (tonal-spatial factor) and time (rhythmic-temporal factor). Decisive for the structure of a piece of music is whether these factors are strictly organized or may be formed freely. In the maqām, the tonal-spatial component is developed so pronouncedly—in contrast to the rhythmic-temporal component, which is subjected to no definite organization—that it constitutes the essential, decisive factor in maqām performance. And herein lies the most inherent characteristic of the maqām: the fixed and binding organization of the tonal-spatial component takes precedence over the freely organized rhythmic-temporal component—totally the opposite of a genre like the waltz, for example, which is first and foremost characterized by the organization of its rhythmic-temporal component, while the tonal-spatial order has no rules to obey.

Most musical genres in the European cultural sphere are not subject to any particularly distinct, well-established tonal-spatial system that would impose clear-cut restrictions on the invention of a musical theme. This, however, has not always been the case. During the eighteenth and nineteenth centuries, for example, the composer of a sonata or a symphony had to observe an established system of tonal-spatial rules. The second theme of the exposition was always written in a higher key than the first, then modulated to a lower register in the development section in order to create a contrast with the recapitulation. In addition, a rhythmic-temporal order was observed that always bore a certain relationship to the chosen recurring rhythmic grouping.

The maqām, on the other hand, is not subject to any fixed organization with respect to time. It has neither an established, regularly recurring bar scheme nor an unchanging meter. A certain rhythm does sometimes identify the style of a performer, but this is dependent upon his performance technique and is never characteristic of the maqām as such.

This lack of fixed meter explains why foreign listeners unfamiliar with this music have sometimes regarded maqām performance as formless improvisation. For the inexperienced ear, a maqām performance appears to have neither beginning nor end. Clearly defined themes and their elaboration and variation during the course of the piece are absent. Furthermore, the Arabian musician performs the maqām without following a musical score.

The maqām, however, does indeed have a form. It consists of structural elements, including melodic passages, phases and tone levels, and emotional content, that can be clearly observed in vocal as well as in instrumental forms.

The Melodic Passage

Characteristic of maqām performance are the long pauses that split up the melodic line into several melodic passages. Every maqām is composed of several such melodic passages during which the tonal-spatial aspect is more fully developed. In each new melodic passage, something musically new happens. The new event is either treated independently or combined with musical material that has previously been presented. If the musician, for example, emphasizes the first tone of the maqām row in the first melodic passage, then the third tone of the maqām may be introduced in the second melodic passage. If the fourth step of the maqām is featured in the third melodic passage, then it can be expected that both of the main tones from the first two melodic passages will also appear in this third melodic passage. There is, however, no binding rule for the order in which the tones are emphasized and for the number of melodic passages within a maqām. Each musician is free to proceed at will.

Phases and Tone Levels

Music played on one tone or within a certain tonal area constitues a "phase" in the development of a maqām. Each melodic passage comprises one or more such phases. The melodic development proceeds gradually from phase to phase from the lower to the higher registers until the melodic climax is reached, at which point the form is completed. The manner in which a phase is realized depends upon the artistic ability of the musician or singer.

The phases of a maqām are based on tone levels that are carefully constructed one after the other during the performance. A tone level is made up of tones that are organized around a melodic axis. A melodic axis results when a central tone, which may be encircled by neighboring tones, has been repeated at least three times. The following example shows a tone level centered on the tone g:

The next example illustrates a tone level that extends over the tonal area from g to g', with the tone d as center. The center tone is encircled by g-a-b♭-c-e-f-g' and is thus emphasized.

It is not unusual for a tone level to have more than one center. The tone f in the same g-a-b♭-c-d-e-f-g' series can form a secondary center, a kind of satellite to the tone d. The entire tone level derives its characteristic color from the intervallic relationship between the primary and secondary centers:

When all possibilities of the musical structuring of such a tone level have been fully explored, the phase is complete. Some musicians develop a particular phase at length; others do so quite briefly. Some extend the tonal area and depart from the central tone; others restrict themselves to a smaller area around the center. But in all cases, the central tone is of utmost importance because it is considered the nucleus of the entire phase. The form of the maqām, which is reflected in the totality of its phases, is defined by the sequence of central tones as, for example, in the following:

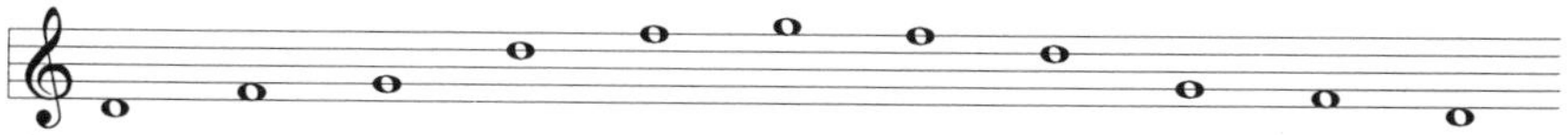

Each tone in this example appears as the center of its own tone level, the duration of which is decided by the musician or singer and is dependent upon his or her musical talent. One musician might need perhaps only seven seconds for the musical elaboration of a given tone level, another possibly forty seconds.

The central tones of every maqām have varying intervallic relationships to one another, but there are always at least two different intervals:

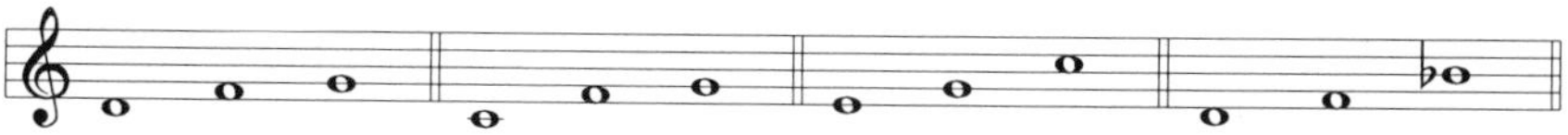

These intervals, which are created from the supply of central tones, conjointly form the nucleus of the maqām. Thus, for example, the eleven central tones in the previous example can be reduced to:

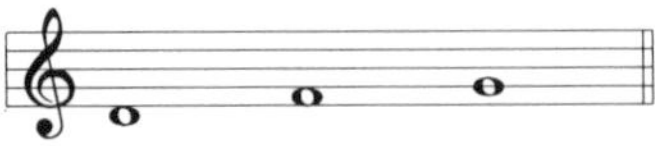

The types of interval that constitute a nucleus determine the emotional content of the maqām. This particular nucleus of a minor third and a major second is the basis of the maqām bayātī. The presentation of the maqām bayātī is thus based—in vocal as well as in instrumental performance—upon the realization of tone levels that rest primarily upon the tones of this nucleus. The first and last tone levels of a maqām always refer to the beginning tone of the mode.

Altogether, then, the presentation of the maqām is composed of melodic passages whose number and length are not previously determined. In each case, one tone level is clearly illustrated and displayed; thereafter, it may be combined, contrasted, or exchanged with one or more addtional tone levels. For each maqām there is a fixed number of tone levels, which can be reduced to a nucleus. Arabian listeners measure the originality and skill of the musician or singer by the way he or she elaborates, combines, and contrasts the tone levels and phases. This applies to the first tone level as well as to the return to the musical point of departure that concludes the musical performance, after the highest tone level—the climax of the maqām—has been reached. In his or her selection and combinaton of tone levels, a first-class musician knows well how to intensify the excitement of the listeners to such an extent that they break into spontaneous applause during the pause following a melodic passage.

For the realization of a truly convincing and original maqām performance, a creative faculty is needed very similar to that of a composer. Yet, the maqām can be regarded as a compositional form only with reservation. Not two performances of the same maqām are ever identical. The compositional aspect is manifest through the predetermined tonal-spatial organization of a specific number of tone levels, while the improvisational phase unfolds during the course of the rhythmic-temporal scheme. This interplay of composition and improvisation is one of the most unmistakable characteristics of the maqām.

The Emotional Content of the Maqām

Every maqām presentation possesses its own emotional content, which is determined primarily by the structure of its nucleus but also by the tones of the maqām row. First of all, however, the tone levels and phases characteristic of the maqām must be worked out. A tone row can have one or two nuclei at its disposal and thereby be assigned to two different *maqāmāt* (plural of *maqām*) and emotional characters. The tone rows of the maqām bayātī and the maqām ʿushshāq turkī are identical:

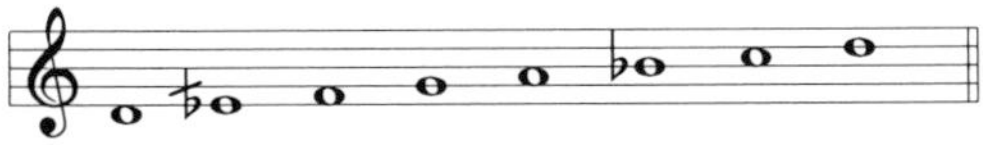

The nucleus of the bayātī, however, is:

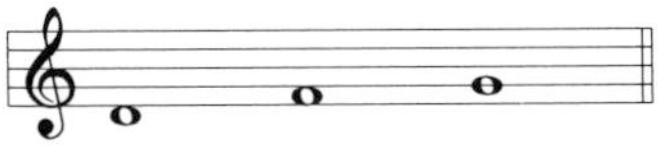

while that of the ʿushshāq turkī has the following structure:

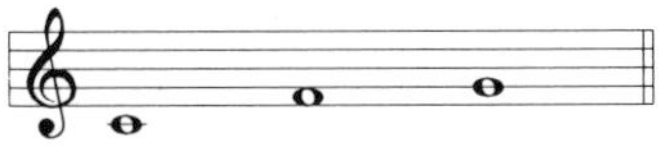

The vocal or instrumental performance of a maqām is inherently linked to the realization of a mood or emotional situation, as the results of a survey among Arabian musicians shows. The maqām rāst, for instance, evokes a feeling of pride, power, soundness of mind, and masculinity. The maqām bayātī, on the other hand, expresses vitality, joy, and femininity, while the maqām sīkāh is associated with feelings of love, and the maqām *ṣabā* evokes sadness and pain. Finally, the maqām ḥijāz conjures up the distant desert.

In an experiment that used an equal number of Arabs and non-Arabs as subjects, the maqām ṣabā was played from a tape recording. During the performance, the listeners were asked to describe, with the aid of four concentric circles, the feelings produced in them by this maqām. The most intensely felt emotion was to be recorded in the smallest, innermost circle, with progressively weaker emotions going in increasingly larger circles. Care was taken not to influence the subjects by allusion to a specific vocabulary.

Whereas the Arabs in the experiment experienced the ṣabā as "sad," "tragic," and "lamenting," only forty-eight percent of the non-Arabs described it thus, with another twenty-eight percent saying that it evoked feeling such as "seriousness," "longing," and "tension." Six percent experienced the ṣabā as "happy," "active," and "very lively," while ten percent couldn't identify any feelings. Thus, only approximately half of the non-Arabs had the same perceptions as the Arabs.

A test page from an Arab and one from a non-Arab are presented below for comparison. The emotions are listed decreasing order from most intense (1) to least intense (5).

Arab	*non-Arab*
1. tearful, expression of the most intense sadness, pain, death lamentation	1. pain
2. compassion, surprise	2. restlessness
3. thirst, unrequited love of a virgin, dark gray, jet-black	3. excitement
4. widow, orphan, garden without flowers, fog	4. loneliness
5. waterfall, white, pink	5. ———

In describing the emotional content of the maqām ṣabā, the Arabs either cited emotional moods directly or resorted to metaphors. Besides using similarly straightforward descriptions, the non-Arabs alluded to colors and called upon the technical language of music, including terminology such as "modally ornamented," "unclean intonation," and so forth.

Within the first few seconds of a maqām performance, whether experienced in concert or as "canned" music, an Arabian listener is immediately certain of the emotional content.

After the first melodic passage, which with approximately three seconds' duration can be the shortest, the Arabian listener is able to say exactly which maqām it is and which mood it conveys. The level of emotional intensity increases during the performance, however, and as a general rule, it is always strongest when the musical event takes place within a traditional context.

Let us nevertheless confine ourselves to the purely modal sound structure of the maqām, which develops formally into melodic passages and tone levels whose central tones can be reduced to a nucleus. Let us attempt to establish why, after just a few seconds, the maqām ṣabā evokes a feeling of sadness in the listener—whether in a vocal or an instrumental interpretation.

Because the Arabian tone system is not tempered, the size of an interval can change during the presentation of a maqām, giving rise to a particular characteristic coloring of a tone level and simultaneously eliciting a specific emotional mood in the Arab listener. The first seconds of a performance of the maqām ṣabā (see below) present a tone level that rests on the fundamental tone (d) of the maqām row. Thus, the tonal area from d to g♭ is fully utilized. The tones e𝄳, f, and g♭ encircle the fundamental tone. The structure of the tonal area from d to g♭ is characterized by a medium second (I: d–e𝄳), which is somewhat larger than a three-quarter-tone, a medium second (II: e𝄳–f), somewhat smaller than a three-quarter-tone, and a minor second (III: f–g♭), which is somewhat smaller than the interval that is known to us as a minor second:

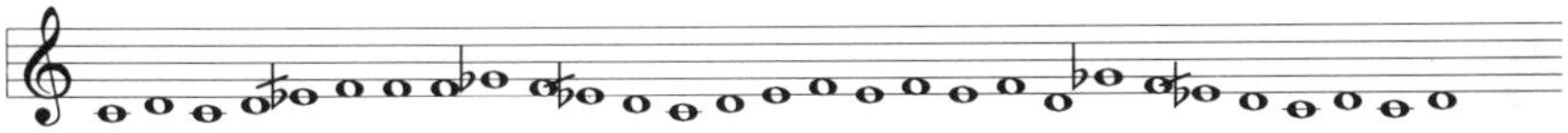

Expressed in cents: d–e𝄳 = 160 cents, e𝄳–f = ± 140 cents and f–g♭ = 95 cents, whereby the tones e𝄳 and g♭ may fluctuate upward or downward somewhat, thus causing a "sadder" or "more sensitive" emotional mood. It is the changeable size of certain intervals in this nontempered tone system that influences the emotional content of a maqām. Such an emotional content, however, becomes lost as soon as the tone system is artificially changed and organized into intervals of equal size.

4

The Rhythmic-Temporal Dimension: Wazn

In Arabian treatises on music from the ninth and subsequent centuries, music theorists expressed the opinion that time should theoretically be divided into very short and very long units. In neither case, however, did this theoretical concept led to a clear and comprehensible segmentation of time, as divisions with not too short and not too long values might have done. The problem of organizing time occupied many Arabian music theorists during the Middle Ages. Thus, in the tenth century, al-Fārābī ascertained that the unit with which time was to be measured should be indivisible. He was convinced that this indivisible unit of measure, because of its shortness, could only be perceived when double its value was presented. He defined the unit of measure as the time span between two beats or tones that would allow room for no other pulse between them. Thus, what is measured is the distance between two impulses, comparable to the distance between two points on a straight line in geometry. When one proceeds from musical practice, musical time can be represented graphically by a straight line that is broken up by points (sound or beat impulses) at more or less regular intervals. To this quantitative dissection of time, music theorists added, as a qualitative factor, accentuation, which gives temporal organization its definitive profile.

In contemporary musical practice, this rhythmic-temporal organization is still carried out in the way music theorists of the tenth century conceived it. Some rhythmic patterns of contemporary Arabian music can be clearly derived from patterns similar to those discussed by al-Fārābī. Already during the time of the Early Arabian Classical School of the seventh to ninth centuries, the singing was accompanied by an underlying rhythmic pattern that was handed down to posterity, together with the song text and the mode of the piece. Especially with the muwashshaḥāt (refer to chapter 5), the practice of identifying the composition by naming the rhythmic cycle can still be found today.

It would not, however, be accurate to state as a general principle that Arabian music is always accompanied by a rhythmic pattern. On the contrary, one must distinguish between genres with a free rhythmic-temporal organization and those with a fixed one.

Genres with a Free Rhythmic-Temporal Organization

Some genres of Arabian music have a rhythmic-temporal structure that lacks regularly recurring measures and motives and does not display a fixed meter (pulse). Defined by a free quantitative and qualitative division of time, the rhythmic-temporal event cannot be reduced to lowest coefficients (as 1, 2, 3) and their combinations within recurring measures (long:short = 2:1, 3:1, 4:1, 3:2, 4:2, 4:3); rather, it can be expressed—independent of recurring measures—only through larger coefficients (5, 6, 7, 8, 9, etc.) and their endless combinations (long:short = 5:2, 7:3, 11:9, 13:5, 14:3, etc.). Decisive for the profile of this free segmentation of time are the personal style and playing technique of the performer—not least because genres with free rhythmic-temporal organization are generally performed as solos, and only rarely are they accompanied by a drone or an ostinato. Here, we experience the maqām phenomenon in its purest form.

Genres with a Fixed Rhythmic-Temporal Organization

Other genres have a fixed rhythmic-temporal organization, with clear, compact, regularly recurring measures, resulting in an organized, easily recognizable segmentation of time. The musical pieces are performed by an ensemble and are the work of one composer. The composition is based upon a rhythmic pattern that is performed by a percussion instrument. The structure of this pattern corresponds largely to the rhythmic structure of the measures.

The rhythmic pattern in Arabian music is called *wazn* (literally "measure") and is also known by the names *uṣūl*, *mīzān*, and *ḍarb*. A *wazn* consists of a regularly recurring sequence of two or more time segments. Each time segment is made up of at least two beats, or *naqarāt* (plural of *naqrah*), which can be long or short, accented or less accented. Because of the quantitative and qualitative setting surrounding each individual beat, the wazn is perceived during the performance as a distinct period. The time segments of a wazn can be equal or unequal in length. A wazn with six beats, for example, could be composed of two equal segments having three beats each (3+3) or of unequal segments having, say, four beats and two (4+2). A wazn containing eight beats could be made up of three different time segments (e.g., 3+2+3). The first beat of a wazn is usually accented.

The Arabian wazn repertoire includes approximately one hundred different cycles, some of which comprise as many as 176 units of time. The longer a wazn, the more difficult it is to recognize it as a cycle. Most *awzān* (plural of *wazn*) appear in Turkish as well as in Arabian music.

Musicians learn the wazn repertoire of traditional Arabian music by memorizing, with the aid of onomatopoetic syllables, the sequence of beats and rests contained in each time segment. Every beat is represented by one of two types of drumstroke: *dum*, which is produced at the center of the drumskin, or *tak*, which is produced at its edge. The notation for these beats is 0 for dum and I for tak. A rest, which is notated with a dot (·), has the same duration as a dum or a tak stroke.

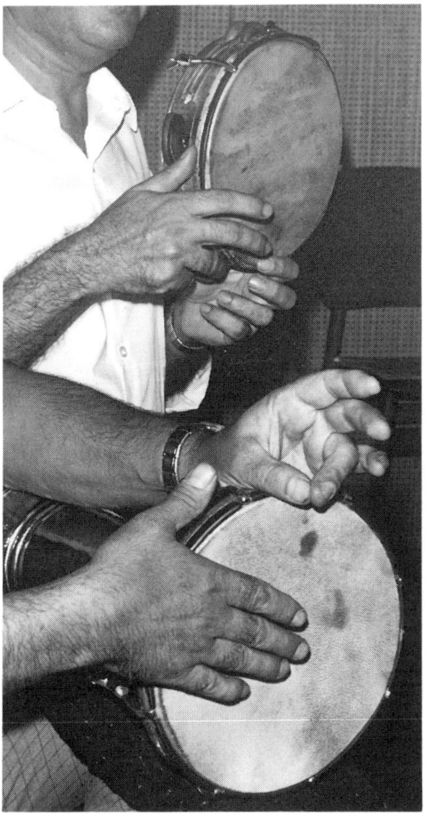

The dum stroke on the darabukkah and riqq. Photo: H. H. Touma.

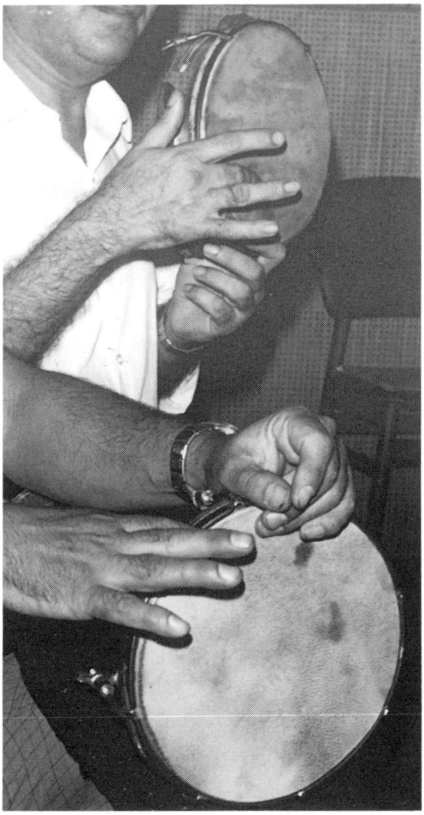

The tak stroke on the darabukkah and riqq. Photo: H. H. Touma.

Two consecutive strokes that are performed staccato must be both dum or both tak. If, however, the second stroke is less strongly accented and played legato, then it is called a *mah* (when it follows a dum) or a *kah* (when it follows a tak). The mah and kah strokes have the same notation (0 and I) as the dum and tak strokes.

Generally only one stroke is played for each unit of time, but occasionally a single unit may encompass two strokes, as indicated in musical notation by a tie (*ribāṭ*) between the two symbols. Wazn structures are performed on the goblet drum (*darabukkah*), the frame drum (*riqq* or *ṭār*), or the pair of kettle drums (*naqqārāt*).

Following are selected awzān of Arabian music:

1. wazn *waḥdah sāyirah* (4/4). Four beats constitute one time segment.

2. wazn *waḥdah* (4/8). Four beats constitute one time segment.

3. wazn *darj* (4/4). Four beats constitute one time segment.

4. wazn *maṣmūdī kabīr* (8/4). Eight beats constitute two time segments (4 + 4).

5. wazn *mukhammas* (16/4). Sixteen beats constitute three time segments (6 + 6 + 4).

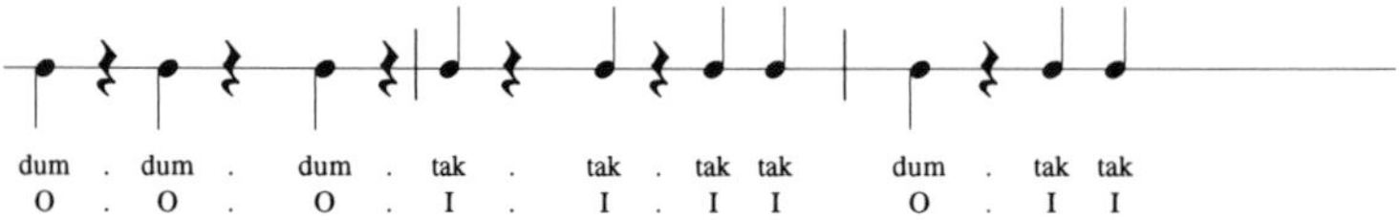

6. wazn *samāʿī dārij* (3/4). Three beats constitute one time segment.

7. wazn *khlāṣ* (6/8). Six beats constitute two time segments (4 + 2).

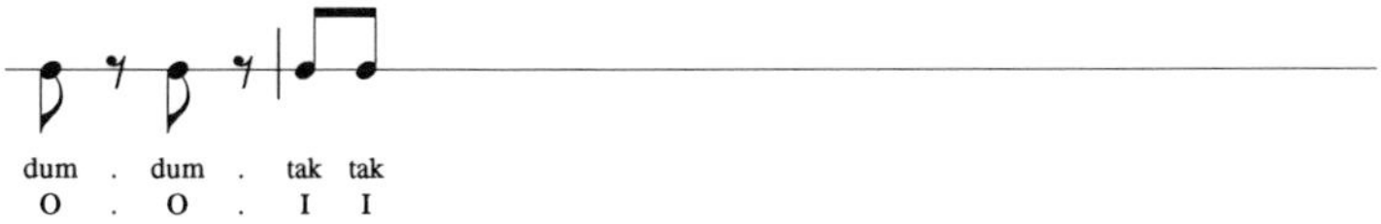

8. wazn *al-basīṭ* (6/4). Six beats constitute two time segments (4 + 2).

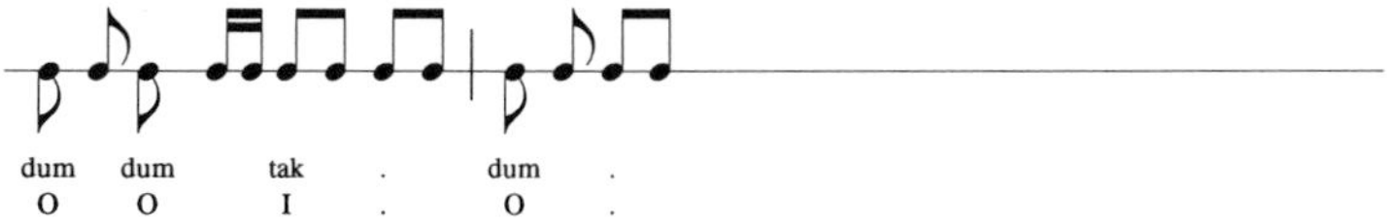

9. wazn *al-qāyim wa-niṣf* (8/4). Eight beats constitute three time segments (3 + 2 + 3).

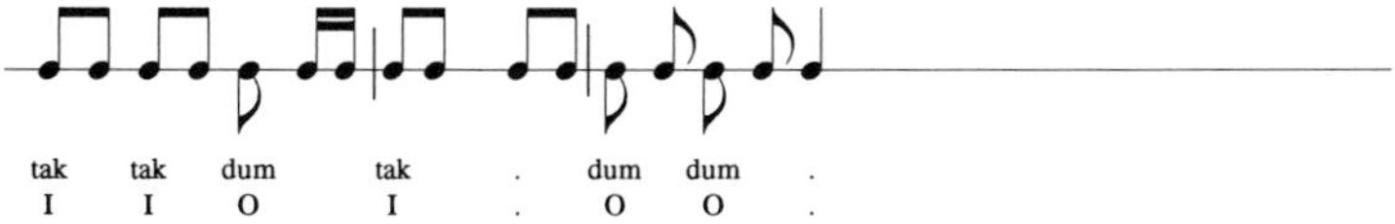

10. wazn *bṭāyḥī* (8/4). Eight beats constitute four time segments (2 + 3 + 2 + 1).

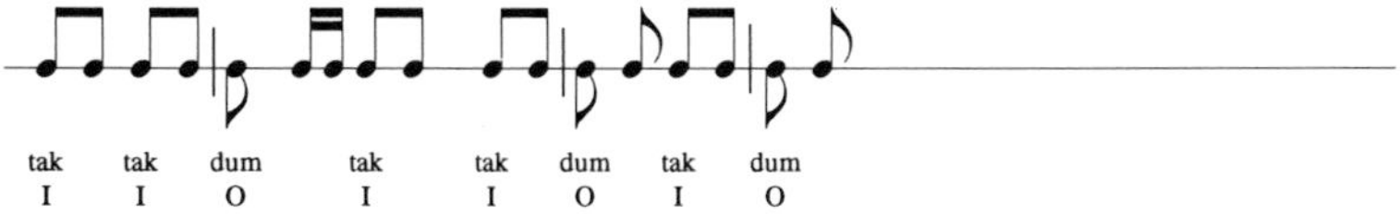

11. wazn *aqsāq* (*aʿraj*) (**9/8**). Nine beats constitute three time segments (**4 + 2 + 3**).

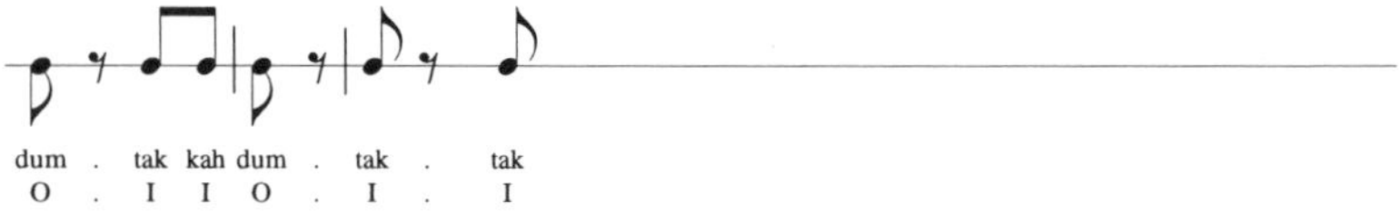

12. wazn *mudawwar* (**12/4**). Twelve beats constitute three time segments (**4 + 6 + 2**).

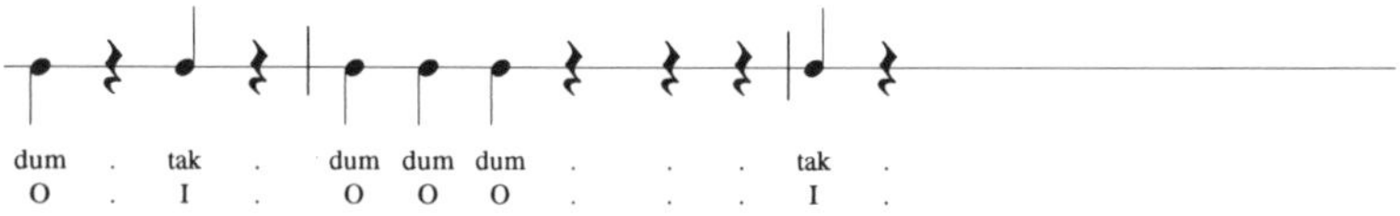

13. wazn *samāʿī thaqīl* (**10/8**). Ten beats constitute two time segments (**5 + 5**).

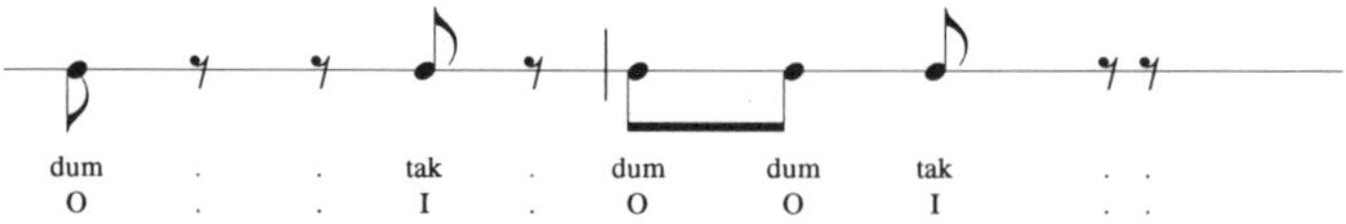

14. wazn *aqsāq samāʿī* (**10/8**). Ten beats constitute two time segments (**5 + 5**).

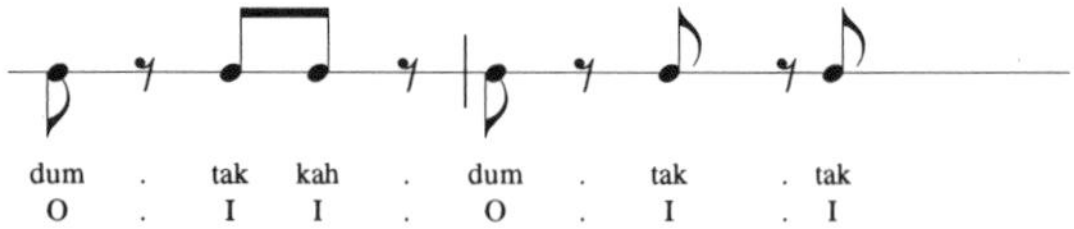

15. wazn *dawr hindī* (**7/8**). Seven beats constitute two time segments (**3 + 4**).

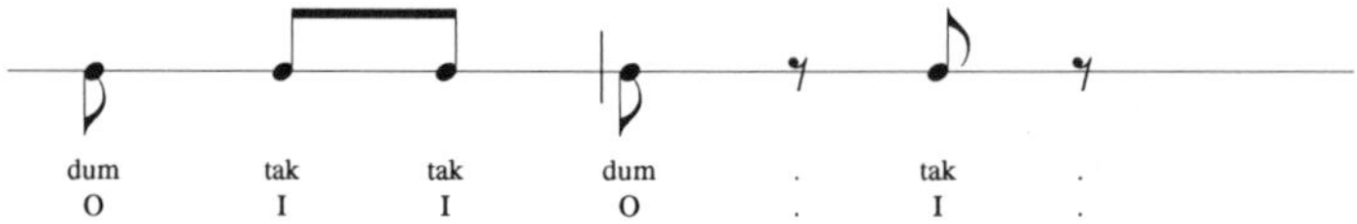

16. wazn *muḥajjar* (14/4). Fourteen beats constitute four time segments (4 + 2 + 2 + 6).

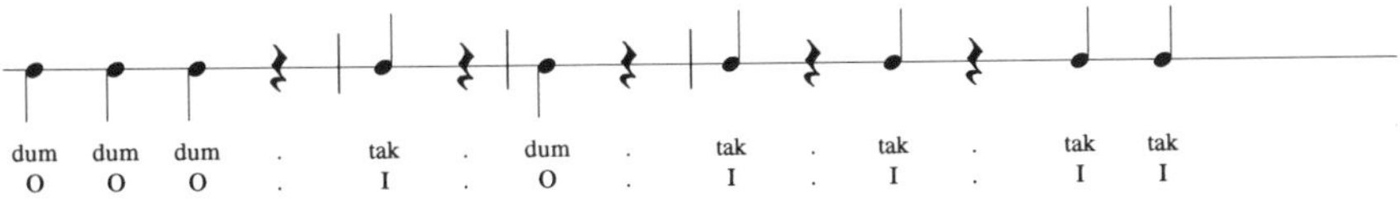

17. wazn *al-ʿawīṣ* (11/4). Eleven beats constitute three time segments (3 + 3 + 5).

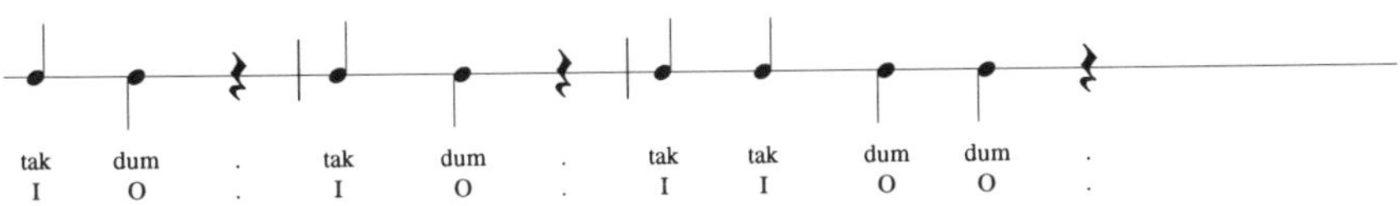

18. wazn *al-murabbaʿ* (13/4). Thirteen beats constitute three time segments (3 + 6 + 4).

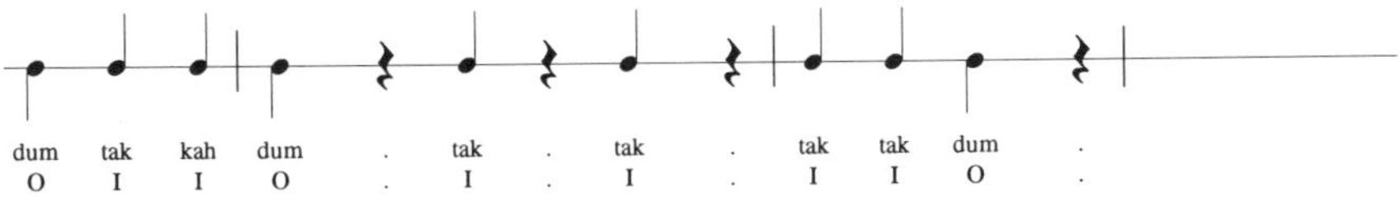

19. wazn *ẓarāfāt* (13/8). Thirteen beats constitute four time segments (3 + 3 + 2 + 5).

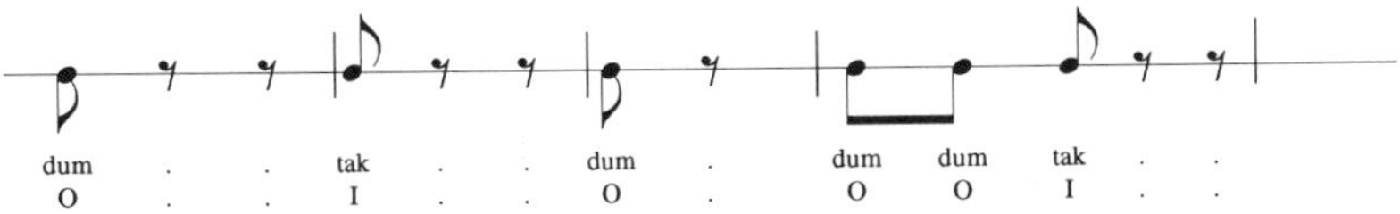

20. wazn *awfar* (19/4). Nineteen beats constitute four time segments (6 + 4 + 2 + 7).

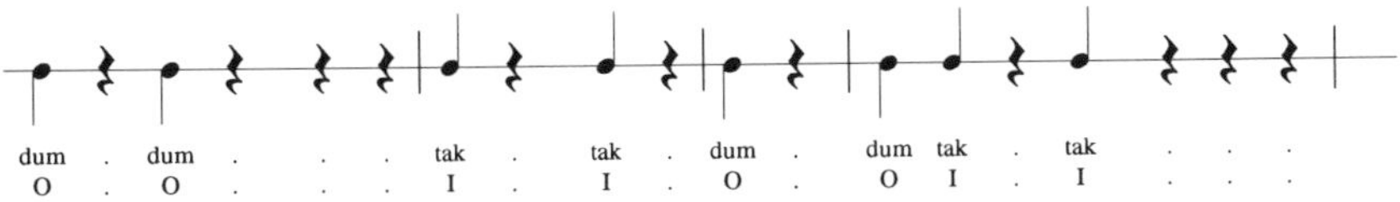

21. wazn *muraṣṣa' shāmī* (**19/8**). Nineteen beats constitute four time segments (**4 + 5 + 4 + 6**).

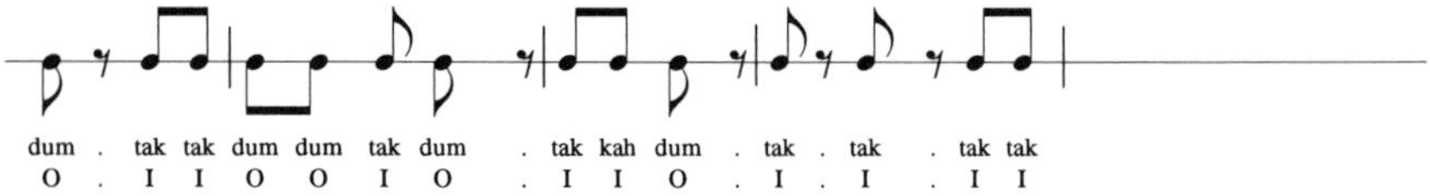

22. wazn *samāḥ* (**36/4**). Thirty-six beats constitute five time segments (**12 + 8 + 4 + 8 + 4**).

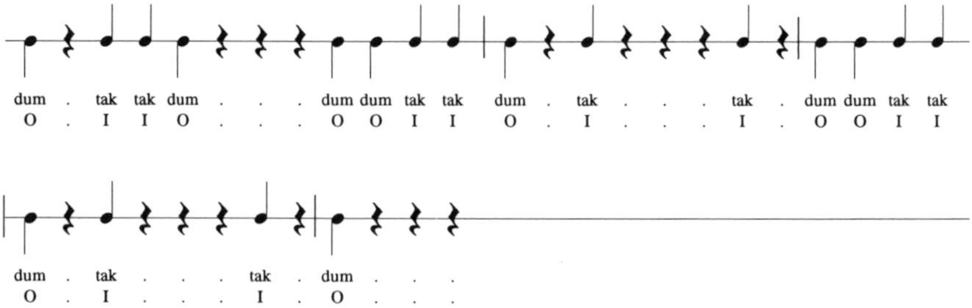

5

Genres of Secular Art Music

Al-maqām al-ʿirāqī

The *maqām al-ʿirāqī* is considered the most noble and perfect form of the maqām. As the name implies, it is native to Iraq; it has been known for approximately four hundred years in Baghdad, Mosul, and Kirkuk. The maqām al-ʿirāqī has been passed on orally through the Iraqi masters of the maqām, who cultivate the form especially in Baghdad. The maqām is performed by a singer (*qāriʾ*) and three instrumentalists playing *sanṭūr* (box zither), *jūzah* (spike fiddle), and *ṭablah* or *dunbak* (goblet drum). Sometimes a fourth instrument, a *riqq* (tambourine), also joins in. *Jālghī baghdādī* is the name of this ensemble, *al-maqām al-ʿirāqī* the name of the musical genre. At the center of a maqām al-ʿirāqī is a sung poem written either in one of the sixteen meters of classical Arabic or in Iraqi dialect. In the latter case, the poem is called *zuhayrī*.

A maqām al-ʿirāqī performance usually begins with the *taḥrīr*, comprising one or more vocal passages that either have no text or consist of Arabic, Persian, or Turkish words (*ākh-khayya, yār yār, amān*). The taḥrīr presents the nucleus of the maqām and establishes its emotional content. Following the introductory passages, the singer and instrumentalists alternately improvise rhythmically free melodic passages through increasingly higher tone levels. In some maqāmāt, the taḥrīr is

Jālghī baghdādī ensemble, Iraq. Photo: H. H. Touma.

preceded by an instrumental introduction of fixed meter. At times it is completely replaced by a *badwah*, a vocal introduction in which short and long tones are juxtaposed by the singer in alternately high and low registers.

As a rule, the first tone level to be presented highlights the beginning tone of the chosen maqām row. Then, one by one, the other phases and tone levels of the maqām are realized. The highest tone level marks the climax of the performance and is immediately followed by the *taslūm*, a descending melodic passage that leads directly to the *finalis* of the maqām row.

Maqāmāt such as the bayāt and ḥusaynī are presented without the rhythmic accompaniment of percussion instruments, whereas performances of maqāmāt such as the ibrāhīmī and nawā always have rhythmic accompaniment. The patterns played by the goblet drum or frame drum sound continuously from beginning to end, as in the maqām sīkāh, or are only intermittently heard, as in the maqāmāt rāst and ṣabā. The wazn yugrig whose rhythmic pattern is organized as follows:

accompanies the maqām jabbūrī with the maqām row:

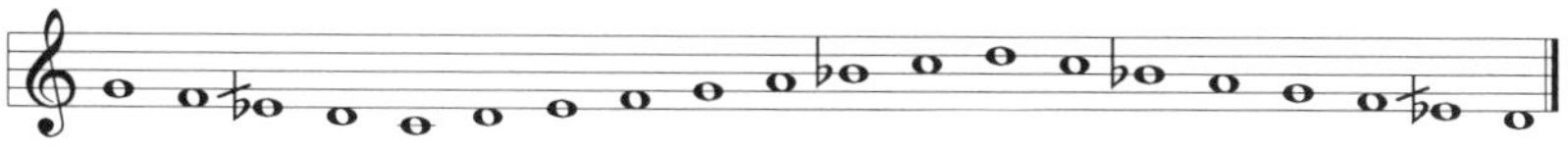

whereas the wazn waḥdah with the following pattern:

belongs to the maqām ūrfah with the maqām row:

There is no correspondence between the free rhythmic-temporal organization of the singer's improvised melodic line and the regular rhythmic organization of the accompaniment.

A complete maqām concert, called a *faṣl*, is composed of a number of maqām realizations whose sequence is fixed. The faṣl is named after the first maqām presented. The Arabian repertoire of the maqām al-ʿirāqī includes five *fuṣūl* (plural of *faṣl*), namely, bayāt, ḥijāz, rāst, nawā, and ḥusaynī.

At the end of each individual maqām presentation within a faṣl, the ensemble sings a song of fixed meter (*bastah*) to give the singer a chance to rest before presenting the next maqām. After all the maqāmāt of a faṣl have been presented, the entire ensemble takes a long break before beginning the next faṣl.

The Repertoire of the Maqām al-ʿIrāqī

The Five Fuṣūl

faṣl al-bayāt and its maqāmāt
- bayāt
- nārī
- ṭāhir
- maḥmūdī
- sīkāh
- mukhālif
- ḥlīlāwī

faṣl al-ḥijāz and its maqāmāt
- ḥijāz dīwān
- qūriyāt
- ʿuraybūn ʿajam
- ibrāhīmī
- ḥadīdī

faṣl ar-rāst and its maqāmāt
- rāst
- manṣūrī
- ḥijāz shīṭānī
- jabbūrī
- khanabāt

faṣl an-nawā and its maqāmāt
- nawā
- msikkīn
- ʿajam ʿashīrān
- panijikāh
- rāshdī

faṣl al-ḥusaynī and its maqāmāt
- ḥusaynī
- dasht
- ūrfah
- arwāḥ
- awj
- ḥakīmī
- ṣabā

The performance of a faṣl lasts three to four hours. In the past, several fuṣūl were performed in one evening. Al-maqām al-ʿirāqī music was performed in a more private setting at the local haunts of famous maqām singers during festive events or on a certain evening of the month, sometimes also the night before a holiday. Alcoholic drinks were served during the performance, as long as it didn't take place during Ramaḍān, the month of fasting. Today the "local haunt" of the maqām singer is in front of a radio microphone or television camera. A great maqām singer is also looked up to as an authority on the subject of the maqām al-ʿirāqī. His musical talent is evidenced first and foremost through his mastery of the entire maqām al-ʿirāqī repertoire and secondly in his ability to give an especially distinctive rendition of a maqām or several maqāmāt.

The musical tradition of the maqām al-ʿirāqī has been passed down orally by the great masters of the maqām in an unbroken chain of transmission leading up to the present. The oldest maqām singer whose biographical data are known to us is Mullā Ḥasan Bābūjidjī (ca. 1760–1840), who counted the famous Raḥmallāh Shiltāgh (1799–1840) among his students. Shiltāgh was of Kurdish or Turkish extraction and was regarded as one of the greatest maqām singers of the nineteenth century. He was instrumental in the development and propagation of the maqām al-ʿirāqī. After his beloved, an Armenian named Yaʿqūb, left him and emigrated to Tiflīs, he created a new maqām, the maqām tiflīs, which is still performed today. Legend has it that Raḥmallah Shiltāgh died just as he reached the highest phase of the maqām ibrāhīmī, on the tone jawāb rāst (c''), when an old wound burst open from the exertion.

An entire generation of maqām singers looked up to Raḥmallah Shiltāgh, among them Aḥmad Zaydān and Mullā ʿUthmān al-Mawṣilī. Aḥmad Zaydān (1833–1912) also created new maqāmāt and developed new forms of the taḥrīr and badwah introductions. A number of twentieth-century maqām singers, including Rashīd Qandarjī (d. 1945) and ʿAbbās Shaykhalī, owe their fame and musical ability to him and the school that he founded. Mullā ʿUthmān al-Mawṣilī (1845–1923) demonstrated his exceptional artistry in the rendition of religious song traditions as well. His performances fascinated audiences in Baghdad as well as in Istanbul, in Damascus as well as in Cairo, where the singer, who had in the meantime become blind, was often wont to appear. Included among the great maqām al-ʿirāqī singers of today are Muḥammad Qabbānjī (b. 1901–1989), Ḥāj Hāshim ar-Rajab (b. 1920), Yūsuf ʿUmar (1918–1986), Majīd Rashīd (b. 1915), ʿAbbās al-Qassām (b. 1917), and Ḥusayn Ismāʿīl (b. 1952).

Analysis of a Maqām al-ʿIrāqī Performance in the Maqām Manṣūrī

The example presented here is performed by the jālghī baghdādī ensemble of the Radio Station in Baghdad.[1] The singer Yūsuf ʿUmar recites a love poem written in classical Arabic with four five-line stanzas following the rhyme scheme:

aaaaz
bbbbz
ccccz
ddddz

The first line of the poem reads: *yā yūsufa l-ḥusn, fīka aṣ-ṣabbu qadīmā* ("Yūsuf, thou beautiful! For a long time I have been in love with you."). The drummers enter with the wazn samāḥ, which consists of thirty-six beats, later changing over to the wazn yugrig, with twelve beats.

The manṣūrī is the second maqām of the faṣl ar-rāst and is presented immediately after the maqām rāst itself. The manṣūrī maqām row reads as follows:

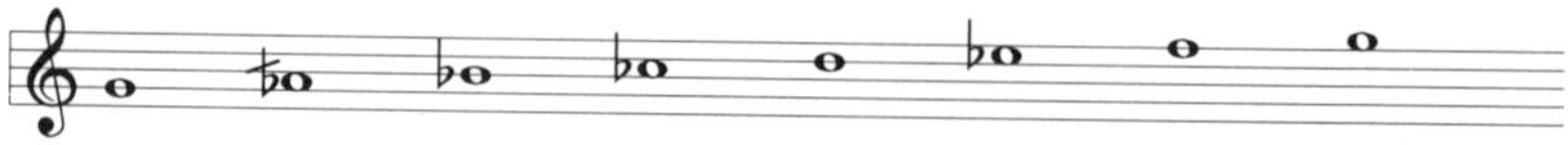

Following the manṣūrī are the maqāmāt ḥijāz shīṭānī, jabbūrī, and khanabāt. Whereas the maqām rāst has the tone c as its *finalis*, the next two maqāmāt, manṣūrī and hijāz shīṭānī, have their cadence on g, and the maqām khanabāt and jabbūri

1 Recording: *Arabian Music: Maqam.* UNESCO Collection MUSICAL SOURCES. Philips 6586 006, Side 2, No. 1.

lead to the *finalis* d. The riqq and darabukkah players perform throughout most of the faṣl; only a portion of the maqām rāst has no rhythmic accompaniment. Whereas the poems for four of the five maqāmāt are written in classical Arabic, a colloquial *zuhayrī* poem is sung to the maqām ḥijāz shīṭānī.

This particular maqām rendition of the manṣūrī lasts fifteen minutes and encompasses eighteen musical structural sections (see the transcription on pages 61–67). The performance begins with an instrumental piece of fixed meter in the wazn samāḥ, which consists of thirty-six beats and is repeated two times. Already in this first section, all seven tones of the maqām row are sounded, and the characteristic structural intervals of the manṣūrī are immediately accessible to the listener. These intervals include the diminished fourth g–c♭, the medium second g–a𝄳 or a𝄳–b♭, the augmented second d'–c♭ and not least, the major whole tone f–g. In this opening section, the tone g, the first tone of the maqām row, is strongly accented. At this point in time, the first tone level of the maqām performance has also already been realized on g.

The following musical sections can be distinguished:

1. The performance begins with an instrumental introduction in the wazn samāḥ.

Instrumental melodic passage in the wazn samāḥ.

2. Next, the soloist, the qāri' al-maqām, enters with the taḥrīr section (0' 59"). He utilizes the tonal area above the melodic axis g, g–c♭, as well as the tonal area below that same axis, g–d.

Taḥrīr.

3. The fixed-meter instrumental opening section is repeated (1' 36").

etc.

4. The first two lines of the first five-line stanza are sung, whereby the singer elaborates upon a selection of the tones that were presented in the taḥrīr (2' 10").

First stanza (first and second lines of verse).

5. The fixed-meter instrumental opening section is repeated again (2' 40").

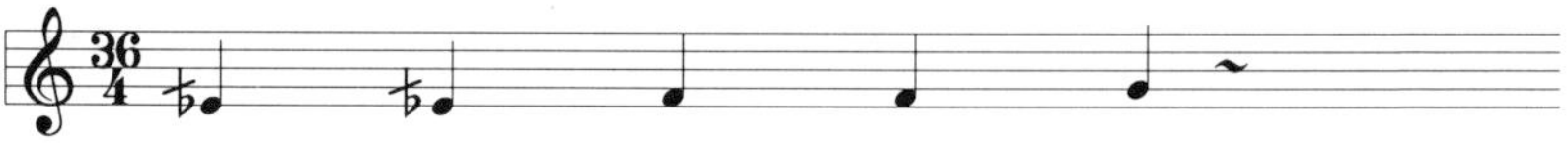

etc.

6. The singer develops a tone level on c and emphasizes the tonal area c'–g. It is within this tonal area that the remaining three lines of the first stanza of poetry are presented—beginning in the maqām bayāt and ending in the maqām manṣūrī. In the manṣūrī section, a tone level on g' later comes to the fore and the singer focuses on the tonal area c♭'–g (3' 09").

The first word of the third line of verse, third, fourth, and fifth lines of verse.

7. The spike fiddle, jūzah, begins with a melodic passage that prepares a tone level on c' and then musically establishes the maqām manṣūrī (3' 54"). The singer presents the entire second stanza of poetry on the tone level g and, in so doing, emphasizes the structural interval f–g, the tonal area c'–g and the tone level c'. At the same time he shifts from the maqām bayātī to the maqām manṣūrī. Thus, here too, the stanza of poetry ends in the maqām manṣūrī. This same process was previously observed in the sixth section.

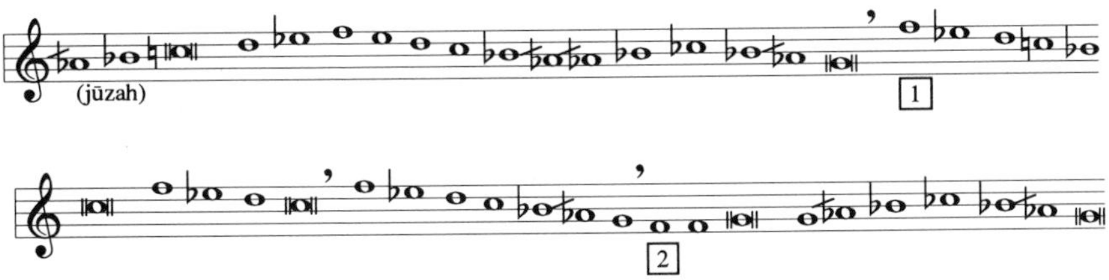

Second stanza:

1 Āy and first word of first line of verse. 2 First through fifth lines of verse.

8. The fixed-meter instrumental opening section is repeated again (6' 21").

9. The entire third stanza of the poem is sung (6' 45"). In its tonal range, its tone-level structures, and its tonal-spatial emphasis, this section is similar to section seven.

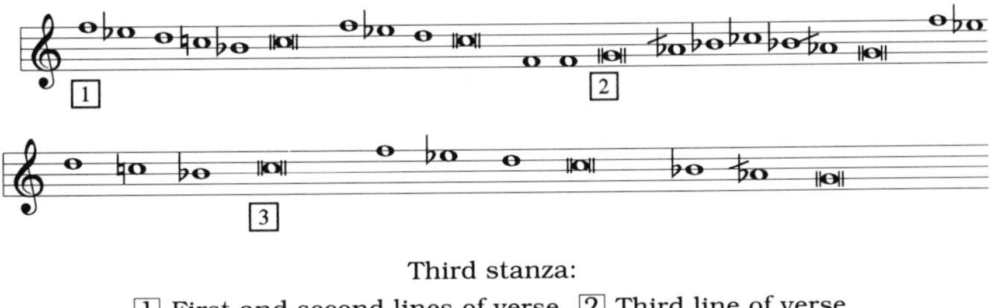

Third stanza:

1 First and second lines of verse. 2 Third line of verse.

3 Fourth and fifth lines of verse.

10. The tone levels built on g and c' are presented anew. At the same time, the first four lines of the fourth stanza of poetry are sung (7' 46").

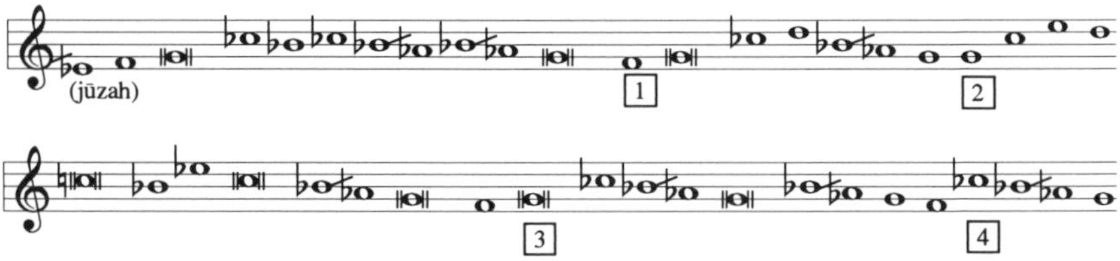

Fourth stanza:
[1] Āy. [2] First and second lines of verse. [3] Third and fourth lines of verse aman. [4] Bidādim.

11. An instrumental intermezzo is performed (9' 28") to rhythmic accompaniment in the wazn yugrig (twelve beats). This is a fixed-meter melodic passage that stands in certain contrast to the succeeding free-meter section. The tone levels d and d–g are emphasized.

Instrumental melodic passage in the wazn yugrig.

12. The fourth stanza of poetry is sung again. In this twelfth section, the maqām performance reaches its first climax (9' 55"). This phase, designated as ṣayḥah, is the first to be presented in a high register. The singer develops a tone level on g' as well as the tonal areas g'–d' and a'–g'. This is in fact

the highest tone level of the maqām manṣūrī altogether. At this point, lines four and five of the fourth stanza of poetry are presented.

First ṣayḥah (mayānah):
[1] Āy wāy. [2] Fourth line of verse. [3] Fifth line of verse of the fourth stanza.

13. The ensemble strikes up the so-called *mathnawī*, a fixed-meter instrumental piece that presents the tone level c' in the tonal region of f'-e♭'-d'-b-a (11' 03").

Mathnawī (instrumental intermezzo).

14. The tone material of the mathnawī section is developed further—here, however, in non-metered form. The fourth stanza of poetry is presented as a whole (11' 23").

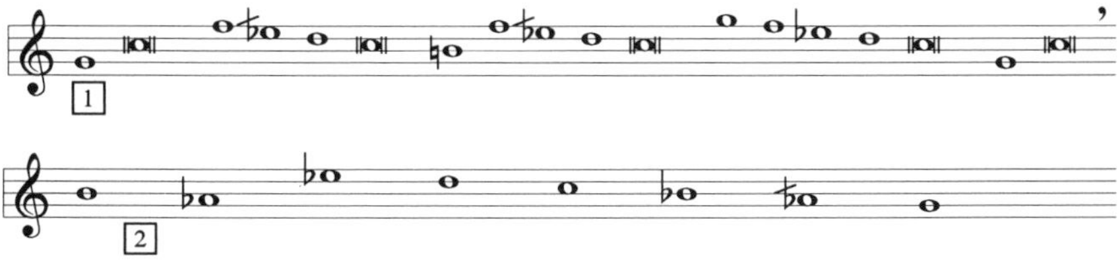

Fourth stanza: [1] First through fifth lines of verse. [2] Amān bidādim.

15. A repeat of the head from section eleven in the wazn yugrig follows (12' 25").

Head of the instrumental intermezzo in the wazn yugrig.

16. This passage is immediately succeeded by the second musical climax of the maqām performance, the second mayānah (ṣayḥah) phase in the upper register (12' 33"). The text sung is the same that was heard together with the first mayānah phase, namely the fourth and fifth lines of stanza four. Whereas that one ended on g in the maqām manṣūrī, this one concludes with the words *amān, amān* on d'.

Second ṣayḥah (mayānah): Fourth and fifth lines of verse of the fourth stanza.

17. The wazn yugrig returns with a vocal passage in which the tonal area d'–g is developed (13' 16"). At this point, the singer resorts to Persian words that do not belong to the actual poem. In place of the Persian *jurdām jūn bābī* ("My soul"), however, the Arabian *mā tadrūn anā maftūn* ("Don't you see how enchanted I am") can also appear. The musicians call this section *mathlath* or *mathlathah* (triangle).

Mathlath.

18. The closing section presents the third and last mayānah (ṣayḥah) on g' (14' 04"). The performance of the maqām manṣūrī finally concludes with a descending melodic line c♭'-b♭-a♭-g, the so-called *taslīm* (*taslūm*), which ends on the maqām's *finalis*, g.

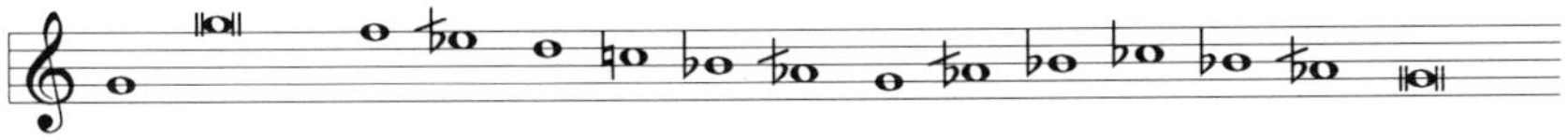

Final ṣayḥah (mayānah) and taslīm (taslūm).

Viewed as a whole, the maqām manṣūrī can be reduced to the following melodic framework:

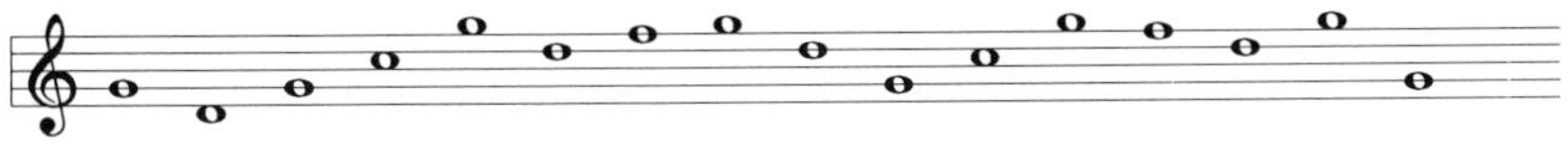

The Andalusī Nūbah

The *andalusī nūbah* (classical Arabic: *nawbah*) is a genre of Arabian music that belongs to the Maghrib states of North Africa (Morocco, Algeria, Tunisia, Libya), as opposed to the Mashriq states (Syria, Lebanon, Egypt, Iraq, and Jordan, as well as the states of the Arabian Peninsula). *Maghrib* means, literally, "place of the sunset" or "time of sunset," whereas *mashriq* means "place of the sunrise" or "time of sunrise." During the ninth and tenth centuries, Baghdad was to Mashriq what Qurṭubah (Córdoba) was to Maghrib: the political as well as the cultural center, where the sciences and, especially among the arts, music flourished. Beside Córdoba, Granada in particular represented the center of cultural life of the Umayads in Spain. In those days, the Arabs called Spain *al-andalus*. Thus, the term *andalusī nūbah* leaves no doubt as to the origin of this musical form.

Today, the andalusī nūbah is an important authentic music tradition in Morocco, Algeria, and Tunisia, a tradition that came to Córdoba and Granada from Baghdad in the ninth century, and with the expulsion of the Arabs from Spain during the thirteenth, fifteenth, and seventeenth centuries, found a new home in North Africa. The musical form of the nūbah consists of several vocal and instrumental pieces. The vocal parts, which are always accompanied instrumentally, predominate. All sections of a nūbah are based on one and the same *ṭabʿ*. The terms *ṭabʿ* and *maqām* denote very similar phenomena. Besides belonging to the same *ṭabʿ*, each section nevertheless has its own specific rhythmic pattern (mīzān).

As early as the ninth century, a musician or singer wishing to perform in front of the caliph was required to wait behind a curtain until he received the order to play or sing from the "curtain man" (*sattār*). It was said that the artist was waiting for his turn (*nawbah*), that is, for his turn to perform the vocal or instrumental piece that he had prepared. The performance piece itself was also referred to as *nawbah*, and the term eventually replaced the word *ṣawt*, which had been used in the early Arabian tradition of the Ḥijāz.

In the ninth century, Ziryāb, the great singer at the court of Hārūn ar-Rashīd, left Baghdad after a quarrel with his teacher, Isḥāq al-Mawṣilī, and emigrated to al-andalus. He founded a music school in Córdoba where he carried on the musical tradition of the Early Arabian Classical School of Baghdad—not, however, without liberating it from its classicism and creating a new form of the nūbah. The singers, in accordance with Ziryāb's instructions, were now required to adhere exactly to a specific sequence of songs and their tempos. During Ziryāb's time, the performance of a nūbah was already realized with a uniform maqām row and with the use of several rhythmic wazn patterns.

Ziryāb's school in Córdoba quickly attained far-reaching influence. In Seville, Toledo, Valencia, and Granada, his teachings were a guiding light, and newly established music schools everywhere turned Ziryāb's innovations into practice. The andalusī nūbah of the present day is still performed in North Africa in the same way as it was described in the literature of Ziryāb's time. Nevertheless, in the current musical practice of North Africa, there are at least three distinct nūbah styles, all of which have been handed down by the great masters of the andalus. In Tunisia can be found the old style of early Seville; in Algeria, that of Córdoba; and in Morocco, that of Granada and Valencia.

In its various formal sections, the nūbah is characterized by a systematic heightening of the rhythmic-temporal intensity. Whereas the tempo within each formal section increases, the awzān assume an ever more simple rhythmic structure.

The formal structure of a nūbah consists of five main sections and varies in North Africa only slightly from country to country. The five main sections are called

in Algeria	*in Tunisia*	*in Morocco*
mṣaddar	bṭāyḥī	basīṭ
bṭāyḥī	barwal	qāyim wa-niṣf
darj	darj	bṭāyḥī
inṣirāf	khafīf	darj
khlāṣ	khatm	quddām

Each of these sections is preceded by a short instrumental piece. The name of a section is taken in each case from the corresponding rhythmic pattern (wazn or mīzān) that identifies the main section in question (see also chapter 4). Thus the bṭāyḥī section, for example, is based on the wazn bṭāyḥī. The nūbah is also known in Tunisia by the name *ma᾽lūf*, in Algeria it is called *ṣanʿah*, and Moroccans speak of *ālah* and *ghirnāṭī*. Originally, twenty-four *nūbāt* (plural of *nūbah*) made up the entire North African repertoire. As early as the nineteenth century, only eleven nūbāt were still known in Morocco, fifteen in Algeria, thirteen in Tunisia, and merely nine in Libya. During the twentieth century, the repertoire has shrunk even further.

The nūbah ensemble is made up of instrumentalists playing the short-necked lute (ʿūd), the bow-necked lute (*rabāb*, *rebec*), the flute (*nāy*), the box zither (*qānūn*), the tambourine (*ṭār*), and the goblet drum (*darabukkah*). The instrumentalists also make up the choir of the ensemble. The vocal sections of a nūbah are sung by a soloist or by the musicians in unison. The poetry performed is in classical Arabic or colloquial Moroccan and describes the love, joy, and sorrow of man, as well as landscapes and drinking scenes.

To start, a free-metered piece is performed either by the ensemble or, less frequently, by one instrumentalist. This piece is variously called *bughyah* or *mishālyah* (in Morocco), *dā᾽irih* or *taqʿīd aṣ-ṣanā᾽iʿ* (in Algeria), and *istiftāḥ* (in Tunisia). The maqām row of the corresponding nūbah is also binding for this introductory piece, which presents the characteristic features of the maqām, or ṭabʿ. Its modal structure as well as the most important phases and tone levels—and with them the emotional mood that characterizes the ṭabʿ—are already present in the opening section. Next comes an instrumental section of fixed rhythm, known in Morocco and Algeria as *tūshyih* and in Tunisia as *mṣaddar*, followed by the previously mentioned five main sections. Each main section theoretically consists of up to forty stanzas, from which a selection is performed. Not until just before each performance does the ensemble select the text to be sung.

The stanzas of the poem that are sung during the performance of an andalusī nūbah have a characteristic form. Those rendered are *muwashshaḥ* stanzas, whose rhyme scheme can look like one of the following:

The Brīhī Ensemble, 1978. Photo: H. H. Touma.

AA bbb AA ccc AA ddd AA . . .
ABAB cdcdcd ABABAB efefef ABAB . . .
ABCABC defdefdef ABCABC . . .

This poetic form, presented here in three variants, is also known by the name *zajal*. Zajal poems, though, are always composed in colloquial Arabic, whereas muwashshaḥ poets avail themselves of classical Arabic.

The Nūbah in Morocco

The following paragraphs focus on the andalusī nūbah of Morocco, with special attention devoted to the nūbah tradition cultivated by the Brīhī school in the city of Fez. Other Moroccan nūbah schools are found in the cities of Rabat and Tetuan.

In Fez, the five main sections of a nūbah are designated basīṭ, qāyim wa-niṣf, bṭāyḥī, darj, and quddām. Also in Fez,

Munshid Muḥammad Bajdūb and ʿūd player Būzubaʿ in 1984; Fez, Morocco. Photo: J. Dietrich.

each section consists of several pieces that are performed vocally to instrumental accompaniment, as well as one or two purely instrumental sections. A cyclic rhythmic accompaniment (called mīzān) with its own characteristic structure identifies each formal section. The rhythmic patterns of the five main sections are organized as follows:

Basīṭ.

Qāyim wa-niṣf.

Bṭāyḥī.

Darj.

Quddām.

 = light stroke

 = heavy stroke

As the outline shows, qāyim wa-niṣf and bṭāyḥī differ in their internal structures, that is, in the distribution of light and heavy beats and rests within cycles of equivalent length. The basic structures form a framework within which rhythmic improvisations are carried out. The sequence of beats, however, remains just as unaffected as the position of the accented heavy beats. The improvisational freedom is rather more clearly felt in the beats containing rests or in those filled by a light drum stroke. The shape of the melody is also tailored to the rhythmic structure of the corresponding section (mīzān).

In the context of oral tradition, the patterns have special didactic functions—as, for example, in the transmission of the nūbah repertoire to the younger generation. Before beginning to learn to sing a ṣanʿah, the student must have a command of the rhythmic patterns, the mīzān. And ultimately the further task of singing the poem clearly while accentuating the rhythmic patterns must be confronted. Students practice in a seated position, using the technique of the *tawsīd*, whereby they strike their thigh with an open hand on the dark strokes and with a fist on the light strokes while reciting in a loud and clear voice. Not until after the completion of this phase of study do they begin to learn the corresponding melodies. At first, the teacher accompanies the student on the ʿūd; later the entire ensemble performs with the singer.

The eleven Moroccan nūbāt are named according to the ṭabʿ in which they are found. The nūbah māyah, for example, is in the ṭabʿ māyah, and likewise the nūbah mashriqī is in the ṭabʿ mashriqī. The tonal hierarchy in the ṭabʿ scale is characteristic of other modal structures in Arabian, Turkish, Persian, and Indian music. The shape of the melody within a nūbah can be influenced considerably by the tonal hierarchy of the corresponding ṭabʿ. A tone that is important in a ṭabʿ can be emphasized by repeating and embellishing it, by reaching it in a leap, and by placing the dynamic accents on it. The ṭabʿ row of the nūbah māyah is as follows:

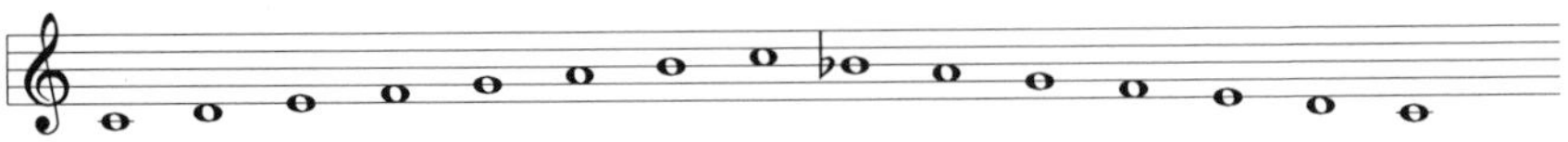

The most important tones of the ṭabʿ māyah are c, e, g, and c'. Although the c' dominates, the e and especially the tonal areas g–e and e–g are clearly in the foreground. For comparison, the tone row of the ṭabʿ mashriqī is presented as follows:

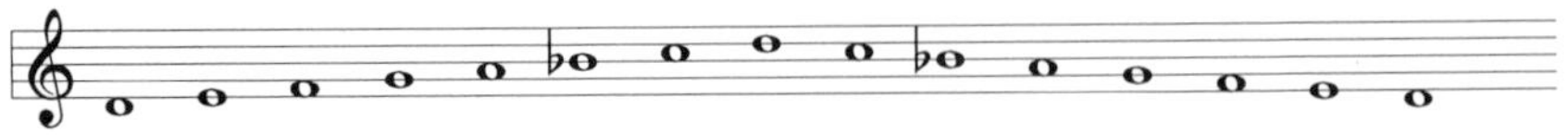

The most important tones here are d, f, and d'. The most prominent position in the hierarchy is occupied by the tone d, followed by f. Less important, though still clearly emphasized, are the tonal area d–f and the tone d'.

The poem that is sung during a nūbah performance is called ṣanʿah ("craft"). The poetic genre of the song text is known as muwashshaḥ. The muwashshaḥ was invented in the ninth century A.D. by Muqaddam al-Qabrī in al-andalus and further developed there as a poetic musical form before it also came to be appreciated in the eastern regions of the Arabian world, the Mashriq states of Egypt, Syria, and Iraq. Characteristic of the muwashshaḥ poem of North Africa is that, although it is composed in classical Arabic, it is not based on any of the sixteen classical meters of Arabian poetry. Furthermore, the muwashshaḥ poem does not exhibit any fixed sequence of stress and arsis; instead, the accents are grouped to conform to a specific musical-rhythmic pattern (wazn). Thus, linguistic and musical rhythm in the North African muwashshaḥ are inseperably linked. The musical form ABA is analagous to the poetic form AAbbbA(AA). The term *ṣanʿah*, however, not only designates the poem but also the musical section in which the poem is sung. In each ṣanʿah, the tones and tonal areas characteristic of the ṭabʿ are developed musically. Here the singer assumes the leading role. Whereas the instrumentalists indeed also sing, the part of the soloist often appears an octave higher than the choir part.

The nūbah form of Morocco may be represented schematically as follows:

The individual sections of a Moroccan nūbah and their performance durations

Basīṭ (6/𝅗𝅥)	Qāyim wa-niṣf (8/𝅗𝅥)	Bṭāyhī (8/𝅗𝅥)	Darj (4/𝅗𝅥)	Quddām (3/𝅗𝅥)
bughya	bughya	bughya	bughya	bughya
1st ṣanʿah	1st ṣanʿah	1st ṣanʿah	1st ṣanʿah	1st ṣanʿah
2nd ṣanʿah	2nd ṣanʿah	2nd ṣanʿah	2nd ṣanʿah	2nd ṣanʿah
3rd ṣanʿah	3rd ṣanʿah	3rd ṣanʿah	3rd ṣanʿah	3rd ṣanʿah
13th ṣanʿah	10th ṣanʿah	13th ṣanʿah	20th ṣanʿah	30th ṣanʿah
14th ṣanʿah	11th ṣanʿah	14th ṣanʿah	21st ṣanʿah	31st ṣanʿah
30–70 minutes	30–60 minutes	40–70 minutes	20–40 minutes	15–30 minutes

Each nūbah section (mīzān) is composed of several *ṣanʿāt* (plural of *ṣanʿah*). During longer performances, the entire text of a ṣanʿah is sung. If time does not allow for such a complete performance, however, the text, but not the melody, may be shortened. The melody of a ṣanʿah is always to be performed in its entirety.

The individual ṣanʿāt follow one another seamlessly without pause or other kind of caesura. For the uninitiated listener, the nūbah appears to be an unending melody, without profile or contrasts. Within each nūbah, however, there are musical passages and text segments that are especially popular among the audience; these are clamored for over and over again during the performance. The continuous increase in tempo within each main section results, moreover, in the last ṣanʿāt being performed in a distinctly faster tempo than was the first.

Analysis of the Basīṭ Section (Mīzān al-Basīṭ) of a Nūbah Māyah Performance from Morocco

The following analysis concerns the first ṣanʿah of the basīṭ section of the nūbah māyah and the free-metered instrumental piece (bughyah) that precedes it.[1] The sections represent an excerpt from a performance by the Brīhī Ensemble (Fez). The director of the ensemble is Ḥāj ʿAbd al-Karīm Rayyis, who also performed on the rabāb (bow-necked lute). Muḥammad Bajdūb participated as solo singer (*munshid*) on this recording.

1 Recording: *Andalusian Music from Morocco.* Harmonia Mundi. EMI IC 2 LP 153 16 9525 3, Side 3.

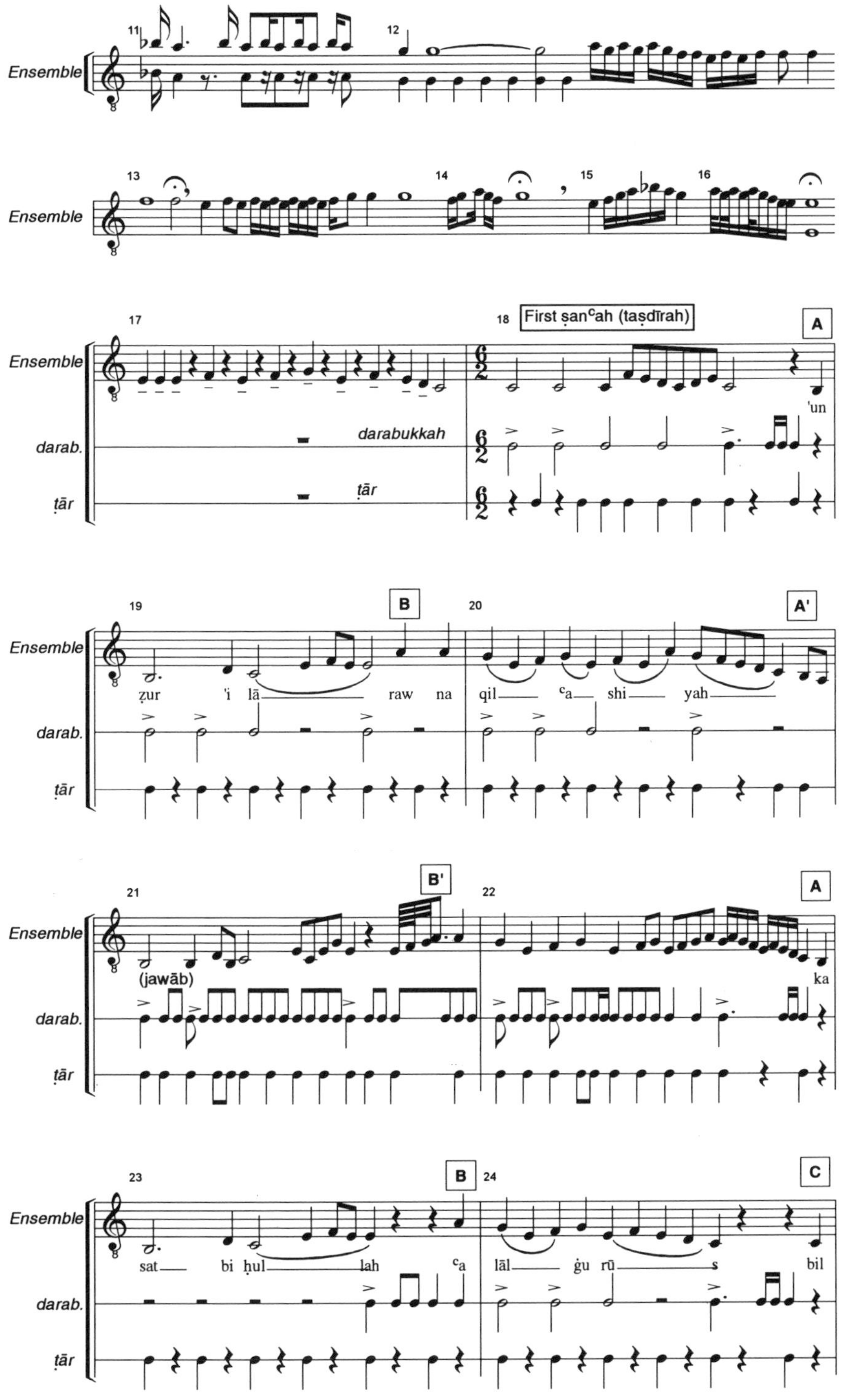
Ensemble
First ṣanᶜah (taṣdīrah)
A
darabukkah
ṭār
darab.
'un
B
A'
ẓur 'i lā raw na
qil ᶜa shi yah
B'
(jawāb)
ka
B
C
sat bi ḥul lah ᶜa
lāl ġu rū s bil

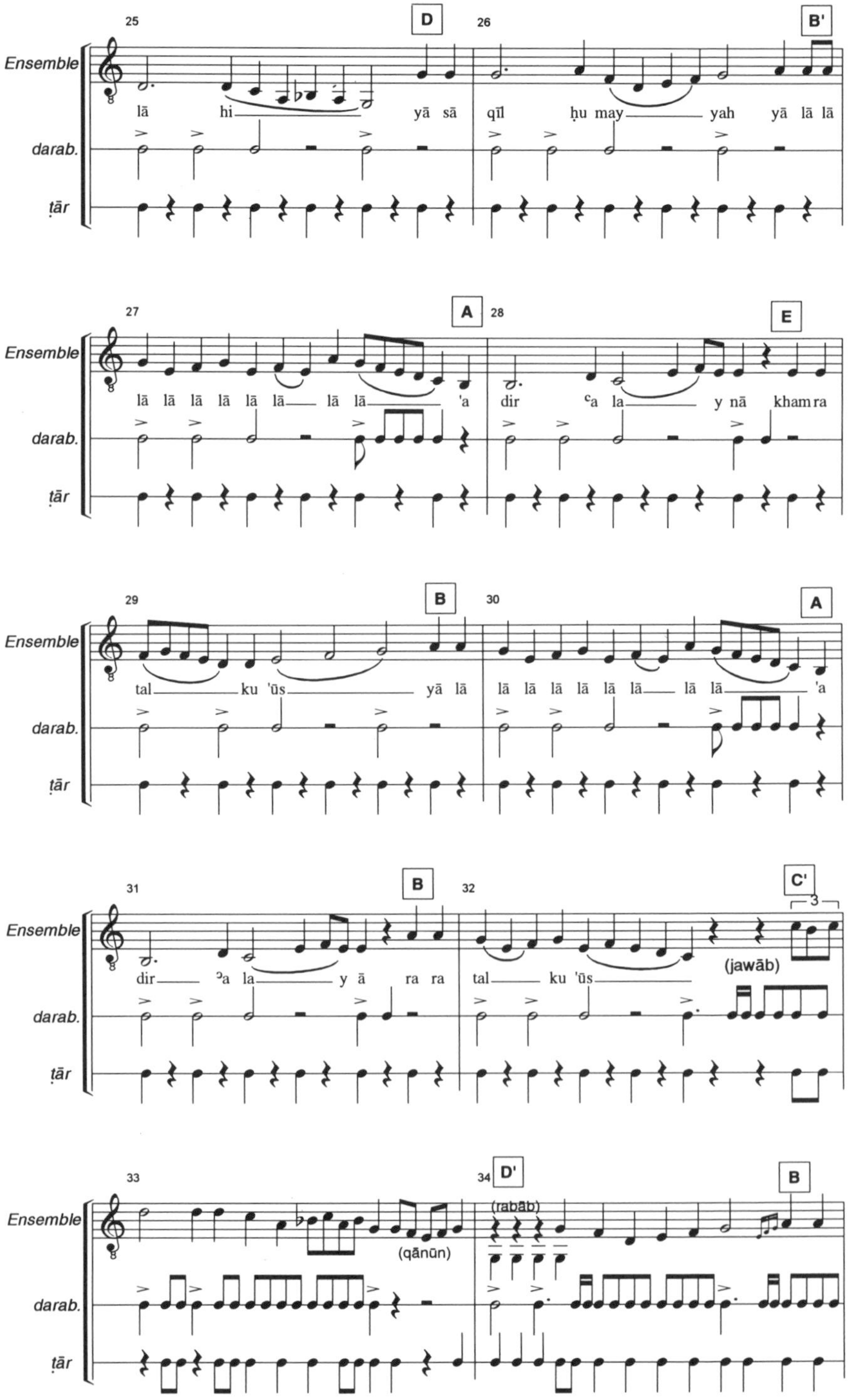
25 D 26 B'
Ensemble
lā hi yā sā qīl ḥu may yah yā lā lā
darab.
ṭār
27 A 28 E
lā lā lā lā lā lā lā lā 'a dir ʿa la y nā kham ra
29 B 30 A
tal ku 'ūs yā lā lā lā lā lā lā lā lā lā 'a
31 B 32 C'
dir ʾa la y ā ra ra tal ku 'ūs
(jawāb)
3
33 34 D' B
(rabāb)
(qānūn)

Ensemble
darab.
ṭār
35
A'
36
E'
37
B''
38
A
39
B'
40
C
da
41
D
ᶜū nī naghnam sā
42
B
ᶜah ha nī yah yā lā
43
A
iā lā lā yā lā lā lā lā mā
44
E
dum tu fī waq

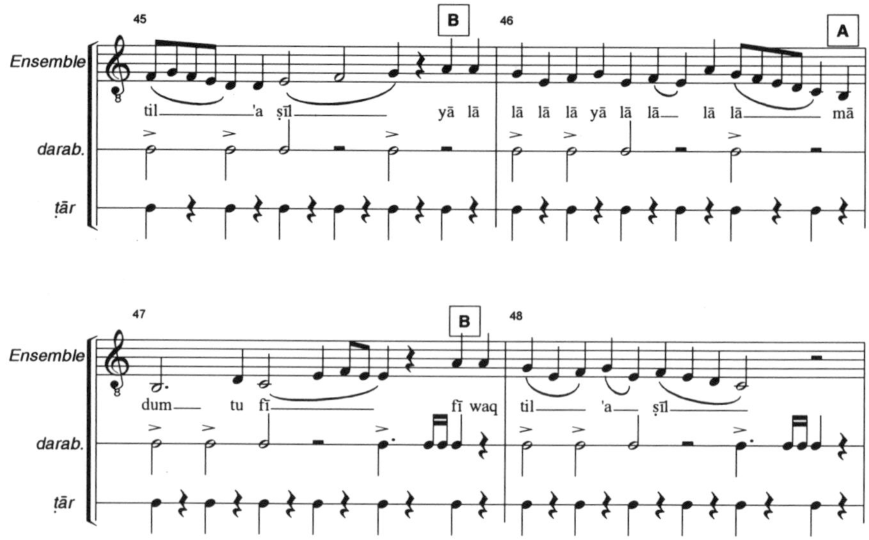

Nūbah māyah: basīṭ.

The nūbah māyah is based on the ṭabʿ māyah with the following tone row:

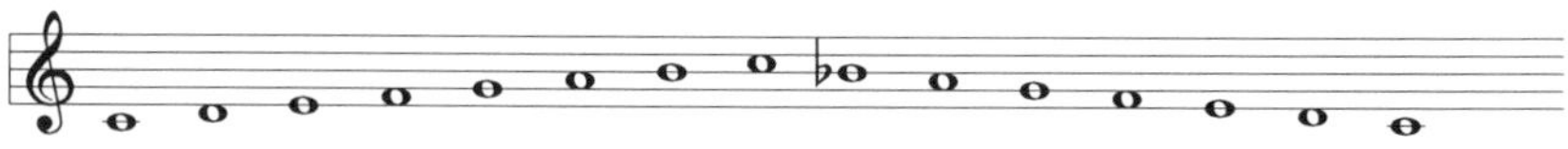

Almost all the stanzas of poetry performed by the singers during a nūbah māyah describe the mood of the evening at sunset. The text sung in this particular ṣanʿah was composed in the muwashshaḥ form and adheres to the following rhyme scheme:

AB AB cd cd cd AB AB

The text of the stanza of poetry reads as follows:

1.	*unẓur ilā rawnaq il ʿashiyyah*	A
2.	*kasat biḥullatin ʿalā al-ghurūs*	B
3.	*billāhi yā sāqī al-ḥumayyah*	A
4.	*adir ʿalaynā khamrata al-kuʾūs*	B
5.	*daʿūnī naghnam sāʿatan haniyah*	c
6.	*mā dumtu fī waqti al-aṣīl*	d
7.	*zāranī ḥibbī waʿṭif ʿalayyah*	c
8.	*mā lir-raqībi ʿalayya sabīl*	d
9.	*saqānī min fīhi al-ḥumayyah*	c
10.	*mawla ad-dībāji waṭṭarfi al-kaḥīl*	d
11.	*shrab waghannā wamāla ilayya*	A
12.	*wadhabulat ʿaynāhu an-naʿūs*	B
13.	*qabbaltuhu qublatan bilā khafiyyah*	A
14.	*waqultu yā rāḥata an-nufūs*	B

Translation:

1.	Behold! The glow of the evening twilight!	A
2.	Like a veil it lays itself over tree and bush.	B
3.	By God! Cupbearer,	A
4.	Fill our wine glasses one after the other!	B
5.	Let us seize an hour full of happiness,	c
6.	While the day draws to a close.	d
7.	My beloved visited and pitied me,	c
8.	Without that anyone could spy on us.	d
9.	From his mouth I drank the wine,	c
10.	As he faced me dressed in silk brocade and with eyelids painted black.	d
11.	He drank and sang and bent down to me.	A
12.	And as his sleepy eyes closed,	B
13.	I gave him without shyness a kiss,	A
14.	And spoke: "Now, take rest, you souls!"	B

The complete stanza of poetry is quoted here. During the performance, however, only the first six lines were presented.

The bughyah piece that opens the basīṭ section is performed in unison by the entire ensemble in a purely instrumental rendition. During the bughyah, all or at least some of the most important tones of the ṭabʿ māyah are introduced. The tone c is emphasized after the lower fourth c-b-a-g has been filled in. Subsequent to this, the series of tones g-a-g-f-e-g-e-g-e are highlighted before the c again comes alone to the fore. Shortly before the end of the bughyah, the rhythmically free melodic line turns into a melody whose rhythm is strictly organized, which then flows into the first ṣanʿah of the basīṭ, the first of a total of fourteen ṣanʿāt.

The first ṣanʿah is performed alternately by the choir, the solo singer, and the instrumentalists. Those places in the transcription where an underlying text is absent refer to purely instrumental passages. Since all participants sing and play in unison, the musical course of events can be notated on a single musical staff.

Musically, the ṣanʿah unfolds from a basis of small melodic elements that are linked together like mosaics. The individual melodic elements are designated in the transcription as A, B, C, D, and E. The tones brought into the foreground within them are e, g, and c. The element A highlights the tonal area b–e and at the same time emphasizes the tone e by the leap c–e and by filling out the interval of the fourth b–e in ascending direction. The element B concentrates on the tonal area g–e, which is established by means of musical repetition and the melodic leap g–e. Both elements are first presented vocally with instrumental accompaniment and then purely instrumentally (AB/A'B'). A renewed vocal rendition of AB follows. The presentation of the element C, which fills in the descending fourth c–g stepwise and emphasizes the corresponding tonal area, now appears. Immediately after this passage, the melodic element D is presented, which by means of repetition emphasizes the tone g—an octave higher than the final tone of element C. With B' and A, both of the opening elements are referred to once again before element E is introduced, filling in the tonal area e–g stepwise with long sustained tones. The unfolding of the basīṭ section once again illustrates the mosaic-like arrangement of all five musical elements: A–B(A'–B')–A–B–C–D–B'–A–E–B–A–B–(C'–D'–B–A'–E'–B''–A–B')–C–D–B–A–E–B–A–B.

Within each individual element, the tonal hierarchy of the ṭabʿ māyah is strictly observed. The complete musical mosaic delineates the modal structure of this ṭabʿ and simultaneously defines the musical form of the ṣanʿah as a whole.

The Muwashshaḥ in the Arabian East

The term *muwashshaḥ* refers not only to the poetic form used in the andalusī nūbah; it is also applied, in the East, to an autonomous genre of Arabian vocal art music that is textually based on the poetic form of the same name (cf. page 70f and page 74f). Whereas in North Africa the term refers to the purely linguistic side of a musical presentation, in Mashriq it designates a poetic-musical product in its entirety. The muwashshaḥ tradition of the Arabian East—from Aleppo in the eighteenth and nineteenth centuries to Egypt in the present—can be further distinguished from that of the Maghrib in that the poets of the East feel bound to the strict rules of Arabian meter, whereas those in North Africa ignore them. Nevertheless, the muwashshaḥ is still universally regarded as andalusī, something that in fact also holds completely true for the musical performance form.

In a muwashshaḥ ensemble, the instrumentalists often also make up the choir. The solo singer's part usually comprises only a few of the lines from the text presented. The instruments played are the plucked short-necked lute (*ʿūd*), the spike fiddle (*kamanjah*), the plucked box zither (*qānūn*), the goblet drum (*darabukkah*), and the tambourine (*daff*). In Aleppo, muwashshaḥāt were composed on several maqām rows, presenting up to three awzān. Moreover, in the B section of a muwashshaḥ, it was also possible to modulate to neighboring maqāmāt.

Before the trend toward modernization decisively influenced music in the Arabian world, it was customary in one concert to perform a complete *waṣlah*, that is, up to eight muwashshaḥāt in succession together with an instrumental introduction (*samāʿī* or *bashraf* [cf. page 99]). Common to all sections of such a waṣlah cycle is the principle maqām row, whereby the combination of pieces can comprise the works of several poets and composers. The muwashshaḥ composition played at the beginning of a cycle has a longer wazn than the muwashshaḥāt that follow. A total of twenty-two *waṣlāt* (plural of *waṣlah*) are known, each named according to the maqām row to which it belongs (for example, rāst waṣlah, ḥijāz waṣlah, and so on). Almost the only place where muwashshaḥ concerts can be heard today is on the radio, where usually only one or two muwashshaḥāt are presented; very seldom is a complete waṣlah performance broadcast.

A specific muwashshaḥ can be more precisely identified by naming the first lines of the poem, the principal maqām row, the accompanying rhythmic pattern, and the names of the poet and composer. If the identities of the poet and composer are not known, as is the case for most of the well-known traditional muwashshaḥāt, one usually encounters the reference *qadīm*, meaning "old."

Regarded as the most productive and original of the muwashshaḥ composers were ʿUmar al-Baṭsh (1885–1950) of Aleppo and Sheik Sayyid Darwīsh (1892–1923) of Alexandria, Egypt. Also during the nineteenth century lived other great muwashshaḥ masters, to whom we are still indebted today for setting countless older muwashshaḥāt to music and passing them on to following generations. Sheik Aḥmad Qabbānī (1841–1902) of Damascus, for example, a student of Sheik Aḥmad ʿAqīl of Aleppo, composed dozens of muwashshaḥāt and handed down a large muwashshaḥ repertoire. Muḥammad Kāmil al-Khulaʿī (1879–1938) of Cairo, a student of Sheik Qabbānī, set several hundred muwashshaḥāt to music. Muḥammad ʿUthmān (1855–1900) of Cairo, student of the great qānūn master Qusṭandī Mansī, created more than 150 muwashshaḥāt. Among the important muwashshaḥ researchers and collectors to be mentioned in particular are the Lebanese Salīm Ḥilū, the late Sheik ʿAlī Darwīsh and his son Nadīm of Aleppo, and Ibrāhīm Shafīq of Cairo.

The following music example is the muwashshaḥ "lammā badā." Based on the wazn samāʿī thaqīl, the principle maqām row is nahawand, and the composer and poet are unknown.

first dawr
lam mā ba— dā— ya ta than nā a—
mā namā namā— namān ḥ— bī ja mā— luh fa ta— nā a—
second dawr
mā n mā namā— namān aw mā bi— lah— ẓi hi as ar nā a—
mā na mā namā— namānghuṣ nun in tha— nā ḥī na- māl a—
khānah
mā n mā namā— namān waᶜ dī wa- yā— ḥī— ra tī man
ghiṭāᵓ
lī raḥīm shak- wa tī fīl ḥub bi min— law— ᶜa tī il
lā ma lī kal- ja māl a— mā na mā na mā— na mān fīl—

Muwashshaḥ "lammā badā."
Text and melody: anonymous; wazn: samāʿī thaqīl; maqām row: nahawand

The Dūr

Among the Egyptian musical forms that developed in the nineteenth century, the *dūr* (*dawr*) may be considered the most important. A singer (*muṭrib*) and a chorus perform a poem composed in classical Arabic or in an Egyptian dialect and set to music by a composer (*mulaḥḥin*). The solo singer himself is often the composer. Originally, three musicians made up the instrumental ensemble (*takht*); later five to six musicians accompanied the singer on the short-necked lute (*ʿūd*), the spike fiddle (*kamanjah*), the end-blown flute (*nāy*), the trapezoidal box zither (*qānūn*), the goblet drum (*darabukkah*) and the tambourine (*daff* or *riqq*).

The dūr is characterized by a unique poetic form that distinguishes it from the other vocal genres of Arabian music. The poem has at least four lines: the first couplet, *madhhab* (A), and the second couplet, *ghuṣn* (B). Up to twelve more lines can be added to the ghuṣn. Usually, the B section is made up of a first ghuṣn (B_1) and a second (B_2). In such a case, one also refers to the first and the second dūr.

The singer is concerned neither with a faithful rendering of the notes written by the composer nor with a variation of the same. On the contrary, he endeavors to paraphrase the composition. In some cases, one might even speak of a metamorphosis of the composition. With such a performance, the singer plays the leading role. He or she highlights some of the words of the poem and repeats them, improvising, while the phases and tone levels of the maqām chosen for the composition are presented in succession.

During the first half of the nineteenth century, the lines of text in parts A and B observed a uniform meter. The singer alone stood in the foreground. Purely instrumental passages were absent from a dūr performance as was a chorus (*muraddidūn*), which didn't appear until later in alternation with the soloist. In addition, parts A and B were musically based on the same maqām row. The performance of a dūr lasted approximately fifteen minutes.

From the second half of the nineteenth century on, poets freed themselves from the strict schema of the dūr poem. The lines of part B now assumed a different meter from those of part A, and the number of lines in both sections increased to three or more. Composers began to set a dūr in several maqām rows and to modulate within a piece to neighboring maqāmāt. As they began to include purely instrumental performance sections, they also called for the appearance of a special group of choristers, a new vocal practice, and the so-called *hank* found its way into the dūr.

Hank denotes the musical repetition schema (*tardīd*) within a dūr performance. In the B part of the dūr, the singer begins to improvise while taking up certain words from the poem anew. After this solo presentation, the chorus and singer together repeat the same thing one or more times, whereupon the soloist sings the same phrase yet again, albeit in altered form. The hank section can extend the performance of a dūr to as much as half an hour.

The most famous singer and composer of the dūr during the first half of the nineteenth century was Muḥammad al-Maslūb. Those who later managed to achieve wide success were ʿAbdū al-Ḥāmūlī (1845–1901) and Muḥammad ʿUthmān (1855–1900), who both created a remarkable number of dūr compositions that they performed as solo singers.

The Fjīrī Songs of the Arabian Gulf

Fjīrī is the term designating the music of the pearl divers and seamen of the Arabian Gulf. Belonging to the *funūn al-baḥr* ("sea music") tradition, it is among the most original music to have been documented in the Arabian Gulf region to date. Fjīrī includes a very rich repertoire and is cultivated along the entire coast, especially in Bahrain, Qatar, Kuwait, Saudi Arabia, the United Arab Emirates, and Oman. Mainly vocal music accompanied by dancing, it is performed by the pearl divers themselves. They accompany their singing with hand-clapping and percussion instruments.

Specific work tasks aboard ship are connected to special songs, which belong to a subcategory of the funūn al-baḥr known as *ahāzīj*. The *mijdāf*, for example, is sung by the seamen while rowing. *Mijdāf* means "oar." The *basseh* and the *qaylamī* are performed respectively when striking the foresail and the mainsail. The *khrāb* is sung while weighing anchor. In these songs, the type of work being carried out has a direct influence on the musical structure of the song. The structure, in turn, can be more clearly understood by knowing what kind of work the song accompanies. Thus, the khrāb is performed by a soloist (*nahhām*) and chorus comprising the rest of the seamen. Here, the seamen sing a kind of ostinato, or drone, two octaves beneath the high voice of the nahhām. Independently of the soloist's part, the choir interrupts the drone with an audible exhale. This moment corresponds to the short pause between two pulling motions while weighing anchor.

The texts of the fjīrī describe the hard life and the plight of the pearl divers, the dangers of the sea and the seabed, and the joy of seeing the family again. They also often contain prayers to Allah, Muḥammad, and ʿAlī. Musically, the fjīrī consists of a series of sections sung by a soloist and a male chorus. Each section is characterized by and named after the specific rhythmic structures that accompany the vocal parts. The underlying rhythmic structure of the first three sections must be developed in identifiable periods. The following sections, as for example the ahāzīj, have a clear, preestablished rhythmic framework made up of shorter patterns.

The nahhām and the mirwās and jaḥlah players during a fjīrī performance, Bahrain. Photo: H. H. Touma.

In the fjīrī, as mentioned previously, only percussion instruments are used: double-headed cylindrical drums, *ṭubūl* and *marāwīs* (plurals of *ṭabl* and *mirwās*); tambourines, *ṭīrān* (plural of *ṭār*); small metal cymbals, *ṭūs* (plural of *ṭāsah*); and water urns, *jaḥlāt* (plural of *jaḥlah*). The *ṭabl*, a drum related to the Indian *pakhawaj*, hangs across the chest of the player and is beaten either with the hand or with the stalk of a palm branch. The *mirwās* is a small double-headed drum. In a fjīrī performance, four to six marāwīs are brought into play. The *ṭār*, whose skin is usually decorated with letter characters as well as with drawings of flowers and the crescent moon, has a diameter of approximately twenty-seven inches (70 cm). Before the performance, all of the frame drums are arranged in a large circle around a fire and heated to increase the tension of the skin. The *jaḥlah* is a water urn, twenty-four inches (60 cm) high, played by beating on its mouth with a flat hand. To the muted tone that results, the musician adds a scratching noise, which he produces on the outer surface of the urn.

The fjīrī is sung not only during long diving trips on the high seas but also during sojourns on land, when the men meet at least once a week in a special house, the *dār*. Some forty

The membranes of the frame drums of a fjīrī ensemble are heated near a fire before being played, Bahrain. Photo: H. H. Touma.

pearl divers and seamen assemble here, usually on Thursday evenings. They drink tea, eat, smoke, tell stories, sing, and dance. During the nineteenth century there were hundreds of such *dūr* (plural of *dār*) scattered along the coast of the Gulf. Today there are significantly fewer. The competition from Japanese cultured pearls and the discovery of oil in the 1930s slowly brought an end to pearl diving in this region. Yet, the contemporary heirs to the musical repertoire of the pearl divers have all at least at one time practiced this profession. The dār, where not only fjīrī are performed but other musical genres as well, is named after the owner of the building and the leader of the group. In each dār, only a specific genre of funūn al-baḥr is cultivated. The dūr differ from one another also in the musical quality of the performances and the richness of the repertoire that the *nahhām*, the soloist, has at his command.

Fjīrī was learned by the pearl divers from their ancestors who have handed down fjīrī repertoire for generations. Nevertheless, the pearl divers from Bahrain tell a fjīrī fairy tale that presents the story of the origins of the fjīrī as follows:

> Once upon a time, there were three friends; two of them came from the island of Muḥarraq, the third from Manāmah (Bahrain). They used to go to a place called Abū Ṣubḥ, some miles outside of the city, where they could sing together without disturbing their neighbors and without being disturbed themselves. One day, on the way to Abū Ṣubḥ, near a mosque that still exists today, they heard some strange singing that seemed to come from a group inside the mosque. They became curious and wanted to see the singers. Just in front of the entrance to the mosque, they were suddenly struck by a shower of stones that came directly from the interior of the building. As they stepped into the courtyard of the mosque, they saw a row of figures sitting; the upper halves of their bodies were human and the lower halves were donkey. One of these creatures asked the young people, "Are you human beings or demons (*jinn*)?" They answered that they were human beings—and very good human beings, at that—and would do no harm to the group. They would just like to spend the evening listening to the singing. One of the

> sitting figures asked the three friends not to utter what was "in their hearts" (that is, not to utter the first verses of the Koran), otherwise the group would disappear before their eyes. This means that the friends had actually encountered demons in the mosque, for at the mention of the name Allah, they would immediately vanish.
>
> The three men then sat down with the others and were allowed to learn their songs—the fjīrī songs—only after they had promised never to tell anyone what they had seen and heard that evening. If they did, it would mean their certain death. Ever since this experience, the three friends met secretly at a cemetery to sing the fjīrī. After many years, two of them died. The third man—the one from Muḥarraq—realized that his own death was approaching. He gathered his family and his friends together and told them what happened on that evening long ago. He sang them the fjīrī, which they also mastered and which has been sung over and over again ever since.

Thus, for the pearl divers, the fjīrī has its origins in a supernatural world.

The rich song repertoire of the funūn al-baḥr can be divided into four parts corresponding to the four stages of a diving trip. During these four stages, four song forms (*fjīrī*, *ahāzīj*, *muwwālah*, and *ḥudwah*) are performed. We thus distinguish between

1. the start of the sea voyage,
2. work at the diving location,
3. passing time on the high seas, and
4. the return from the diving trip.

The Start of the Sea Voyage

The voyage to the diving location begins with prayer recitations ("I say my prayer"). Following this, the ṭabl player strikes up the *fann al-basseh*, the "rope song," to the rhythmic clapping of hands and the crashing of cymbals. While the sailors push the ship off from the shore into the water, they sing a ḥudwah ("Oh Allah! Oh Allah!"). Another ḥudwah sounds when the supplies are loaded, and a mawwāl is sung when the sail is carried from its storage place to the ship. Mawwāl, fann al-basseh, and ḥudwah designate those song genres of the pearl divers that are performed by a leader and a chorus of seamen.

The preparations for the four-month sea voyage extend over approximately three days. The ship gets a fresh coat of paint and is cleaned; the provisions are loaded on board; and sails, oars, lines, and the rest of the gear are placed in readiness. When the ship is ready to set sail, the sailors gather together and receive an advance payment from the captain of the ship. Only after three more days of rest, do they set sail for the high seas.

Work at the Diving Location

At least nine different song genres are performed while the pearl divers carry out their work at the diving location. *Basseh* accompanies the hoisting of the sail, *sūryah* is heard when the sail is set against the wind, *makhmūs* is sung when the mast line is lashed, *khrāb* is sounded when the anchor is weighed, and *ʿashshārī* marks the ship's setting sail for a new dive location.

Passing Time on the High Seas

The songs for the entertainment of the pearl divers include several fjīrī genres, among them, *baḥrī*, *ʿadsānī*, *ḥaddādī*, *mkhūlfī*, and *ḥassāwī*.

The Return from the Diving Trip

The wives of the seamen welcome the homecoming men with the antiphonal song (*mrādāh*) "*tūb tūb yā baḥr*," whose text reads

> "Repent! Repent! Oh Sea! You have carried our men away,
> Oh Sea!
> Have you then no fear at all of Allah's anger? Oh Sea!"

In the following paragraphs, the musical aspects of three genres of the fjīrī repertoire will be examined more closely.[1] First, in the baḥrī section, the nahhām begins with a solo of

1 Recordings: (1) *Fidjeri: Songs of the Bahrain Pearl Divers*. UNESCO Collection MUSICAL SOURCES. Philips 6586 017, Side 1, Nos. 1 and 3. (2) *Bahrain*. UNESCO Collection MUSICAL ATLAS. EMI 3C 064-18 371, Side 2, No. 6.

long recitative-like passages over a rhythmic pattern consisting of sixteen beats. The chorus answers with a melody characterized by long sustained tones, reminiscent of a cantus firmus. Then the ṭabl drummer, accompanied by the hand-clapping rhythm of the singers, develops a rhythmic pattern that extends over three phases. Following the first phase, with four beats per measure in which the third beat of each measure is accented, comes the second, in which eight beats make up each measure. This phase, combined with the four-beat measures of phase 1 results in thirty-two beats (8 + 4 + 4 + 4 + 4 + 8). Of these, the first, ninth, thirteenth, seventeenth, twenty-first, and twenty-fifth beats are accented. Between the twenty-ninth and the thirty-second beats, a double-time hand-clapping pattern, resulting from an interplay of two hand-clapping parts, underscores the four-beat structure. After this, the cycle is repeated. The third phase, in turn, consists of a clear ordering of thirty-two-beat measures with accents on the first, fifth, ninth, and twenty-first beats. Beginning with the twenty-ninth beat, the hand-clapping pattern gives the cue once again, announcing the tutti repetition of the cycle. During this process, the ṭabl player, together with one or two dancers, performs at the center of the circle formed by the singers. The nahhām usually sits next to the jaḥlah or mirwās player.

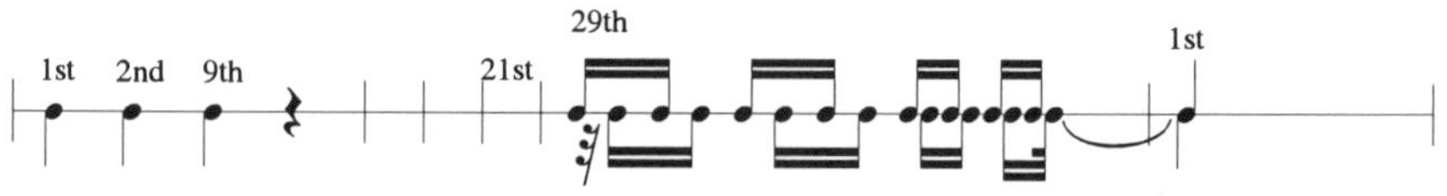

In the ʿadsānī section, the rhythmic structure unfolds in four phases. The first phase is based on groups of four-beat measures; the second, on groups of eight-beat measures; the third on groups of thirty-two-beat measures; and the fourth, on groups of sixty-four beat measures.

The mkhūlfī section has no rhythmic development. The rhythm is based on a series of A and B segments, illustrated by hand-clapping and the playing of drums, cymbals, and water urns. The choir sings a melody in 16/4 meter with variations in every repetition. The melody, which the nahhām sings, is of an improvisatory character.

Beginning of a mkhūlfī

The Qaṣīdah

Qaṣīdah is the term for a poem set to music consisting of ten, sometimes also twenty-five or more lines of poetry. All of the lines are based on one and the same classical meter of Arabian poetry. Religious as well as secular themes are presented. The qaṣīdah performance is not based on any fixed rhythmic formula. A choir and an instrumental ensemble accompany a male or female singer. Musically, no fixed formal construction can be ascertained. Refrain sections can be as much a part of the musical form as are the improvised passages. Formally, however, the qaṣīdah is designed cyclically. Several melodies—usually four in number—are strung together, interrupted only by a refrain, which generally reproduces the first line of the poem. The first line of verse is also referred to in the title of the complete qaṣīdah.

The qaṣīdah is popular among the *ṣūfī* fraternities of Islamic mysticism throughout the Arabian world. The secular form of the qaṣīdah reached its artistic peak during the nineteenth century through the Egyptian singer Salāmah Ḥijāzī (1852–1917). During the twentieth century, the qaṣīdah, again in Egypt, received fresh impetus through artists such as the singer and composer Muḥammad ʿAbd al-Wahhāb (1907–1991), the songstress Umm Kulthūm (1896–1975), and the composers Muḥammad Qaṣabjī (1892–1966), Zakariyyā Aḥmad (1896–1961) and Riyāḍ Sunbāṭī (1907–1985).

The Layālī

The *layālī* is a solo vocal form whose text consists of the words *yā laylī yā ʿaynī* ("Oh my night! Oh my eye!"), referring in poetic metaphor to a beloved woman. Usually, the layālī is performed by a singer who also accompanies him- or herself on the ʿūd. The instrumental accompaniment is often, however, also supplied by a qānūn (box zither) player or even an entire instrumental ensemble, whereby the instrumentalists accompany the soloist individually and in alternating order in his or her realization of the melodic passages. In a layālī, a maqām and its characteristic emotional content are musically presented. Thus, the maqām phenomenon, that is, the realization of phases, tone levels, nuclei, and emotional expressive values is also characteristic of the layālī form (refer to chapter 3).

The Mawwāl

The *mawwāl* is likewise a vocal form that usually follows the performance of a layālī. Only in the Egyptian dūr (see page 86f) does it precede the layālī. As early as the ninth century, at the time of the Caliph Hārūn ar-Rashīd, the mawwāl was described in connection with the working class. The text is still composed in colloquial Arabic today. Four-line (*rubāʿī*), five-line (*aʿraj*), and seven-line (*nuʿmānī*) verse forms are known, all of which are based on the *basīṭ* meter (*mustafʿilun fāʿilun mustafʿilun fāʿilun* – – ∪ – | – ∪ – | – – ∪ – | – ∪ –). The theme of love predominates in the texts. The mawwāl has much in common with the layālī: it is also performed by a solo singer to the accompaniment of a musical instrument, the melodic line likewise dispenses with any division into measures, and the tone levels and phases characteristic of the maqām are also realized, with the highest phase clearly defining the climax of the entire piece. In the structure of its stanzas and in its meter, however, the mawwāl represents a distinct contrast to the layālī.

The Taqsīm

Taqsīm is the term given to the instrumental presentation of a maqām, that is, of its tonal-spatial model. This model focuses melodic development on only a few tones, thus allowing the tone levels characteristic of each maqām to emerge. The rhythmic-temporal structure is not subject to a fixed organization. Specific motivic elements, as part of the repeatedly appearing tone groups of the melodic line, are not characteristic of a maqām; rather they are an expression of the musician's personal style and of the technical possibilities offered the performer by the instrument being played.

Among other things, a taqsīm performance is characterized by the division of the melodic line through long pauses. Such pauses, which can last from two to four seconds, not only possess a formal function; they open up the possibility of communication between audience and musician. Arabian audiences use the pauses, interjecting cheers or shouts, to give their opinion of what was just heard. A first-class taqsīm performer knows how to carry the tension of the audience to such an extreme that, immediately after a melodic passage has died away, applause spontaneously bursts out with cries of *Allah!* ("Oh God!") and *yā salām* ("Oh Peace!").

A taqsīm can be performed on the short-necked lute (*ʿūd*), the spike fiddle (*kamanjah*), the box zither (*qānūn*), or the end-blown flute (*nāy*). Less often, a rhythmic ostinato accompaniment is heard together with the part of the soloist, performed on the goblet drum (*darabukkah*) or tambourine (*riqq*). A genre that stands uniquely alone in Arabian music, the taqsīm places particularly high artistic demands on the musician. Here the maqām phenomenon finds its purest instrumental expression (see chapter 3). The realization of this phenomenon takes place during the course of several melodic passages, whose number is not fixed. Thus, *taqāsīm* (plural of *taqsīm*) can turn out to have different lengths. In the first place, the duration of a taqsīm presentation is dependent upon the performance situation and whether the taqsīm is intended as an introductory piece, an intermezzo, or an independent performance. In the second place, the musicality and virtuosity of the soloist determine the length of the presentation. A taqsīm can precede a mawwāl or muwashshaḥ, and it can also be performed as an intermezzo between two sections of an andalusī nūbah or as an independent performance piece, dedicated solely to the presentation of the maqām phenomenon.

Since Arabian radio and television have enthusiastically embraced the taqsīm, thus making this art form accessible to all, many less talented musicians have succumbed to the temptation of imitating the melodic passages of famous soloists, even quoting them note for note. Because of this, an outsider might arrive at the mistaken impression that taqāsīm are composed pieces. On the contrary, the realization of a convincing original taqsīm requires a creative talent on the part of the performer that is akin to that of a composer. In the hands of a gifted musician, no taqsīm performance is musically the same as any other, for tradition prescribes that the taqsīm be created anew each time. Nevertheless, the taqsīm is not purely improvisational. Underlying its freely unfolding rhythmic-temporal design is a compositional element in the form of its fixed tonal-spatial organization, its predetermined sequence of tone levels and phases. This interplay between composition and improvisation is the essential characteristic of a taqsīm.

The Bashraf and the Samāʿī

Bashraf and *samāʿī* are two instrumental forms of Arabian music that can be traced back to Turkish models (*peshrev* and *semai*). By the time the Ottoman rule over Arab lands came to an end in the year 1918, both had already been known to Arabian music for a long time. In terms of compositional form, there is very little difference between the Arabian and Turkish versions. Bashraf and samāʿī, however, were composed as entertainment music, and their composers furnished them with imaginative new names such as *ʿAzīzah* (maiden name) and *alf laylah walaylah* ("1001 Nights"). Although these pieces represent an unsuccessful synthesis between oriental melody and the musical elements of Western musical cultures, Arabs perform bashraf and samāʿī works by Turkish as well as by Arabian composers. As a general principle, however, Arabian musicians use a different plucking technique on the ʿūd and the qānūn than do their Turkish colleagues, they employ different rhythmic patterns for accompaniment, and they utilize the Arabian rather than the Turkish tone system.

Bashraf and samāʿī are very similar, as far as their musical forms are concerned. Only the layout of the measures occasionally differs. A bashraf is composed of three or four different segments, or *khānāt* (plural of *khānah*). Performed between these segments, not marked off by any pause or other musical caesura, is an unchanging intermezzo (*taslīm*), a kind of ritornello. The musical intensity increases from khānah to khānah but is balanced out again each time in the taslīm parts.

The bashraf is based on a core melody with characteristic intervals and definite rhythmic groupings that reoccur in each khānah and every taslīm in a paraphrased form. All the melodic turns that might perhaps be interpreted as ornaments or arabesques must be considered components of tone levels or tonal areas surrounding a tonal center. It is this center alone that determines the musical structure. Everything else is of secondary importance. If, for example, the tone c forms the center, then the type and extent of the melodic embellishments do not in the least change anything about this, its function.

The samāʿī differs from the bashraf only in a rhythmic aspect. The bashraf unfolds in binary rhythmic units, while the samāʿī is based on a combination of binary and tertiary elements. The ten-part rhythmic structure of the samāʿī has the form 3+2+2+3. Only the last khānah section of a samāʿī follows a six-part measure scheme.

Bashraf and samāʿī can be assigned to the domain of sacred music as well as secular. In the religious context, they are found in the music of the "dancing dervishes," the Mawlawī (*Mawlawiyyah*, in Arabic), whose followers inhabit not only Turkey but also Egypt, Syria, Iraq, and the Maghrib states.

Bashraf and samāʿī are usually performed by an instrumental ensemble, with an accompanying rhythmic pattern played on the darabukkah and the riqq. Sometimes, however, a bashraf or samāʿī composition is presented by a soloist on the ʿūd, the qānūn, or the kamanjah, in which case there is no rhythmic accompaniment so that the solo instrumentalist can have greater freedom in paraphrasing the principal melody. In ensemble performance, the borders are more closely drawn. All musicians must play the same melody. Counterpoint or even just slight deviations from the unison are always the result of carelessness on the part of the musician—they are not intentional. In ensemble performance, the melody is played on the flute, the box zither, and the short-necked lute at an interval of two, or sometimes even three, octaves.

Several Arabian composers have distinguished themselves with bashraf and samāʿi pieces. Among them are Tawfīq Ṣabbāgh (Aleppo, 1892–1964), ʿAlī Darwīsh (Aleppo, 1884–1952),

Jamīl ʿUwīs (?), Ibrāhīm ʿAryān (Egypt, 1850–1920), and Khmayis Tirnān (Tunis, 1894–1964). But the most beautiful and original compositions originate from artists no longer known to us by name, whose works have been handed down with the reference *qadīm* or *ʿarabī qadīm* (namely, "old" or "old Arabian").

Analysis of a Samāʿī in the Maqām Bayātī

The samāʿī bayātī analyzed in this section was composed by the Egyptian Ibrāhīm ʿAryān (1850–1920). The example presented here was performed by the takht ensemble of Cairo.[1]

The tone row of the maqām bayātī is:

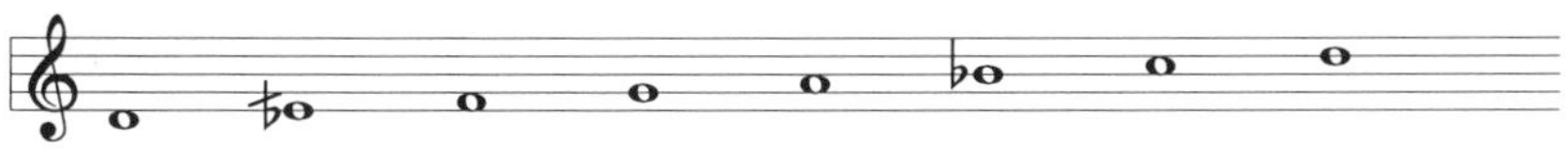

The formal structure of this samāʿī can be represented as A T B T C T D T (where T = taslīm). Each of A, B, C, and T consists of five measures of ten beats each (see wazn *samāʿī thaqīl*, page 52), whereas D extends over ten measures of three beats each (see wazn *samāʿī dārij*, page 51). The entire wazn is performed on the goblet drum and the tambourine.

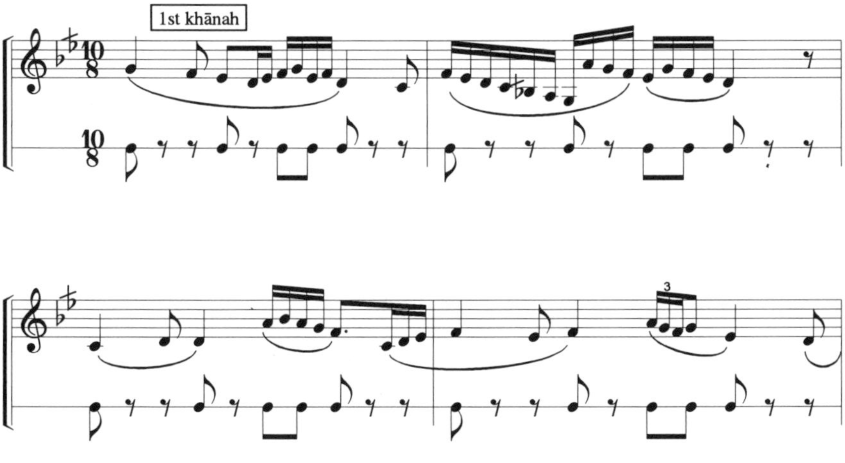

1 Recording: *Taqasim and Layali: Cairo Tradition.* UNESCO Collection MUSICAL SOURCES. Philips 6586 010, Side 1, No. 3.

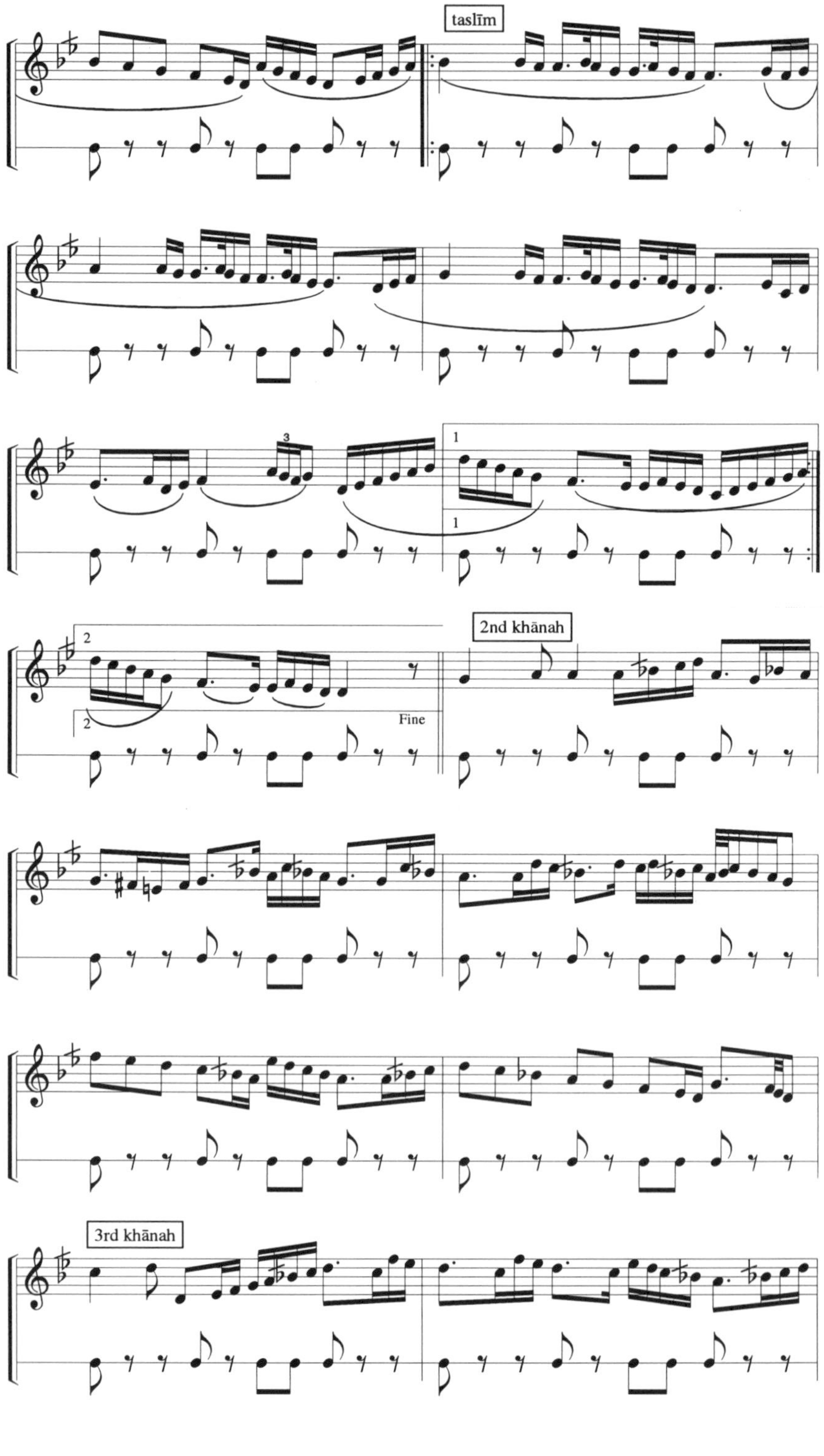
taslīm
1
1
2
2
Fine
2nd khānah
3
3rd khānah

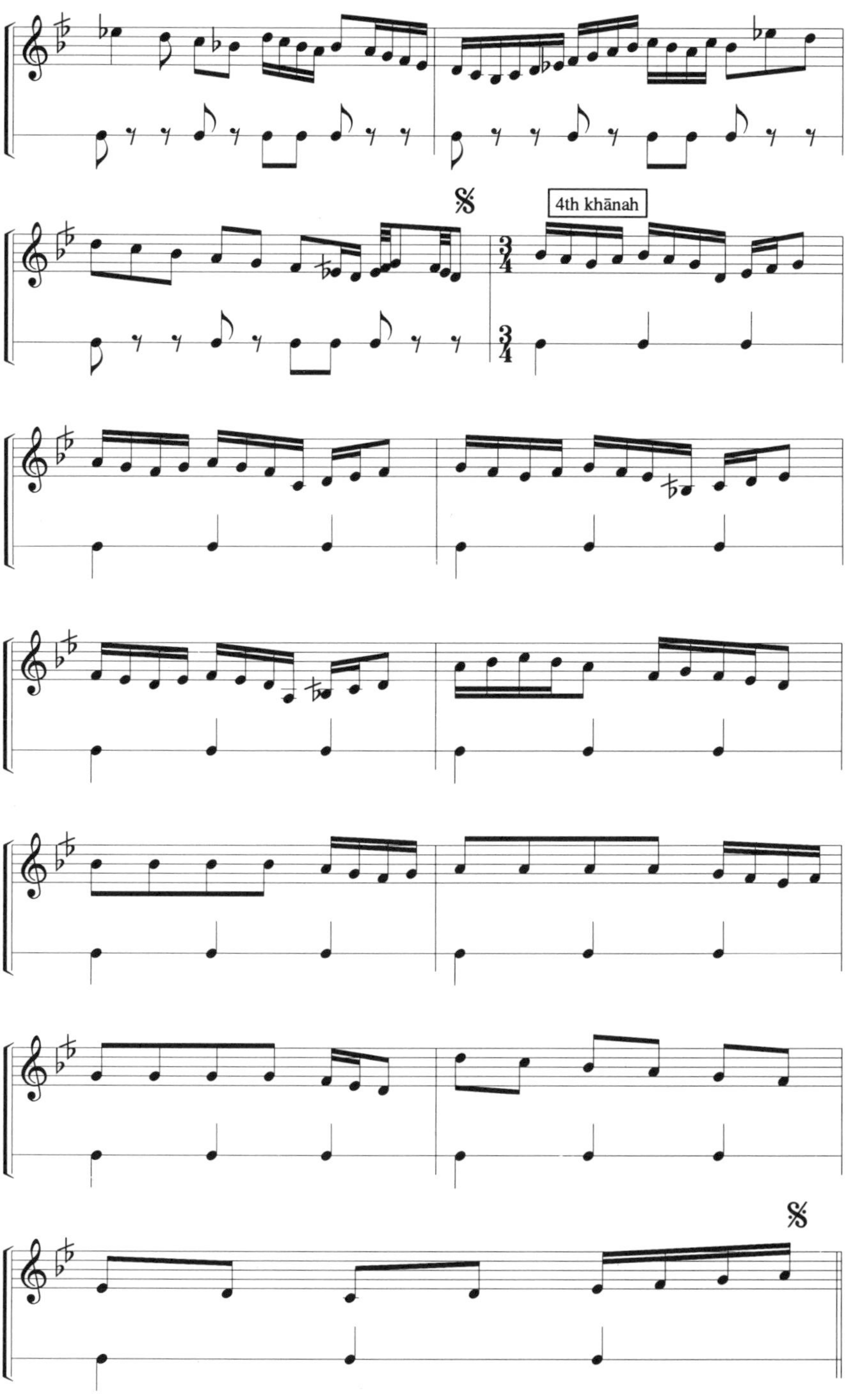

Samāʿī bayātī.
Composer: Ibrahīm ʿAryan (1850–1910).

The metric-rhythmic organization of the melody in this samāʿī is based on the series 3+2+2+3, in which the tones of the first, fourth, sixth, and eighth beats of the measure possess a more important tonal-spatial function than the other beats. The first khānah includes important selected characteristics of the maqām bayātī. Presented here are the tonal areas g–d and f–d, as well as the tones f and d. In the first measure, the stepwise descending melodic line emphasizes the tonal area g–d and reaches its cadence, the *finalis* d, on the eighth beat. With the immediately following leap of a fourth, from c to f, the tone f comes to the fore, which happens again in the second measure, now however, through an octave run with a change of register that is followed on the eighth beat by a cadence on the tone d. Special focus is given to the tonal area d–f in measure 3, whereby the tone a, the fifth of the final tone, also sounds. The same thing happens in the fourth measure. Whereas previously, however, the cadence of the third measure was on the eighth beat, on the tone f, the melodic line of the fourth measure moves on the tenth beat to d, after which it leaps upward to the tone b♭. This leap, encompassing a minor sixth, is considered to be extremely loaded with tension and therefore requires a melodic release of tension, which promptly appears in the form of the stepwise descending minor sixth b♭–d.

The samāʿī performance presented here represents only one of many musical possibilities for performing the composition, for every good musician has an individual musical style and unique preferences concerning musical ornamentation. If the personal elements of the performance are eliminated, however, the first khānah (A) can be reduced to a tonal framework that is strictly observed by every musician, regardless of the embellishments or encircling of the structural tones that are incorporated during the performance. The first khānah can be represented by the following tonal framework:

In a similar way, the taslīm section can also be reduced to a basic musical structure:

The second and the third khānah (B and C) display modulations to neighboring maqām rows. For this reason, it is not possible to compare their structural framework to that of the first khānah (A) and that of the taslīm (T). The fourth khānah (D), however, is again in the maqām bayātī.

The characteristic structural elements of the maqām bayātī now become clearly evident when one compares the basic musical structures of khānah 1, khānah 4, and the taslīm to one another. The musical essence of the maqām bayātī is expressed in the tonal areas d–f, f–d, d–g, b–g, and g–b♭.

The Taḥmīlah

Taḥmīlah is the name given to a genre of instrumental music native to Egypt that has been forced into the background today by newer, non-authentic musical forms. The *taḥmīlah* depicts a kind of musical contest between the takht ensemble and its individual instrumentalists. It is based on a traditional, easily remembered melody in two-part time, which extends over eight to twelve measures and is composed in an easily recognizable maqām row. At the beginning of the performance, this melody is played in unison on the ʿūd, the kamanjah, the qānūn, and the nāy, with rhythmic accompaniment by the darabukkah and the riqq. Seamlessly following this unison presentation, one of the ensemble musicians begins a solo improvisation. A question and answer play emerges between the soloist and the ensemble, wherein the beginning melody forms a kind of refrain that the ensemble repeats before the part of soloist is passed on from one musician to the next. In this way, each melody instrument has one solo during which the musician is expected to improvise freely on the principal melody, presenting variations, paraphrases, or metamorphoses of it. Such improvisation requires a high degree of musical ability. A taḥmīlah performance ends the same way it began, with the ensemble performing the beginning melody one last time.

The Dūlāb

Dūlāb is the term for a short introductory instrumental piece that a takht ensemble uses to precede a vocal performance, especially when it does not intend to perform any longer instrumental introduction such as the bashraf or samāʿī. The *dawālīb* (plural of *dūlāb*) are based upon traditional melodies in 2/4 time, during whose animated performance, a certain lightness is expressed. The dūlāb melodies are based on a maqām row and are performed to the rhythmic accompaniment of the wazn waḥdah. The dawālīb, at the same time, also serve as practice pieces for musicians who are specialized on a melody instrument.

The Ṣawt

The *ṣawt* is a song form known in all lands of the Arabian Gulf as *ṣawt baḥraynī, ṣawt kuwaytī, ṣawt qaṭarī*, and so forth. In Bahrain and Kuwait, it is the melody and the rhythmic accompaniment, more than the sung text, that impart the unique character to a ṣawt performance. Both are selected by each ṣawt singer (*muṭrib*) for his own individual performance, whereas the poem that is sung does not undergo any appreciable change from singer to singer.

A ṣawt comprises three melodic sections that belong to a

specific maqām row. In addition, the ṣawt is characterized by a unique, characteristic form of rhythmic accompaniment that is shaped by playing on the small double-headed cylinder drums (*marāwīs*) and by the hand-clapping (*ṣafqah*) of two groups of men. Two rhythmic accompanying patterns are differentiated. The first consists of twelve beats, organized as follows:

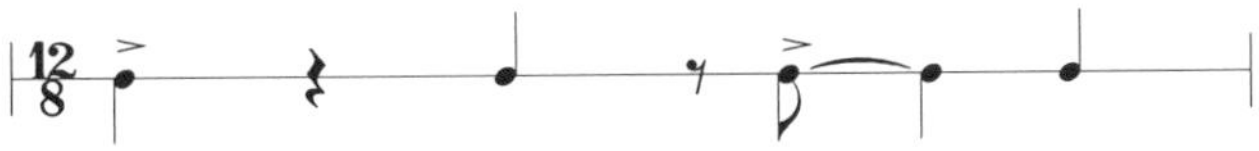

The second consists of eight beats, arranged as follows:

The hand-clapping marks the fundamental rhythmic beats until a rhythmic structure of particular density is created by the interplay of the clapping patterns performed by the two groups of men.

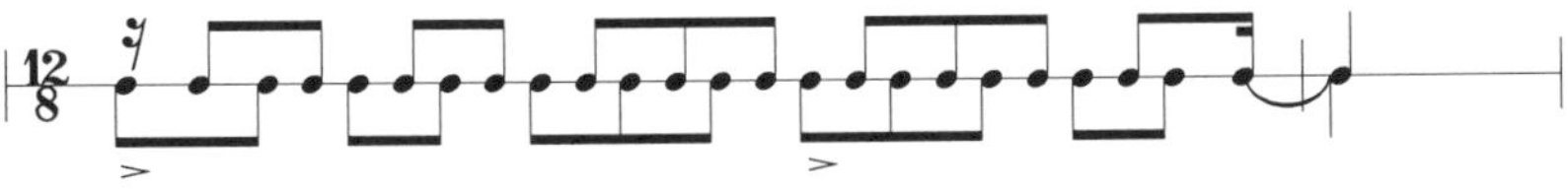

or

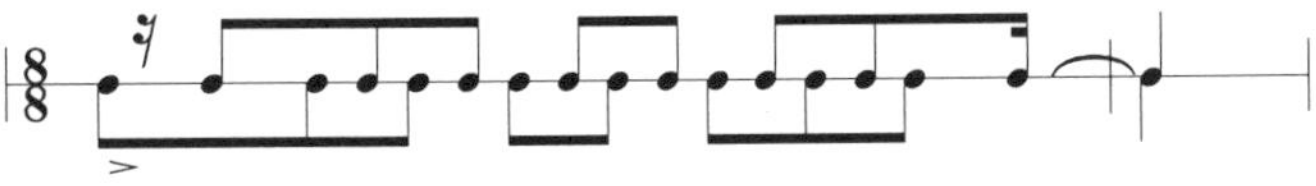

A ṣawt poem consists of several lines of verse (*abyāt*, plural of *bayt*), whose number is chosen to fit the context. There are usually about nine to twelve double-verse lines. The final part of a ṣawt is called *tawshīḥah*. To conclude, the tawshīḥah is repeated by the group of men in chorus.

The cyclic form within whose framework several aṣwāt are performed is called *samrah*. In a narrow sense, *samrah* is the name given to those concerts that present the ṣawt repertoire after one of the communal banquets held in connection with weddings and other festivities. To start, the singer performs a ṣawt ʿarūbīyah (12/8), without a tawshīḥah section. Following this, among others, comes a ṣawt shāmī (8/8), named after the Shām region of Syria; a ṣawt mrūbaʿ (12/8) (*mrūbaʿ* meaning "square"), and a song named *bastah*. The sequence of the aṣwāt can essentially be chosen freely, except that the ṣawt *khatm*, the "final" ṣawt, must always be played at the conclusion of the cycle. The text of the ṣawt khatm has either religious or humorous content, and its rhythmic accompaniment is the wazn *yamānī* (8/8):

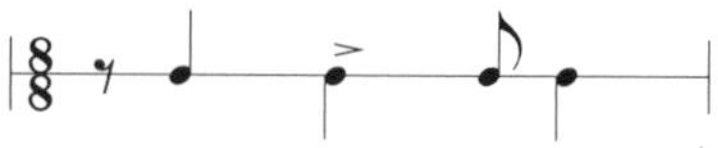

Some ṣawt singers enjoy great prestige in the lands of the Arabian Gulf. During their performance, they accompany themselves on the ʿūd. Considered among the greatest singers of the ṣawt in the Gulf region are ʿAbdullāh al-Faraj (1836–1901), Muḥammad Fāris Āl Khalīfah, and Ḍāḥī Bin Walīd. The singing style of these three "fathers" of the ṣawt stands out for its high degree of originality. Other singers found it impossible to imitate their performances, which for the Arabs, as always, attests to the high quality of the musical original. Muḥammad Fāris was introduced to singing and composition by ʿAbd ar-Raḥmān Yamānī. Yamānī, as his name implies, hailed from Yemen. Because of the economic relations between the Gulf States and Yemen before the discovery of oil, Muḥammad Fāris also lived there. Consequently, it is not surprising that the ṣawt boasts Yemenite features. As early as 1928 and 1932, Fāris and Ḍāḥī Bin Walīd made recordings in Iraq and Pakistan for Bayḍaphon Records.

6

The Musical Instruments

As early as the tenth century A.D., Arabian scholars such as Ibn Zaylah, the Ikhwān aṣ-Ṣafā' (the "pure brothers"), and Ibn Sīnā devised a special classification system for musical instruments that led to their subdivision into percussion, plucked, bowed, and wind instruments. In addition to these classifications, it was important for the systematization whether the duration of the tone produced by the instrument was short, long, or sounded continuously, and whether the neck of a stringed instrument was equipped with frets.

From time immemorial, the Arabs have preferred to make music in small ensembles. The only exceptions to this were presented by the splendid court orchestras in Iraq, Morocco, and Egypt, as reported to us by historians. Up to one hundred musicians were said to have performed in these orchestras on drums, timpani, trumpets, horns, and oboes.

Stringed Instruments

The ʿŪd and Other Forms of Lute Instruments

The ʿūd is a fretless, plucked short-necked lute with a body shaped like half a pear. The ʿūd can indeed be considered the very embodiment of Arabian musical culture. Music theory, in particular the Arabian tone system, was and still is illustrated

The ʿūd player Munīr Bashīr, Iraq. Photo: H. H. Touma.

with it; it is regarded as the cornerstone of Arabian art music in concerts, on the radio, and in the domestic sphere. It is not without reason that the Arabs call the ʿūd the "Sultan of the Musical Instruments." Both men and women perform on this instrument, and small instruments are manufactured especially for children. Since the beginnings of Arabian musical history, the lute enjoyed immense popularity and was not absent from any festive and jovial social gathering. Still today, the tender and sweet sound of the ʿūd fascinates the Arabian listener, who occassionally compares the tone to the voice of a nightingale. The ʿūd is as widespread in North Africa and the Near East as, for example, the piano is in Europe. At any rate, its area of distribution is not limited to the Arabian world alone but reaches far off into Central Asia and the regions south of the Sahara.

Already during the Middle Ages, the ʿūd was finding its way toward Europe, with the returning crusaders as well as through Spain in the West and Byzantium in the East. Troubadours, trouvères, and wandering minstrels took up the instrument to accompany their singing. Not until the sixteenth century, however, did the popularity of the lute reach its peak. All the European names for the instrument—*laute, alaude, laud, luth, liuto,* and *lute*—can be derived from the Arabic word *al-ʿūd*, calling to mind the Golden Age that this essentially Arabian instrument experienced in the Occident.

ʿŪd literally means "wood." The explanation for this name is simple: relatively late—not until the end of the sixth century—the Arabs of the Ḥijāz adopted the wooden-faced lute from the city of Ḥīrah, in Iraq, in place of the old skin-faced instrument known in pre-Islamic times by the names *mizhar, kirān,* and *muwattar,* and used in varying sizes. In pre-Islamic times, Ḥīrah was considered the center for literature as well as, of course, for music. Here is where the famous Persian King Bahram Ghur (430–438) received his education. It is possible that the ʿūd was influenced by the four-string Persian lute *barbaṭ*; it is also feasible, however, that the term *barbaṭ* at that time was merely a synonym for ʿūd.

In the ninth century, Ziryāb further developed the lute from a four-stringed to a five-stringed instrument. Up until the fifteenth century, the Arabs differentiated between the *ʿūd qadīm*, the "old ʿūd" that was strung with four strings tuned in fourths, and the *ʿūd kāmil*, the "complete ʿūd," which had five strings. The four strings of the ʿūd qadīm were identified with the four body humors and the four temperaments of man known to the medicine of classical antiquity. Ziryāb colored the highest string yellow (*zīr*), which symbolized bile; the second highest was red (*mathnā*), for blood, the third white (*mathlath*), for phlegm, and the lowest string black (*bam*), for black bile. The additional fifth string, inserted by Ziryāb between mathnā and mathlath, symbolized the soul, since the four body humors, as he maintained, could not exist without the soul. Furthermore, instead of plucking the strings of the ʿūd with the wooden plectrum customary up until then, Ziryāb began to use the quill of an eagle feather, as is still common throughout the Arabian world today. Be that as it may, those at the beginning stages of learning nowadays use a featherlike plectrum made of plastic. Today the ʿūd is strung with five double strings, of which the three highest are made of gut or nylon and the two lowest of silk wound with copper wire. The double strings are tuned thus:

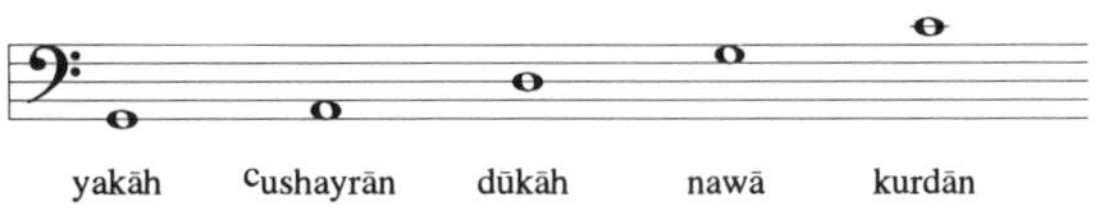

Altogether, the instrument encompasses a tonal range from G to c'' (*yakāh* to *jawāb kurdān*):

Some especially virtuosic ʿūd performers even attach a sixth string next to the *kurdān* string (c'), usually tuning it to f' (*māhūrān*). Iraqi ʿūd performers, however, prefer the tuning F (*qarār jahārkāh*) or E𝄳 (*qarār sīkāh*). Hence, the tuning variants that result are:

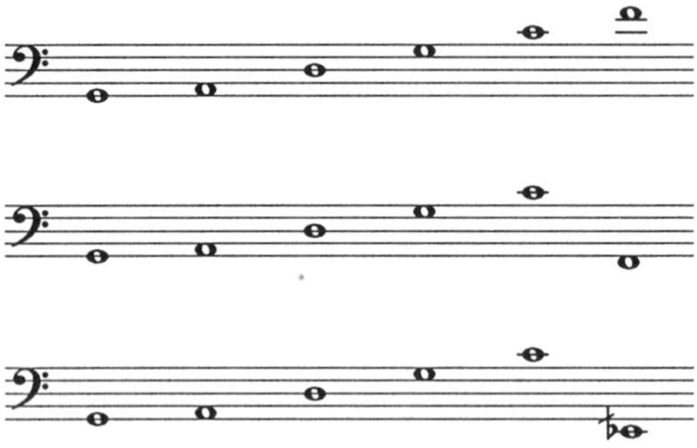

The plectrum named *rīshah*, the quill of an eagle feather, is held by the ʿūd performer between thumb and index finger. It is plucked in one (∨∨∨∨) or in two directions (∨∧∨∧). The strings can be plucked in regular (∨∧∨∧∨∧∨∧) or irregular upward or downward motions (∨∨∧∨∨∧∧∧∨∨). A good ʿūd player is not only celebrated for his large repertoire of maqāmāt, but also for a well-balanced application of regular and irregular motions when plucking with the plectrum. In the style and manner of plucking, a certain individuality of the musician's personality can express itself. Every ʿūd player strives to do his best here—especially in the taqsīm, where he can apply his plucking technique to the utmost, since the music is not bound to any temporal order. The musician further demonstrates his technical ability in the clean and rapid execution of passages in the high registers of the instrument, in quick changes between the high and low register (usually at an interval of an octave), and in the "hocketlike" realization of two or even three voices. Hocketlike voice lines result when the musician, by rapidly repeated plucking on a high open string—usually the c-string—creates a drone and simultaneously plays one or two melodies:

If the drone string must also be stopped, additional technical problems arise.

The ʿūd player occasionally desists from plucking with the feather in the right hand, and instead stops a string with the index finger of the left hand while striking it with the middle, ring, or small finger of the same hand. A kind of echo effect is thereby produced. This technique is especially popular in Egypt and is referred to there as *baṣm*.

The solo repertoire of the ʿūd is principally made up of the taqāsīm of the individual maqāmāt. In the layālī vocal form, the ʿūd is looked upon as a preferred, if not a completely irreplaceable, accompanying instrument to the solo song.

Instrument builders who manufacture the ʿūd are found in almost every Arabian land, especially in the big cities like Baghdad, Aleppo, Beirut, Damascus, Cairo, Algiers, and Rabat. Fāḍil ʿAwwād of Baghdad, Nazīh Ghaḍbān of Beirut, and Naḥḥāt of Damascus pride themselves, however, in being the best ʿūd builders in the Arabian world, and indeed, because of the excellent sound of their lutes, most ʿūd virtuosos buy their instruments from them.

In North Africa, musicians are familiar with another type of short-necked lute with four pairs of strings, called *kwītrah* in Morocco and Algeria. The kwītrah is similar to the ʿūd, though its body is approximately the same length as its neck. The tuning of the strings is G-e-A-d. The ʿūd in its classical form is also played in Tunisia, although a four-stringed lute, on which the tones are stopped at frets, is also known there. The tuning of this instrument is D-d-G-c. And in Morocco, a two-stringed, sometimes three-stringed, spike lute known as *gumbrī*, *jnbrī*, or *gnbrī* is popular. Its body, a wooden box or a tortoise shell, is covered with lambskin. Its strings are tuned to the notes G-D or G-D-A.

The *nashʾatkār* is a short-necked lute that is played in Syria and is heard as a solo instrument during taqsīm performances. Its five pairs of strings are tuned the same as the ʿūd's (G-A-d-g-c'), but because it is strung with wire, it sounds more like the long-necked lute, *buzuq*.

The body of the *buzuq* recalls that of a mandolin, its neck, on the other hand, that of a guitar. This hybrid instrument was built for the first time in the nineteenth century in Turkey and is popular today among the gypsies of Syria and Lebanon. The frets on the neck of the buzuq are movable. Thus, before making music, the buzuq player must not only tune the strings of the instrument but must also move specific frets to the exact positions that enable fingering of the intervals characteristic for the piece at hand in such a way that entire melodic passages can be performed rapidly and cleanly on one string. The strings are plucked with a tortoise shell plectrum in a manner similar to the way ʿūd is played. But because its two, or sometimes three, pairs of strings are steel, the buzuq has a more metallic sound than that of the ʿūd. The three-stringed instrument is tuned to intervals of an octave and a fourth. Belonging to the solo repertoire of the buzuq are, above all, the taqāsīm. The instrument is also often used in the musical accompaniment of a singer. The buzuq does not, however, belong to the traditional takht ensemble of the Arabs.

Jnbrī player, Morocco.
Photo: J. Dietrich.

Buzuq player Jamīl al-ʿĀṣ, Jordan. Photo: J. Dietrich

The Kamanjah and Other Stringed Instruments

Kamanjah is the name used in the Arabian world today for the European violin. The Arabians, however, do not use the European tuning, but rather:

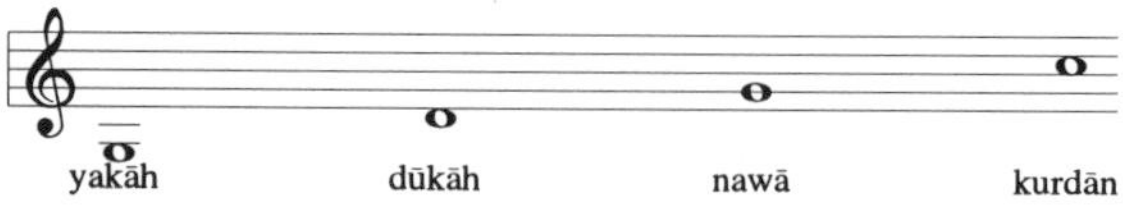

In performance, the kamanjah is generally held like the European violin; only in Morocco is it held vertically and supported on the musician's knee. The European violin illustrates in an exemplary way the musical influence of Europe on the Orient. Until the beginning of the twentieth century, the Arabs

Alto (viola) player of the Brīhī Ensemble of Fez, Morocco.
Photo: H. H. Touma.

were only familiar with the Arabian kamanjah, whose body consisted of half a coconut shell covered with the skin of a sheep or fish. When played, the instrument was held in the lap of the performer, who was seated on the floor in a cross-legged position. Musicians who advocated the so-called new Arabian music, after having acquired experience with European music, were of the opinion that the Arabian kamanjah should be replaced by the European violin. They maintained that the violin possessed a better sound. During the trend of widespread admiration for everything European, the violin did, in fact, supplant the Arabian kamanjah.

As early as the tenth century, al-Fārābī described a stringed instrument, which he called *rabāb*, that may be considered the precursor of the European violin. Its tones were produced, according to al-Fārābī, by "drawing" several (bow) strings over the strings of the instrument. The string bow to which al-Fārābī's description refers must indeed have been discovered much earlier in the Asian realm, if not in the Near East itself. The violin, that most important of European orchestral instruments, can thus be traced back to Asian origins.

The solo repertoire of the kamanjah consists exclusively of taqāsīm. Furthermore, the instrument possesses an essential function in the takht ensemble. The Arabian kamanjah is still played in the Iraqi jālghī baghādī ensemble today. It is known there by the term *jūzah*.

In Tunisia, Algeria, and Morocco, musicians perform on a two-stringed instrument (rabāb), that has a narrow, concave wooden body and a neck for the pegs bent at a right angle to the back. Body and neck are formed from one piece of wood and merge into one another. The string bow is held like a European contrabass bow. The strings are tuned to the interval of a fifth (G–D). Single-stringed instruments are also familiar to the Arabs. The *rabāb ash-shāʿir*, the "rabāb of the poet," has as its body a rectangular wooden frame through which the neck is run, with lambskin covering both front and back of the sound box. The rabāb ash-shāʿir is played primarily by impoverished musicians, usually to accompany epic songs based on such famous epic poems as the "*Abū Zayd al-Hilālī*" or the "*ʿAntar ʿAbs.*" The tonal range of the instrument is limited to a fourth (*yakāh–rāst*/G–c).

Rabāb player, Tunisia.
Photo: A. Danielou.

The rabāb player ʿAbd al-Karīm Rayyis, leader of the Brīhī Ensemble of Fez, Morocco.
Photo: H. H. Touma.

Jūzah player of the jālghī baghdādī ensemble, Iraq. Photo: H. H. Touma

Rabābah player, Aswan, Egypt. Photo: H. H. Touma.

Playing position of the qānūn player, Palestine. Photo: H. H. Touma.

The Qānūn

The body of the *qānūn* (plucked box zither) has the form of a right trapezoid. The number of diatonically tuned strings varies between sixty-three and eighty-four. As a rule, seventy-two strings of gut or nylon are stretched across the top, arranged and tuned in sets of three, so that every three neighboring strings produce the same tone. An instrument with seventy-two strings thus has a total of twenty-four tones at its disposal. The Egyptian version of the qānūn, however, has seventy-eight strings and can accordingly produce twenty-six different tones. The tonal range extends from *qarār-jahārkāh* to *jawāb-kurdān* (F^1–c''):

The trapezoidal box has a wooden surface that does not completely cover the body but leaves open an area extending over the entire width of the instrument to the right of the musician. Stretched across this open area are five rectangular pieces of skin on which the feet of the wooden bridge (*faras*) rest. To the left, along the oblique side of the instrument, are the tuning pegs, arranged in groups of three. Near the pegs are 156 attachable and detachable metal bridges (*ʿurab*), which can be placed beneath the strings to alter their length and, thereby, their tuning. Six such ʿurab are available for each of the twenty-six sets of identically tuned strings. The tuning is generally diatonic and reflects the structure of the maqām row chosen for the piece about to be performed. The qānūn is plucked with tortoise-shell plectra affixed to rings that are worn on the right and left index fingers.

The ʿurab allow for a quick retuning of the qānūn, which may be necessary not only between two performance pieces but also in the middle of a piece when modulating to a new maqām row. However, to increase the tension of a string and thus raise its tone, a skillful qānūn player will sometimes, with delicately measured pressure, quickly apply one finger of the left hand to the string while plucking it with fingers of the right hand.

During performance, the qānūn lies horizontally in the lap of the musician. During the 1920s, it was customary for the qānūn player to sit on the ground in cross-legged position; today the performer sits in a chair. While plucking the strings, the fingers wearing the plectra are held at the interval of an octave, and the left index finger follows the right one somewhat displaced temporally. The result is a synchopated, heterophonic two-voice composition in parallel octaves.

The qānūn appears under that name in Arabian sources as

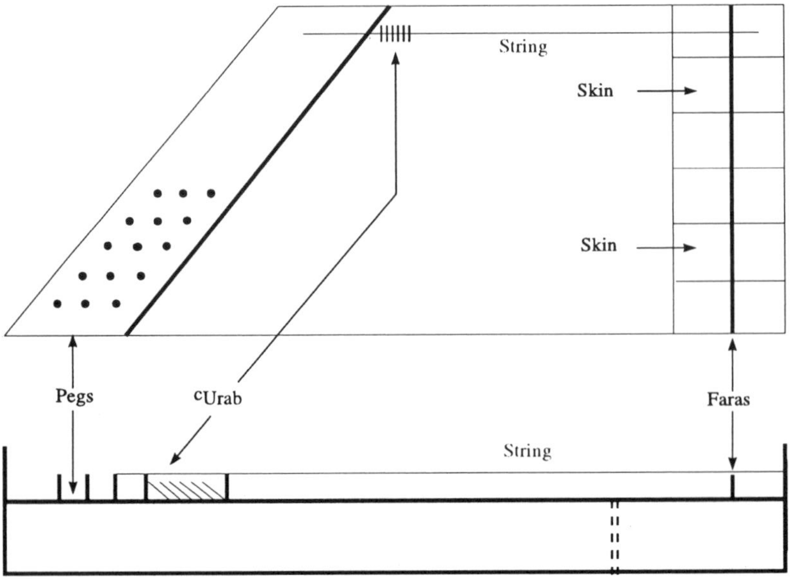

Qānūn player, Morocco. Photo: H. H. Touma.

early as the tenth century. In his "Great Book of Music" (*Kitāb al-mūsīqā al-kabīr*), al-Fārābī already discussed the tuning of the forty-five-stringed instrument of the time. Ṣafī ad-Dīn al-Urmawī, however, did not speak of the qānūn but called the zither *nuzhah*. Today, the qānūn is popular everywhere in North Africa and the Near East as the instrument of traditional Arabian art music. It is primarily men who make music with it; female qānūn performers are seldom encountered. Like the ʿūd, the qānūn has a solo repertoire consisting mainly of taqsīm pieces, and it is also used to accompany layālī singing. The Egyptians, in particular, can look back at their centuries-old tradition of qānūn building with pride that the most accomplished builders have been among their ranks.

Sanṭūr player, Iraq. Photo: H. H. Touma.

The Iraqi Sanṭūr

The Iraqi *sanṭūr* is a trapezoidal box zither with a walnut body and ninety-two metal strings. The strings, which are tuned to the same pitch in groups of four, are struck with two wooden mallets. The tuning of these twenty-three sets of strings extends from the low *yakāh* (G) up to *jawāb jawāb ḥusaynī* (a''):

The name *sanṭūr* is derived from the Greek *psalterion.* Native to Persia and Turkey as well as to Iraq, the instrument came to Europe with the Arabs by way of North Africa and Spain during the Middle Ages. In China, at the beginning of the eighteenth century, it was referred to as the "foreign *qin.*" Iraq has produced entire generations of famous sanṭūr virtuosos.

Although of the same type and name, the Persian sanṭūr differs from the Iraqi in the number of strings and the arrangement of bridges on the resonating surface. Whereas the Persian instrument has only eighteen sets of unison strings and two rows of bridges, the Iraqi boasts twenty-three sets of strings and three rows of bridges.

Parallel to the oblique side of the Iraqi sanṭūr are twelve bridges, which divide alternate sets of strings so that exactly one-third of their vibrating length is to the left of the player, and two-thirds is to the right. The tone to the right side of the bridge is therefore an octave lower than that to left (oscillation ratio 2:1). When being played, both parts of the string are used alike. Toward the right side of the sanṭūr, beneath the remaining sets of strings, are eleven to fourteen bridges arranged in groups of seven, eight, nine, or ten, and four. The bridges in the larger group divide their sets of strings so that one-third of the vibrating length is to the right and two-thirds to the left. Their function is thus similar to the twelve bridges to the musician's left, but in this case the strings may only be struck to the left of the bridge. The four remaining bridges partition off the distance between the right edge of the instrument and the row of twelve bridges. Here again, one-third of this distance is to the right of the bridge and two-thirds to the left, and also again, the strings may only be struck to the left of the bridge.

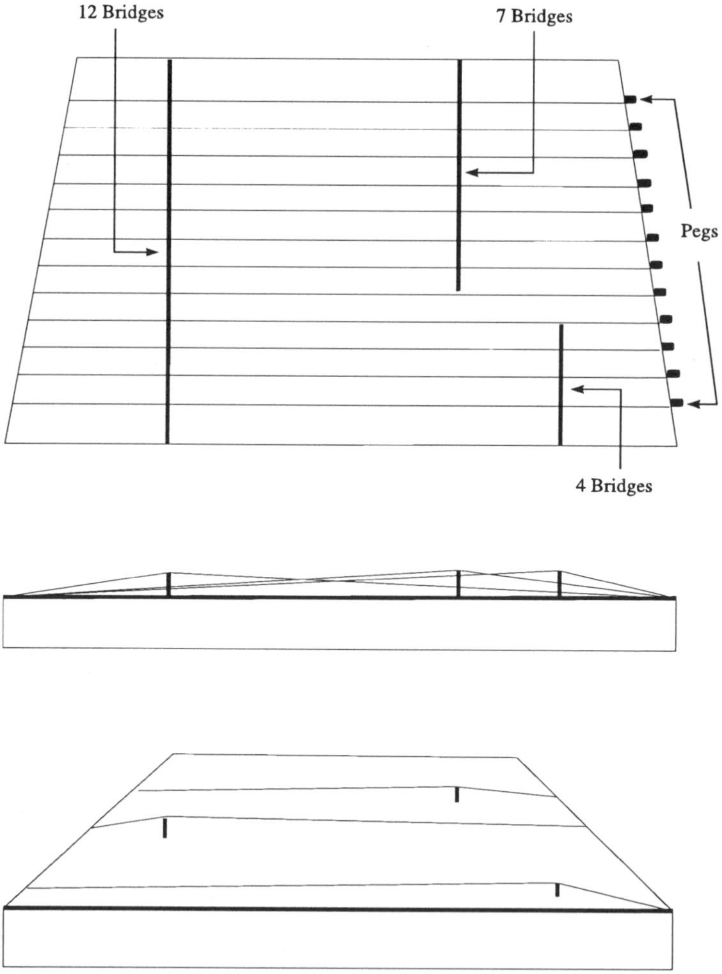

In view of this arrangement of the bridges and the basically diatonic tuning of the sanṭūr, the following tones are available to the instrument:

1. The four sets of strings with bridges placed furthest to the right yield

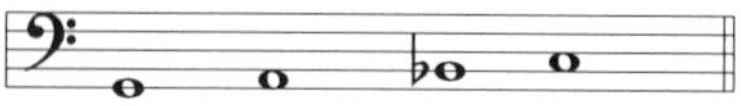

2. The remaining seven string sets with bridge positions on the right yield

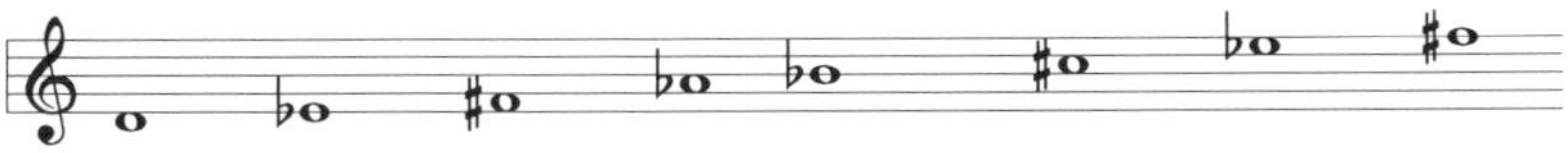

3. The twelve string sets with bridge positions on the left yield

   a) struck to the right of the bridges

   b) struck to the left of the bridges

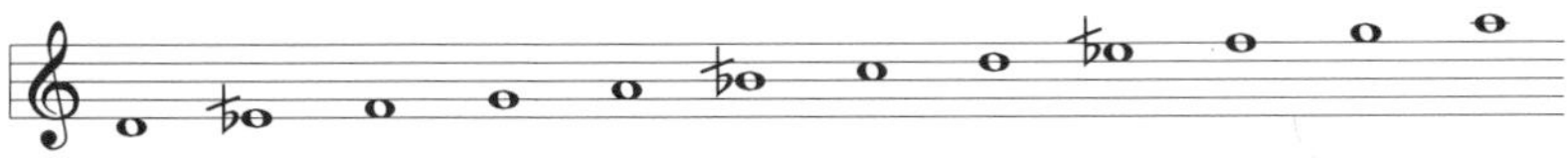

All the metal strings of the sanṭūr have the same gauge, which is why the pitch of each string is solely dependent upon its tension. The bridges are called *dāma* ("chessmen") because they look like pawns. The strings do not rest directly on the wood of the bridge but on a nail lying across the upper part of the bridge, hence the pure metallic sound of the sanṭūr. Belonging to the repertoire of a sanṭūr player are the taqāsīm and the complete literature of the maqām al-ʿirāqī.

Wind Instruments

The Nāy

The *nāy* is an end-blown flute that is open at both ends. It is constructed in different sizes, traditionally from bamboo or cane. In various places of late, however, plastic pipe has been used in place of the traditional material. The musician blows against the edge of the pipe opening. This instrument, which is also a part

Nāy player, Tunisia. Photo: J. Dietrich.

of many other musical cultures, has attained in the Arabian a special degree of refinement with regard to performance technique and sound, though in its structure it is a relatively simple instrument. The nāy generally has one finger hole on the underside and six on the front. Through the technique of over-blowing, the musician can play a range of more than three octaves. The fundamental tone of a nāy depends upon the length of the flute pipe. One differentiates, for example, between the large nāy (*dūkāh nāy*) with *dūkāh* (d) as the second lowest tone and the small nāy (*nawā nāy*) with *nawā* (g) as the second lowest tone. Dūkāh nāy and nawā nāy are the most frequently played *nāyāt* (plural of *nāy*).

Players often have nāyāt of several different sizes on hand during a performance so that they can easily execute pieces lying in different maqām rows. In general, though, a nāy virtuoso is perfectly capable of producing all the tones of the maqām row on a single instrument. To do this requires considerable finesse: the lip and head position must be changed while blowing and the finger holes must be opened or closed in diverse combinations. In this way, it is possible to modulate within a piece to the neighboring modes as well as to the distant ones without having to change instruments. The solo pieces performed on the nāy are primarily taqāsīm. On the other hand, nāy players also number among the members of the takht ensemble. The nāy is performed exclusively by men.

Other Wind Instruments

Aside from the nāy, no other wind instrument has been able to assert itself in the traditional art music of the Arabs. Instruments like the *shabbabah*, *sūrnāy*, *mijwiz*, *arghūl*, and *qirbah* all belong to the domain of folk music. *Shabbabah* is the term used in Syria, Lebanon, and North Africa for a split-core flute. It was already known in Arab-occupied Spain by the name *axabeba*. The *sūrnāy*, a double-reed instrument that is popular throughout the entire Near East as well as in North and West Africa, is played to drum accompaniment in processions on holidays. In North Africa, the sūrnāy is known by the names *al-ghayṭah*, *al-ghaydah* and *zukrah*. The *mijwiz* and *zummārah* are a kind of double clarinet, whose two pipes are of equal length and have the same number of finger holes. If, however, the pipes are of different lengths, then one refers to an *arghūl* or *yarghūl*. The pipe without finger holes, which produces a drone, can reach a length of over two meters in some instruments. *Qirbah* and *ruwāqah* are the names given to the bagpipe. Horns and trumpets are found less frequently in Arabian music, although instruments of this kind are mentioned in historical accounts as *būq* and *nafīr*. Nafīr trumpets are still played occasionally today in North Africa at festive parades during Ramaḍān, the month of fasting.

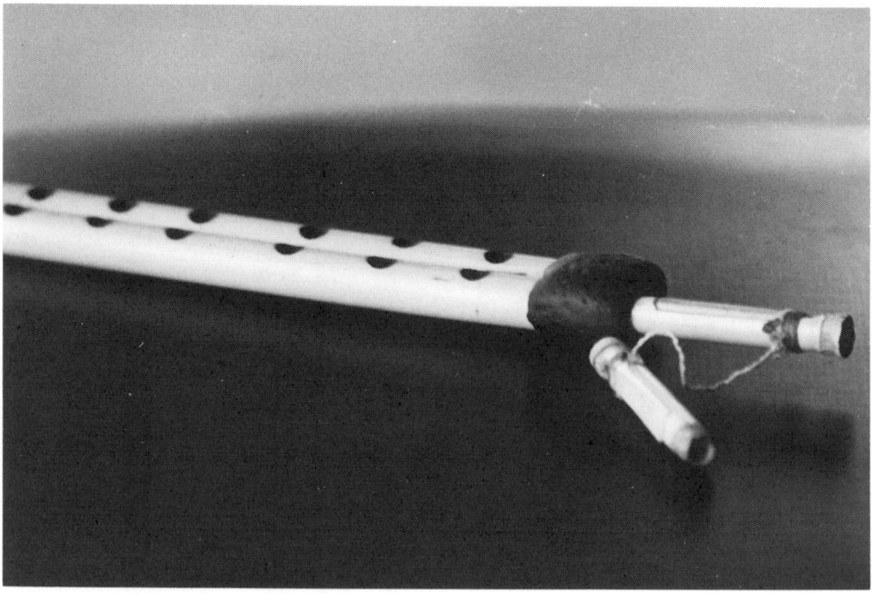

Mijwiz from Iraq. Photo: H. H. Touma

Mijwiz player from Lebanon. Photo: J. Wenzel.

Arghūl player from Upper Egypt. Photo: J. Dietrich.

Percussion Instruments

The Riqq

The *riqq* is a single-headed tambourine with a diameter of approximately eight inches (20 cm). The frame is mounted with ten pairs of cymbals set inside vertical pairs of "cymbal windows" that are cut out of the frame in a symmetrical arrangement. The riqq is held in the left hand by the thumb and the fingers in such a manner that the fingers can also strike the rim of the frame. The right hand maneuvers at the center as well as at the edge of the membrane. These two positions correspond to a light drum beat, *tak*, and a heavy one, *dum* (see page 48). The frame of the riqq is covered with small colored mosaic tiles made of mother-of-pearl, bones, horn, or wood. A precious instrument—that is, one that professional musicians prefer to use—is covered with fish skin, while an ordinary riqq, as found mostly in the hands of lay musicians, is equipped with a simple goatskin membrane.

Riqq players perform in the traditional takht ensembles. There they take on an indispensible function in the performance of Arabian art music. The musician must perform the awzān, the accompanying rhythmic patterns, exactly, thereby earning him the name *ḍābiṭ īqāʿ* ("he who performs the rhythm exactly"). All the wazn patterns belong to the repertoire of the riqq player, who must be prepared to improvise on them during a performance.

The riqq is popular in all Arabian lands, chiefly as an instrument of art music. In Iraq, however, the term *daff zinjārī* is common, while in the lands of North Africa one speaks of *ṭār*. Riqq instruments are manufactured in all big cities of the Arabian world; nonetheless, professional musicians prefer to buy instruments from Damascus and Cairo because of their presumed special quality.

The single-headed frame drum is found in the Arabian lands in still three other forms, which differ from the riqq in size, method of production, performance technique, and context in which they are used. In addition, the ethnic, social, and religious position of the musician and his listeners could in each case be different. The following sections discuss the three drums *daff*, *mazhar*, and *bandīr*.

A ṭār player of the Brīhī Ensemble of Fez, Morocco. Photo: H. H. Touma.

A ṭār player of a ma'lūf ensemble, Tunisia. Photo: J. Dietrich.

The Daff

The *daff* (*duff*), like the riqq, is a tambourine. This instrument, however, has a larger diameter—approximately twelve inches (30 cm)—and a shallower frame. Furthermore, the daff has only five pairs of cymbals, although these are likewise set symmetrically into the "cymbal windows" of the mosaic-covered frame. When played, the left hand holds the instrument while the right one strikes it. Now and then the cymbal-adorned instrument is shaken to produce tremololike effects, and sometimes it is struck against the body of the musician.

The daff is not used to perform wazn patterns; its primary function is to accompany female dancers in the Oriental cabarets of the big cities. The fact that the frame drum was chiefly played by women in the Near East has already been supported by documentary evidence from early times. Such documents can chiefly be found in Egyptian and Jewish history. The Jews called the frame drum—and still call it today—*tūf miryam* ("Miriam's drum"). Also among the Arabs of the jāhiliyah, an instrument of this type was reserved exclusively for women. The first man whose frame drum playing was reported by Arab historians of the Ḥijāz was Ṭuways, who belonged to the group of mukhannathūn, effeminate men who behaved as women.

The Mazhar

The *mazhar* (*mizhar*) is a frame drum without cymbals of approximately twenty-four inches (60 cm) in diameter. The frame, which is 2.4 inches (6 cm) wide, is not covered with mosaics but instead is equipped with small iron-ring chains hung inside of the frame. The instrument rests upright in the left hand while the right strikes the middle of the membrane. The use of the mazhar is reserved for ritual occasions, since each instrument is dedicated to a saint. The mazhar is played at the dhikr ceremonies of some sūfī sects such as the *Rifāʿiyah* and *Qādiriyah*, and at other religious occasions such as the birthday of the Prophet, funerals, and healing ceremonies. The instrument is also played in the mosque.

The Bandīr

Bandīr (*bindīr*) is the name given to a single-headed frame drum of approximately sixteen inches (40 cm) in diameter. The frame, approximately four inches (10 cm) wide, has an opening into which the thumb of the left hand holding the instrument is placed. Two snares run directly underneath the drum's membrane. The bandīr is struck like the mazhar and likewise belongs to the sphere of religious music. It is very common in all Arabian lands and is chiefly played by sūfī musicians.

The Darabukkah

A single-headed drum in the form of a cup or goblet is known in Arabian music by the name *darabukkah*, *durbakkih*, or *dirbūkah*. When played in a standing position, the darabukkah is held under the musician's arm; when played in a sitting position, the instrument rests on the thigh. The membrane is struck with both hands. The heavy principal dum beats, as with the frame drum, are produced at the center, whereas the light secondary tak beats are produced near the rim. Differentiating the sounds in this way, the darabukkah player is able to present the wazn patterns of traditional Arabian compositions.

The darabukkah has a clay body. In recent times, however, instruments made of brass or metal, with a tension ring and a tightening device that serve to regulate and fix the tension of the membrane, have come into use. With the clay darabukkah, the membrane is heated and stretched near a fire or by rubbing it with the hands. Professional musicians use instruments covered with fish skin. Goat or sheepskin, on the other hand, characterize the simpler darabukkah forms.

The darabukkah is a musical instrument that is extremely popular in the Arabian world and may not be absent from any Arabian festivity. It is an instrument of folk music as well as art music and is played at wedding celebrations in the village and the city as well as in the ensembles of Arabian art music. Whereas women are also allowed to make folk music with the darabukkah, only men play the instrument in Arabian art music. A good darabukkah player, like a riqq player, must have a command of the entire wazn repertoire.

The darabukkah player Sāmī ʿAbd al-Aḥad, Iraq. Photo: H. H. Touma.

The Naqqārāt

Naqqārāt (singular, *naqqārah*) are a pair of kettle drums consisting of clay or copper kettles with camel skin stretched over them. The musician sits cross-legged on the floor and strikes the drums, which are placed in front of him, with two sticks. The heavy main beats *(dum)* are performed on the drum to the right, the light secondary beats *(tak)* on the one to the left. In this way, the entire wazn repertoire can be presented on the naqqārāt.

Naqqārāt player from Iraq. Photo: H. H. Touma

Naqqārāt exist in different sizes. The large specimens, called *naqāryah*, are mounted onto the right and left sides of a camel. The musician plays while riding the camel. The medium-sized naqqārāt are called *naqrazān* and are carried by a donkey. Both types of instrument are chiefly used in processions.

Other percussion instruments, which are encountered primarily in the folk music of the Arabs, include double-headed drums of different sizes (*ṭabl*); a double-headed rectangular frame drum; copper castanets (*ṣājāt*), which are played by both male and female dancers in public performances; and cymbals (*ṣunūj*), which are played during religious musical exercises.

Instrument Construction

The musical instruments of Arabian art music are manufactured by specialists in the big cities of the Arabian lands. The instrument builders, of course, also supply lay musicians. Orders for custom-made construction are only taken from the professional musician in order to fulfill the particular needs of the artist concerning the size of the instrument, the material for the body and membrane, and the workmanship and decoration. Primarily the nāy players take pride in being able to construct their instruments themselves.

Many Arabian musical instruments are produced in quantity and sold to lay musicians and tourists at the markets of Arabian cities. In addition, the small urban factories also export their products to other Arabian lands or even to countries outside the Arabian world. In the urban instrument-building workshops, it is often possible, for a modest sum, to acquire a new instrument in exchange for an old one or to borrow a musical instrument.

In the secular sphere of Arabian musical life, the value of an instrument is measured according to purely musical criteria. It is different, however, in the religious sphere. Here, through the blessing of a Shaykh or an Imām, the esteem in which the musical instrument is held can increase considerably. The fact that an instrument belongs to a mosque can also enhance the measure of appreciation it is shown. An old mazhar drum, for example, which was once blessed by a Shaykh and which is the property of a mosque, despite its ripped drumskin, means more to musicians than a newly manufactured instrument without any religious relevance.

The Art Music Ensembles

The Takht Ensemble

Takht literally means "bed," "seat," or "podium." The takht ensemble, which truly embodies the ensemble of Arabian art music, consists of the following musical instruments: the ʿūd, the qānūn, the Arabian kamanjah (later two), the nāy, the riqq, and the darabukkah. The melody instruments either sound together heterophonically at intervals of one or two octaves or step to the fore as soloists. If vocal compositions are being perfomed, a male or female singer assumes the principal musical role, supported by a group of four to six singers who perform the refrainlike sections. Takht ensembles with this instrumentation exist in Egypt, Syria, Lebanon, and Jordan. The repertoire of the takht includes vocal forms such as the dawr, muwashshaḥ, layālī, maʾlūf, qaṣīdah, and mawwāl, together with instrumental forms such as bashraf, samāʿī, taḥmīlah, and dūlāb.

The Jālghī Baghdādī Ensemble

The *jālghī baghdādī* ensemble, which is native to Iraq, includes the sanṭūr, the jūzah, the darabukkah (also called *ṭablah* or *dunbak*), and the riqq (known in Iraq by the name *daff zinjārī*). Together with a vocalist (*qāriʾ*) and a choir, the jalghī baghdādī ensemble performs the entire repertoire of the traditional maqām al-ʿirāqī.

The Andalusī Ensemble

Andalusī music, which is popular over all of North Africa, is noted for its own special ensemble formations that include a ʿūd, a kamanjah violin, a darabukkah, a rabāb (bow-necked lute), a viola, and a ṭār (tambourine).

The Big Orchestra of "Modern" Arabian Music

When speaking of the music of the Arabs, one cannot by any means disregard the large professional ensembles at the radio, television, and theater houses that exist today in all Arabian lands and which make up more than ninety percent of all music programs broadcast in Baghdad, Cairo, Tunis, and Rabat. They are financed by the state or sponsored privately, since they are in fact the "pride" of many Arabs. The size and makeup of the orchestra depend upon the attitude of the music directors at the television and radio stations toward the question of the "modern" in Arabian music. Musical instruments "made in Germany," "made in Great Britain," "made in France," and also "made in Russia" have found a place of honor in the contemporary "big Arabian orchestra." They have stripped the Arabian musical instruments of their traditional function in the ensemble or at least have forced their sound more and more into the background. These Western musical instruments have destroyed the principles of the Arabian tone system and, for all practical purposes, have eliminated the traditional takht ensemble and its intimate sound character.

The "big Arabian orchestra" of the present, which many an Arab looks upon with obvious pride, is fundamentally a hybrid, neither traditionally Arabian nor authentically European in its structure. It includes, among other instruments, the ʿūd, the qānūn, and the nāy; a string section of approximately twenty violins, five cellos, and two contrabasses; clarinets, oboes, and trumpets; accordion, electric organ, and synthesizer; as well as the riqq, the darabukkah, timpani, and a glockenspiel. With a huge racket, it plays together in unison or—if it is an "up-to-date" orchestra—in multi-voiced harmony, offering nothing better than a poor imitation of European orchestral style. Often, the orchestra accompanies a male or female singer who croons a pop song into the microphone. Through the mass media, and especially through Egyptian feature films, such singers have managed to achieve immense popularity. Hence, for traditional Arabian music—for its song forms, rhythmic wazn cycles, and much more—there is hardly a place left in public musical life. The tradition is falling more and more into oblivion. Today, in place of the wazn patterns are the samba, rumba, and foxtrot.

7

Musician and Composer and the Problem of Cultural Identity

Living in a society that is struggling to preserve its identity, and thereby having to grapple with problems that have arisen since the end of the nineteenth century and particularly since the end of the First World War, the Arabian musician today is bewildered. In his book *The Arabs in History* (London 1950), Orientalist Bernhard Lewis summed up the situation:

> In these problems of readjustment the Arab peoples have a choice of several paths; they may submit to one or other of the contending versions of modern civilization that are offered to them, merging their own culture and identity in a larger and dominating whole; or they may try to turn their backs upon the West and all its works, . . . or finally—and for this the removal of the irritant of foreign interference is a prerequisite—they may succeed in renewing their society from within, meeting the West on terms of equal co-operation, absorbing something of both its science and humanism, not only in shadow but in substance, in a harmonious balance with their own inherited tradition.

The Arabian musician is confronted by the same problem of readjustment. Like Arabian society, he has not devoted himself totally to either the capitalist West or the formerly socialist

East, to the Third World or to his own tradition and culture. In his creative work, he follows no clear course. He cultivates a music that does not convincingly represent the essence of either the Arabian spirit or the foreign. The music appears to be largely influenced by the laws of the music market, or popular taste, and the new trends that govern this music market are looked upon as real progress. But the new developments give rise to nothing more than a monstrous distortion of the traditional musical resources of the Arabs. Such a distortion was created by the use of non-Arabian instruments, rhythms, and compositional forms, by the tendency toward harmonization and orchestration of Arabian music, and by a performance practice that is, along with everything previously mentioned, foreign to its nature.

Advocates of the "new," the *jadīd*, observe that Arabian society has developed itself further through the adoption of the technological achievements of the West. The Arab cooks Arabian food today on electric stoves without sacrificing the essence of Arabian cuisine. Why then shouldn't one also make use of the "perfected" musical instruments and other aspects of Western musical practice? Arabian music, as the supporters of new musical developments argue, should not rest content with the time-honored forms alone but should develop new forms of expression. Strictly speaking, however, the musical forms of the jadīd are based on the same fundamental cyclic principle as the *qadīm*, the so-called old. Melodies are strung together with or without a refrain, allowing for the possibility of a convergence with such traditional genres as the taqsīm and layālī. But with respect to the traditional Arabian tone system and rhythmic-temporal organization, the new music has irresponsibly compromised the essence of Arabian music. While the performance of Arabian vocal genres of earlier times was based on the maqāmāt, rhythmically accompanied by wazn patterns, today's composers avoid writing music on the basis of maqām rows—especially if they contain medium seconds (intervals of approximately 155, 173, or 182 cents). They prefer to use, if any, diatonically constructed maqām rows that are playable on Western instruments, even though the equally tempered intonation of the instrument completely adulterates the characteristic

Arabian mode. The same is true for the wazn patterns, which must give way to the 3/4 and 4/4 rhythmic meters of the foxtrot and samba.

The number of Arabs espousing the "new" in music is large, while the influence of those pleading the cause of the "old" is minimal. Those who have not yet lost their identity, however, have recently achieved some first successes in their efforts to preserve what is genuine and old. In their view, musical change should represent a true further development of the handed-down genres of traditional art music. Moreover, appearing on a wider scale since approximately the 1960s in many Arabian lands is a growing movement to preserve and cultivate authentic music. Ministries of Culture, and even radio and television stations, are beginning to support the representatives of a traditional Arabian musical practice.

Coupled with the neglect of older musical genres has been a growing demand for new compositional forms that depart in structure from the strict rules of tradition. Arabians have distanced themselves from their own musical legacy—which is now rather smiled at—in order to set about creating a "new" Arabian music. If one observes critically what survives today in the way of traditional compositional forms—those based on the strict rules of the Arabian musical tradition—then one encounters genres such as the muwashshaḥ, dawr, bashraf, samāʿī, and taḥmīlah. Among the early handed-down musical forms, the qaṣīdah is the only one that allows the composer a relatively free hand in setting preexisting text to music. For this reason, contemporary composers concentrate their creative efforts on the *ughniyah* ("pop song"), an embodiment for the Arab of the new Arabian music.

The contemporary Arabian ughniyah cannot be compared to a Schubert lied or an operatic aria. The Arabian composer does not set his works down on paper and hence is not dependant upon a publisher to publish them. Music publishers virtually do not exist in Arabian lands. The singer does not learn the new ughniyah from a score but rather studies it together with the composer during joint music making. Later, the song is always performed by the same singer in concerts and on radio and television broadcasts, and before long, it is inevitably connected with his or her name by the public. The amount of payment for the composer is calculated according to the popularity of the singer for whom the ughniyah is intended.

The transmission of music without recourse to visual means is nothing unusual in Arabian music. For centuries, Arabs have been handing down their vocal and instrumental music by oral means alone. One argument against adopting the European system of notation is that a written transcription of Arabian music will always be inexact and incomplete, given the limited number of symbols in the Western system.

In the process of devoting themselves to the jadīd, Arabian musicians and singers have relinquished their dual function as creators and performers and have become one hundred percent interpreters in the Western sense. Whereas they do not in general have a command of notation, they do possess an enormous power of recollection, which enables them to perform their part from memory. And once a composition has been preserved on tape, it becomes easier to learn a new piece or to freshen up one previously stored in the memory when an occasion calls for it.

In contrast to many other professions, that of musician is met with only limited esteem in Arabian society. At the beginning of a career, musical activity is nothing more than a sideline. Not until after success has come, after the musician has won over the public through concerts, radio and television broadcasts, and recordings, can he begin to earn his livelihood through music alone. The social prestige of Arabian musicians also suffers from the fact that there are so far no unions to look after their interests.

The musical career of a singer or musician begins with performances in private settings. Small public concerts follow. Employment in an ensemble or at a radio station and the making of a recording mark the next stages of the musical career. An artist must generally pay for all production costs of the first recording. If the record sells well, or if a permanent job materializes, then the artist has achieved a remarkable position—one, however, that doesn't necessarily benefit artistic development, considering that what is played or sung thereafter is dictated by the radio station or the director of the ensemble, based entirely on the demands of the marketplace, that is, of popular taste.

The composer of traditional Arabian music is often its interpreter, as well. Furthermore, the performer does not just interpret a musical text: in forms such as the maqām al-ʿirāqī, the nawbah, the taqsīm, the layālī, and the mawwāl, for example, the artist also functions in a musically creative way within the preexisting framework set by tradition. In paraphrasing traditional musical material the performer becomes composer. For other musical forms of traditional art music, such as the muwashshaḥ, dawr, and qaṣīdah, however, the border between composer and interpreter is much more clearly drawn.

Since the beginning of this century, there has been a noticeable tendency to overrate the importance of composing, as distinctly separate from the function of performing, in a way not previously known to the tradition. As a result, traditional musical genres in which the name of the composer was not usually a part of the information handed down, have receded into the background. To this day, they are labeled qadīm. The overrating of the composer ultimately manifests itself as well in the tendency to adopt Western attitudes—stimulated by both the capitalist West and the formerly socialist East.

Contemporary composers can be grouped into three categories. In the first category are those who write compositions that can be classified between entertainment music and serious music. For them, the entertainment value is paramount. They create a kind of pop music that is produced for radio, television, records, and the concert stage. Formally, it is based on the principles of the ughniyah, the qaṣīdah, and the instrumental forms bashraf and samāʿī. The temporal organization of the bashraf and samāʿī, and the names of the genres, however, have been changed. The composers choose new titles for their works: the name of a girl, for example, or that of a city—or they name their compositions with an arbitrary word. As previously mentioned, representatives of this type of modern music take pride in the "big Arabian orchestra."

Belonging to the second category is a group of approximately ten to twenty composers who have studied composition at conservatories in Europe or America and whose works combine art music of an Oriental color with Western counterpoint and Western harmony and rhythms. Although they have created symphonic works, piano music, and so on, these composers have not mangaged to become anything more than shadows of their European models. Nevertheless—as their argument goes—one can't be expected to wait until Arabian society has evolved so far on its own initiative that it will be possible to write Arabian symphonic works at Arabian music conservatories for Arabian orchestras. But until Arabian society rediscovers its identity and serious Arabian composers are able to shake off their feelings of inferiority, the question will remain whether, in fact, Arabian society needs symphonic works at all.

Composers in the third category want to preserve the traditional music of the Arabs and pass it on to succeeding generations. They believe that true Arabian music should be created within the framework of the tradition and according to conventional standards. The creation of authentic musical material, based on the modal structures of the maqām al-ʿirāqī, taqsīm, layālī, and nawbah, has met with great interest on the part of Arabian audiences.

One of the most original of these composer-interpreters is the Iraqi musician Munir Bashir (see page 110). He has satisfactorily and convincingly solved the ostensibly unsolvable problem of the further development of traditional Arabian music by creating something new without destroying the old. Munir Bashir's music is directly descended from traditional Arabian music. Its authenticity is underscored by its embedment in the Arabian tone system, by its adherence to the traditional characteristics of form and style, and by the instrument that serves him when he performs, the ʿūd. In stark contrast are the supporters of the jadīd, who have caused great damage to the Arabian music tradition by seizing a fundamentally foreign genre that originated in a very different cultural sphere and making it completely their own. Their creations thus became foreign substances within the framework of Arabian musical practice.

The maqām performances of Munir Bashir are deep meditations, philosophizing on the lute with mystical expressive content. Whereas a taqsīm performance today does not, as a rule, last longer than ten minutes lest it bore the listener, Munir Bashir's exciting taqsīm presentations can last more than forty minutes. In a conventional taqsīm, only one musical climax—

the highest tone level—is usually presented, but Bashir's taqāsīm have several such highpoints, which are developed spatially, dynamically, and agogically. While the dynamic level of traditionally performed Arabian music typically lies unchanging in the medium range, the dynamics of Bashir's taqāsīm range from *ff* to *ppp*. Also new in Bashir's taqāsīm are his use of harmonic tones, which expand the tonal range of the lute by two octaves, and his stopping of strings in different positions, which reveals new timbres on the instrument. Furthermore, the long pauses between the melodic passages of his taqāsīm possess an extraordinary tension.

All these elements, paired with a high degree of musical originality and virtuosity, put a unique stamp on the music of Munir Bashir. He is concerned not with mere reproduction of the traditional but rather with further development while maintaining authenticity. Bashir's music is just as Arabian as Beethoven's is German or Borodin's, Russian. Because Bashir, in the words of Bernhard Lewis, freed himself "of the irritant of foreign interference" and "met the West on terms of equal cooperation" (see page 142), his music has achieved success—not only in Arabian lands but in Europe and the United States as well—to an extent that has not to date been equalled by any composer in the other two categories.

In the domain of singing, a phenomenon that has thus far surfaced approximately every two hundred years in Arabian music history is encountered in the person of Umm Kulthūm (1896–1975), the prima donna of Arabian vocal music. Her outstanding artistry can truly be compared to such legendary singers as Ziryāb and Ḥāmūlī (ninth and nineteenth centuries). Umm Kulthūm was born in an Egyptian village in the year 1896. Her father, a Shaykh, used to perform religious songs and praises to the prophet Muhammad in the mosque. At the age of five, she could already recite from the Koran. Still as a small girl, she appeared as a singer at village festivities and assisted her father at his performances. From 1918 on, she gave public concerts in Cairo. These were broadcast regularly by Cairo Radio, starting in 1937. In the year 1923, Umm Kulthūm moved to Cairo.

Umm Kulthūm's originality is evident in her inimitable

vocal interpretations, which are based on a musical phenomenon that can only be described as improvisatory-compositional. Attentive listeners can discern how Umm Kulthūm changes the tempo of a qaṣīdah, how she stretches or shortens phrases, how she unexpectedly repeats words or entire lines of verse, and how she throws the substance of a text segment into relief by long improvised melodic passages. By a certain play of gestures, by sighing, or by a mere movement of the hands, Umm Kulthūm was able to convey the content of a song so well that the audience would be swept away by her performance. Moreover, the songstress's voice, judged according to the standards of Arabian music aesthetics, had all the characteristics of perfection; it was regarded as beautiful, radiant, ravishing, and dreamlike.

Umm Kulthūm's concerts usually took place in a large garden in Cairo on the first Thursday of every month during the concert season. The program consisted exclusively of *qaṣā'id* (plural of *qaṣīdah*) that had been expressly written and set to music for her. The premiere of a qaṣīdah was always a big and exciting musical event, not just for the public assembled at the open-air concert, but also for the millions of listeners throughout the Arabian world who were seated in front of their radios.

The musical experience imparted to the listeners by performers like Umm Kulthūm and her ensemble is called *ṭarab*. The intensity of ṭarab depends primarily on the voice and performance style of the singer, as exemplified by Umm Kulthūm. Her performances often only approximately followed the fixed rhythmic-temporal organization of the melody. She would strip some melodic passages of their strict rhythmic form in order to repeat, vary, and paraphrase individual sections in an improvisatory way or transform the musical material more dramatically within the framework of traditional modal principles. Her presentation thus hovered between that which she performed and that which she created herself. The musical contrast between the familiar and fixed on the one side and the new, freely structured though related on the other creates, in general, a tension whose up and down evokes ṭarab in the listener. The emphasis of this contrast represents the most striking stylistic element of Umm Kulthūm's artistry.

As is common in contemporary Arabian vocal music, one

speaks of the qaṣā'id of Umm Kulthūm; that is, one uses the name of the singer without describing the composition more specifically. For the majority of the music-loving public, the person of the composer remains unknown. His contribution to the musical event appears to be irrelevant to the listeners. Only a few people, mostly musicians, know the names of those who, in certain circles, are highly desired.

Approximately ninety-five percent of the programs offered by radio stations in Cairo, Baghdad, Damascus, or Rabat, however, consist of pop songs, whose popularity lasts only three or four months, after which they usually fall into complete oblivion. Musical products such as these cannot be clearly assigned either to the domain of art music or to that of folk music. Thus, ninety-five percent of the radio programs bear witness to the unhealthy situation that prevails in Arabian musical life today: fixation on the musical "new," the jadīd. A constructive music critique in this direction is completely lacking.

In recent years, Arabian musicians have sought to find more recognition within their own society by performing on European stages. Not until the early sixties did musicians and singers begin to recognize and exploit this possibility. But the only Arabian artist who can survive in a European concert hall is one who appears before the audience as a representative of traditional Arabian musical culture. Inferior Arabian compositions in a European style and musical genres of the jadīd, neither of which convincingly represents either the European or the Arabian, have no chance here. Arabian musicians on the European stage have the possibility of winning over the audience by performing traditional Arabian music and fully using their artistic expressive powers. Musicians who manage this are also assured of wide acceptance in their homeland.

The Arabian musician has always been not only composer and interpreter in one person but also teacher. Consequently, many excellent musicians and composers are active today as teachers in the music conservatories that have recently been established in almost every big Arabian city. There one can learn to sing or to play an Arabian instrument, and anyone with musical talent can earn a diploma from one of these conservatories. The graduates go on to work in urban music ensembles or at the local radio station, or they give private music lessons—usually, however, outside the big cities.

Imitation of European teaching programs and methods in the music schools, however, has also led to the familiar problems with relation to the preservation and further development of traditional Arabian music. Instruction in classes or groups includes subjects such as music history, music theory, and ear training. Teaching methods developed in Europe for the study of the violin, flute, and so on, were transferred to the study of Arabian musical instruments and, in a modified form, to the study of voice. In the beginning are simple exercises, followed by short compositions, and not until after one or two years are bashraf, samāʿī, and muwashshaḥ pieces studied.

Prerequisite for studying at a music conservatory is a command of European notation. Modal structures, however, must be learned without written notes, through intensive listening or oral instruction. When musical forms such as the taqsīm and layālī are rendered in European musical notation, they leave the reader, especially one less familiar with the music, too much free play in interpretation. The student therefore listens to and musically imitates the teacher until able to find his or her own musical forms of interpretaion and expression. Thus, the transcription of Arabian music in European notation appears to be hardly more than an unavoidable evil with which the Arabian musician must live today.

8

Religious Music

The religious music of the Arabs encompasses the music of Christians as well as that of Moslems. We will confine ourselves here to the music of the Moslems, which is based on the same structural elements as secular Arabian music. The church music of the Christian Arabs, on the other hand, has its roots in foreign musical cultures: in Catholic, Greek Orthodox, and Anglican, as well as in Coptic and Maronite church music. Although the latter two likewise have their origins in a Near Eastern realm, they should nevertheless be viewed more as representatives of the music of the Eastern churches than as attributable to a specific Arabian music culture.

Religious music is performed by Moslems in the mosque during the *dhikr* ceremonies, during the *mawlid* festivities, and at various other religious occasions. Central to this music is a sung text that glorifies God (Allah), his prophet Muhammad, and the Prophet's family (*ahl al-bayt*). Musical instruments, especially the melodic instruments, are seldom played. During processions or for the musical accompaniment of a religious festival, however, the sounds of cymbals and hand or barrel drums are often heard.

A discussion with a Moslem holy man about the "music of Islam" would quickly prove to be problematic. Vocal forms with religious content such as the *mawlid, qaṣīdah, dhikr, madīḥ*, and so on, are not defined as music by the Moslems. Throughout the various epochs of Arabian history, Islamic legal scholars and theologians have by no means been in agreement about the value and function of singing and instrumental performance in either a religious or a nonreligious context, that is, about the value of listening to music itself. Influenced by prevailing moral and religious attitudes, some praised and glorified the musical vocation, while others condemned any kind of singing and performing. But despite such negative sentiments, a distinctive Islamic musical practice was nevertheless able to develop.

The Reading of the Koran

The Koran itself is often presented in the form of a song that represents its own vocal genre. Such a Koran performance requires a beautiful voice and great musical skill. Nevertheless, the one who presents the Koran is never referred to as a *mughannī* (singer), although he of course actually does sing, but as a *muqri'*, *tālī*, *murattil*, or *mujawwid* (reader or reciter). No Moslem would ever use the word *singing* in reference to a recitation of the Koran. Terms such as those named above are only applied to the Koran recitation, which is to say, the field of religious music in general. The differentiation between reading and singing is justified by the fact that the Koran does not, in fact, have to be sung but can also be recited or read in a plain manner and style. Even so, the best Koran readers are always excellent singers as well, and thus the singing of the Koran must be clearly differentiated from secular song forms.

The reading of the Koran has a liturgical and sacramental, indeed even a mystical, function. It is a permanent part of every devotional service of the mystical brotherhoods. The Koran, the holy book of Islam, embodies a treasure of eternal truths that are realized anew with each reading. It contains the words of God as imparted to the prophet Muhammad by the angel Gabriel. The Koran is thus by no means a literary product of the Prophet himself but rather is of divine origin. It consists of 115 chapters, the suras, which are sub-divided into verses. The entire book contains approximately four hundred pages, with the suras arranged in such a way that the longer ones precede the shorter ones. Immediately following the opening sura, *al-fātiḥah*, comes a sura with 286 verses, the longest in the Koran;

the last sura, with only three verses, is the shortest.

The reading of the Koran is the art of recitation of the holy book according to established rules for pronunciation, intonation, and caesuras. These rules were laid down by the Prophet himself and passed on from generation to generation. Already during the lifetime of the prophet Muhammad, some of his followers (*ṣaḥābah*) had distiguished themselves in the reading of the Koran. They spread the art of reading among their fellow believers. Not until the eighth century A.D., that is, the century after the birth of Islam, did seven great Islamic scholars lay down the rules for the so-called seven ways of reading, which are still valid today. The reading of the Ibn Ḥafṣ, though, was propagated most widely among Moslems. Eventually, during the ninth century, the faithful began to "sing" the Koran without, however, departing from the rules of the seven ways of reading. Since that time, Koran reciters have received their religious and musical education at one of the many Koran schools.

The reading of the Koran is performed as a solo and begins with the two mandatory formulations presented one after the other: "God protect me from the wicked devil!" and "In the name of Allah the merciful, the compassionate." It concludes with the mandatory phrase "The great God has spoken the truth." A reading can start in the middle of a sura and finish before the end of a sura.

The musical structure of the reading is defined, first and foremost, by the musical talents of the reader and by the expressiveness of his voice. Thus the same sura can take on several musical forms. A reciter who pays special attention to pronunciation and caesuras can perform a sura on one, two, or three tones, or the presentation can be clothed in an artistic, musically complex form. In the latter case, the reading can resemble a complete maqām performance. In each case, however, the paramount rule is to pronounce the words clearly and to partition the verse in a way that is syntactically logical and corresponds to the rules. Thus, everyone who has a command of the reading rules—and they are taught orally to every Moslem in school—may read the Koran without having to sing at the same time. Good Koran readers are generally engaged at the larger mosques in the cities.

The Koran text contains no marks, such as the neumes and the taʿamīm of the Old Testament, that suggest the shape of the melody. Nevertheless, approximately twenty-six symbols, partly in color, are used underneath, above, or beside the individual letters. These are small circles, rectangles, dashes, and letter symbols of the alphabet. They indicate how a consonant is correctly pronounced, whether a blending with a neighboring consonant may take place in the pronunciation, whether recitation pauses are forbidden at a particular place, or if caesuras are possible in the text. Musical matters are not referred to.

Viewed from a musical standpoint, the Koran performance (*tartīl, tajwīd, taghbīr*) is based on one of the many maqām rows of Arabian secular art music. Not infrequently, the reading actually involves a complete maqām presentation. It differs from the secular performance forms, however, in that the structure of the melodic line is largely shaped by the rules of reading that must be taken into account. The Koran reading also involves the musical design of melodic passages with different lengths. Their temporal expansion, however, is essentially defined by the caesuras in the text. In every melodic passage, just as during a secular performance, the performer realizes a tone level centered on one tone of the maqām row. The presentation of the mandatory phrases at the beginning and end of the Koran reading is always restricted to the first tone of the maqām row. Other characteristics are the relatively slow tempo of the singing, the many long sustained tones, the melismas on consonants as well as on vowels, the register changes at the interval of an octave, and the long pauses of up to ten seconds between melodic passages. During these pauses, the faithful burst into spontaneous applause, especially when an excellent Koran reader, by modulating to neighboring maqām rows or by abruptly finishing a melodic passage on a high tone, manages to heighten the inner tension of the listeners until they have no choice but to release it with exclamations praising God.

The Koran reading generally takes place on Fridays—in the mosque during the holy service by the muqriʾ, at home with the family during religious festivities, and recently also on the radio and on television in front of a microphone and camera. What is heard in each case is a chapter of the Koran—complete or in

The First Ninety Seconds of the Sixty-Seventh Sura al-mulk *("The Empire")*

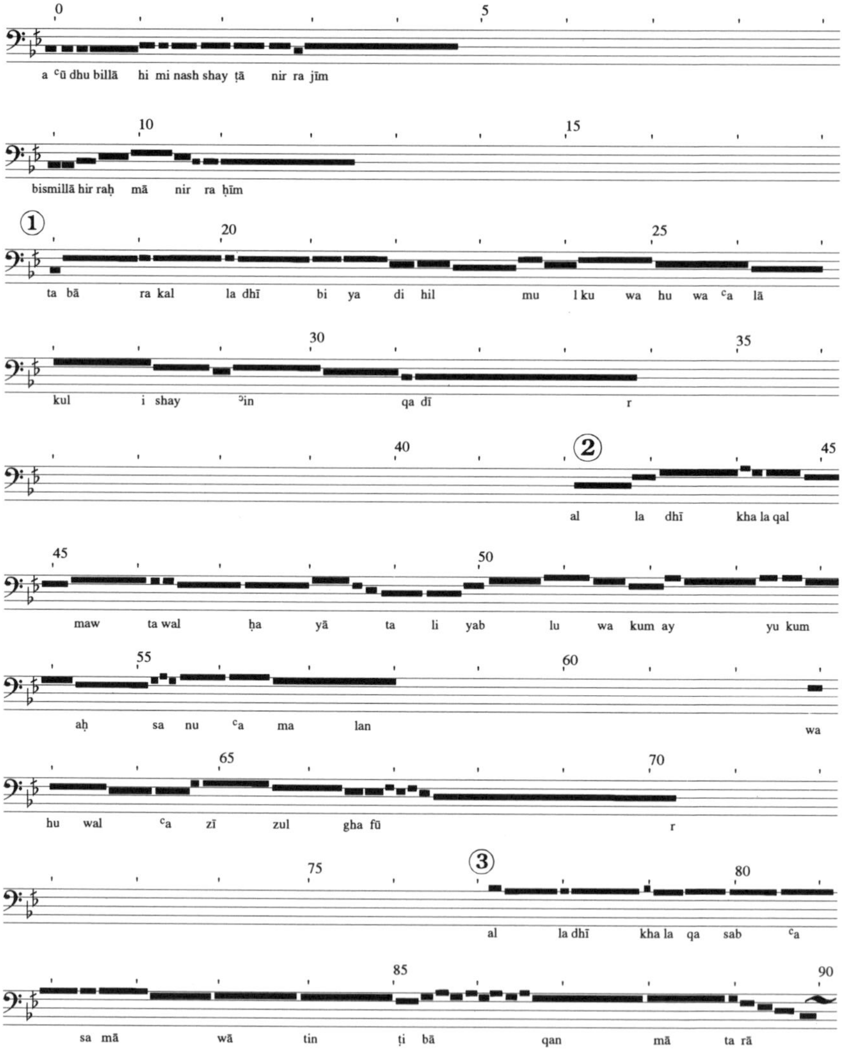

The melodic line is represented here using a five-line system, but in contrast to the Western method of notation, with beams of different lengths. The duration of a tone is determined by its absolute length in seconds (occuring as vertical dashes in the transcription) and expressed by the length of the beams. The above recitation is based on the maqām bayātī. It is from a recording that appears on the record "Union Records U 132" in Cairo.

excerpts. Furthermore, during each of the five prayer times prescribed throughout the day, every believer recites *al-fātiḥah* (the opening sura) and other selected short suras. This is done in the mosque, within the circle of the family, at the workplace, or at any other location. The publicly presented reading of the Koran, however, should be viewed as a highly developed art form that presupposes a mastery of the maqām repertoire and the rules of the tajwīd as well as a full-sounding voice in a high register.

The Adhān

The *adhān* is the name for the call to pray from atop the minaret. With this, the believers are called to the Friday holy service and to the five prayers prescribed for the day—in the morning, at noon, in the afternoon, at sunset, and in the evening. Shortly before the beginning of the holy service the *mu'adhdhin* (muezzin) climbs atop the minaret or the roof of the mosque and loudly and distinctly sings the text of the call to prayer, which for orthodox Moslems comprises these seven formulations:

1. God is most great.
2. I witness that there is no God but Allah.
3. I witness that Muhammad is the messenger of God.
4. Come to prayer.
5. Come to salvation.
6. God is most great.
7. There is no God but Allah.

These seven phrases are repeated one or more times according to fixed rules, with a longer singing pause following each phrase. Already during the lifetime of the Prophet it was customary to announce the holy service in this manner.

The musical structure of the adhān is defined by the principle of contrast, which gives an individual musical profile to each repetition of a phrase as well as to the different phrases. Whereas, during the first appearance of a phrase, the melodic line ordinarily turns out short, is less melismatically elaborate, and has a limited tonal range, the repetition can be clothed in an extended, richly embellished melodic passage, whose tonal range can extend over an octave.

Altogether, the adhān is made up of twelve melodic passages that move between two tonal centers in the same maqām row, separated by a fourth or a fifth. Each adhān can thus be unmistakably identified, quite apart from the details of the melodic line, by the position of these two melodic poles. The tempo of the adhān is usually quite slow; only at sunset is it performed at a faster tempo and with fewer melismas. For festive occasions it is customary for two *muʾadhdhinayn* (dual of *muʾadhdhin*) to perform the adhān antiphonally. With skilled *muʾadhdhinīn* (plural of *muʾadhdhin*), such as those engaged at the large urban mosques, the call to prayer can become a highly developed artistic musical form.

The Mawlid

Mawlid means "birthday" and denotes the public performance of the story of the Prophet's birth. In the mosque or in domestic spheres, a solo singer and a choir perform the text of the mawlid, which is composed in rhymed prose. The mawlid may thus be ascribed to the genre of the *madīḥ nabawī* (see page 159), which is exclusively reserved for praises of the Prophet or the Prophet's family and is widespread in all Islamic lands.

The official occasion for the performance of the mawlid is the birthday of the Prophet—according to the Islamic calendar, the first day of the month Rabīʿ Awwal. On this day, the faithful come in droves to the mosque to hear the mawlid story. The mawlid can also be performed at any other festive occasion in the mosque, as well as in a private setting. Such performances take place at the special wish of a believer, who is responsible for covering the costs of the singer. The preferred time of day for such a mawlid performance is the time after the evening prayer.

The oldest mawlid text known to us probably has its origins in twelfth-century Persia. From there, manuscripts spread to all parts of the Arabian world. Today, at least forty versions of the text are known in the Arabic language. They come from different epochs and vary considerably in style and form. In essence, however, they all illustrate versions of the story of the birth of the Prophet. Among the authors of the mawlid texts were leaders of the various Islamic sects and other shaykhs, who not infrequently added new elements to the actual story, things that appeared to benefit their limited political and economic objectives. In North Africa, the mawlid is usually based on the text of the Imām Barazanjī, while in Iraq, that of the ʿUthmān al-Mawṣilī is preferred.

The musical performance of the mawlid is undertaken by a solo singer with a resounding voice who has a command of the maqām repertoire. He is assisted by a chorus of eight to sixteen men. The chorus sings in unison and, following certain segments of the mawlid text, inserts new verses of poetry as well as prayers or blessings for those present. The musical structure of the mawlid is borrowed from the musical forms of secular art music: in North Africa, the mawlid calls to mind the style of the ma'lūf, that is, the andalusī nūbah; in Egypt, the dūr; in Syria, the muwashshaḥ; and in Iraq, the maqām al-ʿirāqī.

The Madīḥ an-Nabawī

The *madīḥ an-nabawī* is a widely popular song form in the Islamic world whose texts eulogize the Prophet and his family. At the same time, the madīḥ an-nabawī represents a genre in the belletristic literature of the Arabs, wherein the deepest religious feelings of the Moslem can be expressed. The *madā'iḥ* (plural of *madīḥ*) owe their propagation to Sufism (Islamic mysticism) and the poets who fully cultivated this genre.

The earliest madā'iḥ, however, came into being in A.D. 632, immediately after the death of the prophet Muhammad. Thus, one might justify the perception that the madīḥ an-nabawī is actually a kind of death song. But since Moslems continued to devote their thoughts and address their prayers to the prophet Muhammad after his death as if he were still alive, the term madīḥ ("praise") was considered the only legitimate one. The first madā'iḥ were written by Ḥassān Ibn Thābit, the scribe of the Prophet. The poems of Ibn Thābit served as a model for later poets—as, for example, ʿAlī Ibn Abī Ṭālib, the son-in-law of the

Prophet and also the fourth Islamic Caliph, who also included the Prophet's family (ahl al-bayt) in his songs of praise.

The special sympathy and the compassion that the Moslems offer the ahl al-bayt, harkens back to A.D. 660, when 'Alī lost the battle over the caliphate to Mu'āwiyah, an Umayyad. This compassion was further intensified in the year 661, a year after the murder of 'Alī, and reached its zenith after the murder in 680 of Ḥusayn, the son of 'Alī, who was also a grandson of Muhammad. The blood that was unjustly shed by the family of the Prophet has stirred the passions of Moslems for centuries. Those tragic events are the basis for the intense manifestations of sympathy by the Shiites who, from that day until this, on the tenth of the month muḥarram, the so-called *laylat 'āshūrah* ("'āshūrah night"), mourn the anniversary of Ḥusayn's martyrdom at Karbala in Iraq.

The most beautiful madā'iḥ, by poets such as Kumayth (seventh century), Da'bal (ninth century), Sharīf ar-Raḍiy (tenth century) and Mihyār, testify to a deep religious conviction and a great love of the Prophet and his family. Nevertheless, the masterpiece of the madīḥ literature did not appear until the thirteenth century, when the ṣūfī poet al-Būṣīrī created the poem *al-burdah*, the title of which refers to the Prophet's outer garment. Al-burdah comprises 182 verses and enjoys great popularity among Moslems. Selected lines of verse are recited into the ears of those suffering from certain illnesses for the purpose of healing. In principle, the performance of the burdah poem is possible at any time; it is, however, explicitly mandated every Friday evening at the graveside of Ḥusayn as well as for special religious occasions. After each line of verse, the person reciting is to insert a line of text called the *mawlāya ṣallī*. The supplementary text is always the same: "Lord, bless your beloved (the Prophet), the best of all men, and grant him salvation to the end of all time."

The burdah verses have had an enduring influence on the madīḥ poems. Poets imitated the model by using the same poetic meter and the same end rhyme, by replacing half of a line composed by al-Būṣīrī with their own poetry, or by creating all conceivable combinations of original text with the newer poetry. As a result, the madīḥ repertoire of today includes a great

Shiite preacher in Karbala, Iraq. Photo: H. H. Touma.

abundance of poetic works, from popular poetry to highly developed art poetry.

Musically, the following religious song forms are to be added to the madīḥ repertoire: *tanzīlah* (revelation), *ibtihāl* (supplication), *tawassul* (beseechment), *tawshīḥ*, and *muwashshaḥ*. The musical performance of a madīḥ is undertaken by a solo singer and a group of men, which forms the chorus. The participants also accompany their singing with frame drums. The instruments are known by the name *mazhar* or *bandīr*. The musical building block of the madīḥ is a melodic passage that the listener can encounter in different variations, paraphrases, and transformations. The chorus generally sings the text of a line of refrain in strict rhythmic organization, whereupon the soloist answers by improvisationally varying, paraphrasing, or transforming the same line of text. In so doing, he emphasizes the characteristics of the respective maqām rows. He thus realizes a modal improvisation in a free rhythmic-temporal organization. The chorus then answers again with the refrain. In place of the refrain, however, a long sustained "Allah" can also appear on one of the tones characteristic of the maqām. As a general principle, though, the madīḥ observes the rules of the secular art music of the Arabs.

The Dhikr

Dhikr literally means "pronouncement" or "remembrance." In Islamic mysticism (Sufism), the dhikr is a ceremony whose liturgy can include recitation, singing, instrumental music, dance, costumes, incense, meditation, ecstasy, and trance. As early as the eighth century, small groups of pious Moslems came together in organized circles to recite out loud the suras of the Koran and other religious texts. In these meetings, the essential core of the institutionalized forms of the dhikr and the *samāʿ*, the so-called spiritual concert, can be seen.

Sufism is also based on the Koran and the moral philosophy of Islam. It gained enormous popularity in view of the fact that it made possible an individual and intuitive approach to

Bandīr player, participant in a dhikr of a ṣūfī brotherhood in Meknes, Morocco
Photo: J. Dietrich.

religion and its questions, and in this way coincided with the religious mentality of the masses. Too many were disappointed with the abstract teachings of orthodox theology and found in Sufism new spiritual gratification and room for a religious experience that, moreover, did not put the believers in conflict with Islamic dogma. Besides the prayers that were prescribed five times a day, the Sufis began to practice devotional exercises that they called dhikr, with reference to the content of sura 33, verse 41, which reads: "Oh, true believers, remember God with a frequent remembrance, and celebrate his praise morning and evening."

The Islamic ascetics used to dress themselves in woolen robes, according to accounts originating from the tenth century. The woolen robe thereafter became the definitive "trademark" of all Islamic mystics. The term *ṣūfī* itself is derived from the Arabic word for wool (*ṣūf*). Many Moslems freely subjected themselves to the rituals and hierarchical ordering that characterized religious life in mystic circles. They enjoyed visiting the homes of the Sufis and participating in the discussions, litanies, and exercises that took place there. In time, organized brotherhoods developed out of these voluntary gatherings, with a shaykh, an important religious authority, at their head. The followers flocked around the shaykh to let themselves become educated in his teachings. The shaykh, they believed, enjoyed the blessing of God. He passed his knowledge on to the youth who later, in turn, conveyed the mystical doctrine, the *ṭarīqah*, to others. In this way, the number of followers grew very fast.

The literal meaning of *ṭarīqah* is "way" or "path." The different *ṭuruq* (plural of *ṭarīqah*) therefore originally signified the various mystical teaching concepts that were linked to the person of the shaykh. *Ṭuruq* later became the generic term for the religious orders that were being established everywhere during the twelfth and thirteenth centuries and later, the main objective of which was to win over new members. The converts were to be initiated into the ṭarīqah of the founder of the order and then to continue participation in the required devotional services.

There are still a great many ṭuruq in the Islamic world today: their members are encountered in all Arabian lands. Now, as from the beginning, the ṭuruq differ from one another in individual aspects of their religious doctrine and in the kind of devotional exercises they practice. The dhikr ceremony, in particular, can be structured differently from ṭarīqah to ṭarīqah; that is, a particular ceremonial aspect might be neglected in one but emphasized in another. For example one ṭarīqah might focus on movement and dance, another on meditation and trance, and a third on the act of self-flagellation.

Viewed from a musical standpoint, the dhikr ceremony represents a large-scale musical form that can last several hours and is laid out as a cycle that can include several genres of secular Arabian art music. The fundamental goal of a dhikr ceremony is to bring about God's presence (*ḥaḍrah*) during the devotional service. It is therefore the ḥaḍrah, the presence of God among the believers, that marks the climax of the ceremony of all ṭuruq, regardless of the formal structure of the dhikr cycle. The state of the ḥaḍrah is evoked when those in attendance have called out the name of Allah so often that they fall exhausted into a trance.

The tasks that present themselves during the realization of a ceremony are assigned to individual brothers of the order within the ṭarīqah, in accordance with the prevailing hierarchy. These brothers, who are concerned in this way with different duties, are referred to as *fuqarā'* or *aḥbāb*, the "beloved" (of the shaykh). The assignment of duties applies to the main office of the shaykh just as much as to the simple office of the cleaning person of the mosque. There are supervisors, choir singers, solo singers, Koran readers, dancers, instrumentalists, sword dancers, and so on. In their various functions, all contribute in their own way to the achievement of the common goal, the ḥaḍrah, or ceremonial climax.

On a fixed day of the week, the followers of a ṭarīqah assemble either in the mosque or in the so-called *zāwiyah* ("corner") outside the mosque to hold the dhikr ceremony. The muqri' begins with the recitation of a Koran sura. This is followed by the madīḥ section, whose content and music, even within a ṭarīqah, can be shaped very differently from land to land. The vocal and instrumental pieces and the rhythmic patterns correspond largely to the apparent musical forms of secular art music as practiced in the respective lands. Thus, the musical elements of the madīḥ section in the Iraqi dhikr (maqām rows, wazn patterns, music and poetic forms, style elements) are taken from the maqām al-ʿirāqī repertoire. The same applies to the madīḥ in relation to the nūbah in North Africa, to the dūr in Egypt, and to the muwashshaḥ and qaṣīdah in Syria. In Syria, the madīḥ section is made up of a chain of qaṣā'id and muwashshaḥāt, which are accompanied instrumentally. All the texts, of course, have a purely religious content.

The ḥaḍrah section, as a rule, consists of a continuous repetition of the name of God, which forms a kind of ostinato on top of which a soloist renders a hymnlike, richly ornamented song. At many ṭuruq, the ceremonial climax is reached through the unrelenting cries "Allah! Allah!" or "hū hū" ("He! He!"), again meaning Allah. This melismatic singing is accompanied by deep exhaling and inhaling of the participants. When exhaling, the participants bend forward, while inhaling, they stand straight again. While the name of God is articulated by those present in a manner that is rhythmically accentuated, emphatic, and at one with the inhales and exhales, the speech and breath patterns transform during the course of the ḥaḍrah as follows:

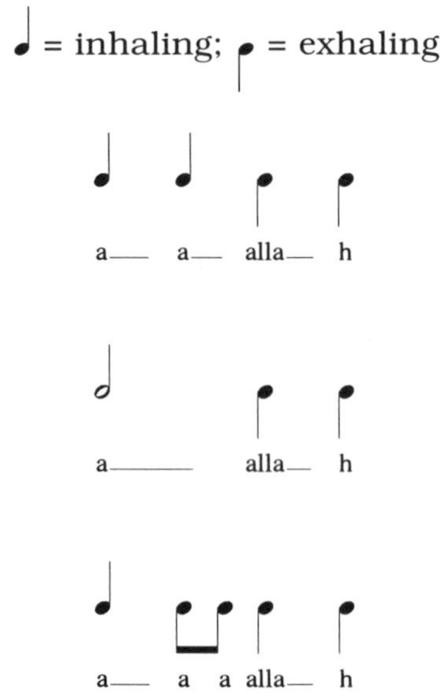

Gradually, the shaykh speeds up the tempo, resulting in a simple

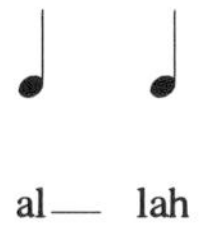

and, finally, the participants change over to a fast

that is forced out while exhaling. Together with the breathing rhythm, the body movements of the believers also accelerate, although they remain in their places during the entire ceremony. The point of culmination has now been reached. The state of trance sets in among the participants. With a song of prayer, the ceremony ends.

9

Recent Publications on Arabian Music

The history of research in Arabian music is as old as Arabian cultural history. Already in the eighth century, Arabs wrote treatises on Arabian music. The earliest work written by a European giving information on this theme is *Cartas sobre la música de los árabes* (1787), by Juan Andres of Venice. This chapter, however, discusses only more recent publications on the music of the Arabs, publications that have appeared since the end of World War II.

As extensive as the European-language literature on Arabian culture may be, there are few treatises in which Arabian music is explored by Western musicologists and ethnomusicologists. The politically unstable situation in many parts of the Arabian world may be to blame, but the almost inexhaustible volume of material and the lack of preliminary studies may be a contributing factor. In contrast, the number of publications by Arabian scholars in the Arabic language is large, even though only a few of these works are capable of furnishing sound, hitherto unpublished, scholarly information. More often, information and hypotheses already published by Western musicologists are merely repeated. It must be pointed out, however, that in the Arabian world, the subject of musicology is seldom if ever taught at a university. The only exception is the Institute of Musicology at the University Saint Esprit in Kaslik (Lebanon).

The practical education of musicians, on the other hand, is provided for at many institutions in Arabian lands.

Publications on Music Theory

Arabian music scholars conducted their research chiefly on the basis of a purely theoretical, mathematical way of thinking, completely independent of the practice. Theory always had precedence over practice. An example of this is the book *Falsafat al-mūsīqā ash-sharqiyah* (The Philosophy of Oriental Music) by the Syrian philosopher and mathematician Mīkhā'īl Allāhwīrdī, published in Damascus in 1948 (Allāhwīrdī 1948).

In the fifth volume of his extensive work *La musique arabe* (d'Erlanger 1949), Baron Rodolphe d'Erlanger deals with the different theories of the Arabian tone system that were discussed during the Cairo Conference in 1932. A detailed discussion of the modal tone system follows. The total of 120 modes are divided into sixteen genres; each individual mode is analyzed independently. A transcribed taqsīm illustrates the text in each case. The analyses are based on the assumption that the mode can be understood as a chain of tetrachords. This tetrachord theory is as old as Greek music theory. It cannot, however, explain why modes with the same tetrachordal structure sometimes have different names and are assigned to different genres in d'Erlanger's modal system.

The sixth volume of *La Musique Arabe* appeared in 1959. Here, d'Erlanger deals extensively with the rhythmic-temporal organization of Arabian music and the individual musical genres (d'Erlanger 1959). Each of the 110 wazn patterns is analyzed and explained. Transcription examples from the field of art music are provided and, together with the song texts, likewise examined. These two excellent volumes by d'Erlanger are therefore capable of providing a comprehensive picture and are indispensible for anyone looking for more detailed information on Arabian music.

Since 1969, two other important works in this field have appeared. One of these is *Qiyās as-sullam al-mūsīqī al-ʿarabī* (Measurement of the Arabian Scale), a book by the Egyptian

Yūsuf Shawqī, former director of the Cairo Symphony Orchestra, who was also a research fellow at the Center for the Publication of Arabian Manuscripts (Shawqī 1969). Shawqī critically discusses the efforts of musicologists, specifically around the year 1932—the very year in which the Cairo Conference on Arabian Music took place—to measure the Arabian scale exactly. The author presents a detailed concept for systematic measurement using electronic instruments. Independent of the more hypothetical, purely theoretical measurements of the past, Shawqī wants to clarify whether the octave in Arabian music actually contains twenty-four tones or whether, in fact, there are fewer. He is also concerned with establishing the exact size of the intervals as determined by musical practice. Although twenty-four tones do theoretically exist, the practice is familiar with many fewer pitches.

The second of these important works is a book by an Indonesian, Liberty Manik, but published in Germany: *Das arabische Tonsystem im Mittelalter* (The Arabian Tone System in the Middle Ages; Manik 1969). Manik's work—submitted as a dissertation at the Free University in Berlin (Manik 1969)—is based on a critical examination of fifteen music treatises that were written between the eighth and thirteenth centuries and are preserved today in various libraries and museums of Europe and the Near East. Manik's investigation of the Arabian tone system is therefore based entirely on the theories developed in the Middle Ages. Because all the treatises that Manik took into consideration have already been published in translation, the value of his work lies more in the fact that he subjects the works to a comparative study. In comparing the mode rāst of the Middle Ages with the modern form, he comes up with an explanation for the fact that, in contrast to the Turks and Persians, the Arabs tend to divide the octave into twenty-four pitches. To this day, the Arabian tone system is based on the pure Arabian system of al-Fārābī from the tenth century, whereas the Turkish and Persian tone systems are derived from the Pythagorean system of Ṣafī ad-Dīn al-Urmawī from the thirteenth century.

Music theory in the second half of the thirteenth century is investigated by O. Wright in *The Modal System of Arab and Per-*

sian Music A.D. *1250–1300* (Wright 1978). The work deals with the analytical procedure of followers of the Systematist school of Ṣafī ad-Dīn al-Urmawī (d. 1294).

The most comprehensive work on questions of Arabian music theory was done by Amnon Shiloah in his book *The Theory of Music in Arabic Writings (c. 900 to 1900)* (Shiloah 1979). In the form of a catalogue, Shiloah presents more than six hundred treatises that are preserved in forty European and American libraries. Three hundred forty-one of the treatises are analyzed in detail. Those topics covered in the source catalogue include acoustics, call to prayer (*adhān*), literature (*adab*), earth sciences, dance, modes, musica speculativa, musicians, notation, phonetics, rhythm, and meter. This truly excellent publication of Shiloah, which was published in the International Source Lexicon of Music (RISM) series, does not, however, take into account the manuscripts in the holdings of libraries and archives in India, the former USSR, and the Arabian lands.

Bibliographies and Glossaries

The bibliography *Rāʾid al-mūsīqī al-ʿarabiyah* (Guide to Arabian Music) was compiled by ʿAbdulḥamīd al-ʿAlwajī (al-ʿAlwajī 1964). The work lists more than a thousand writings on Arabian music that have appeared, chiefly in the Arabic language, during the last seventy years. The entries are organized according to headings (music, song, dance, singer biographies, music listening, musical instruments), and the headings are further subdivided according to authors' names. A subject index as well as an author and title index considerably facilitate work with this bibliography. Al-ʿAlwajī also published *Al-murshid ilā an-nitāj al-mūsīqī* (A Guide to Musical Work) (al-ʿAlwajī 1975). The bibliography contains 865 entries supplemented by an alphabetical name and book index. Listed here are books and articles from the time between 1964 and 1975. The work thus complements the author's earlier publication.

With *The Sources of Arabian Music*, Henry George Farmer published an annotated bibliography of all Arabian musical treatises written between the eighth and seventeenth centuries

(Farmer 1965). Farmer specifies the place where each treatise is kept, along with its classification number at the library in question. Also noted is whether the work has been published and translated. All entries are ordered chronologically according to author.

Neuere Bücher zur arabischen Musik (Recent Books on Arabian Music) is the title of an article by Eckard Neubauer (Neubauer 1971). In it he discusses Henry George Farmer's work *The Sources of Arabian Music* in addition to predominantly more recent publications that have appeared in the Arabic language on the music history and music theory of the Arabs. Neubauer's catalogue, nonetheless, encompasses a total of fifteen hundred years of Arabian cultural history.

Wilhelm J. Krüger-Wust's bibliography *Arabische Musik in europäischen Sprachen* (Arabian Music in European Languages), with over two thousand entries, encompasses all areas of Arabian music—art and folk music, music theory and musical practice, instrument construction, Islam and music, as well as biographies of composers, interpreters, and music theorists (Krüger-Wust 1983). The bibliography is arranged alphabetically according to author, with a subject index facilitating use. Because publications on Spanish-Arabian music are taken into account as well, the bibliography also represents an important contribution to the research of this area of Arabian music and European music of the Middle Ages.

An annotated dictionary of Arabian music terminology is presented by Lois Ibsen al-Fārūqī in her *Annotated Glossary of Arabic Musical Terms* (al-Fārūqī 1981). The tradition of glossaries of musical terms in the Arabian culture reaches back approximately 1500 years. The alphabetically ordered entries in Arabic, English, and German, compiled from over 150 works on Arabian music, have been carefully commentated and critically examined by al-Fārūqī. For every entry, the source is named. Concluding with five extensive appendixes, this annotated specialized Arabic-English dictionary is currently the only one of its kind.

Editions of treatises from the Middle Ages

Publications of musical treatises from the Arabian Middle Ages make up a large part of the recent music history research of the Arabian world. But because the publishing projects are rarely in the hands of musicologists, the commentaries are usually limited to brief descriptions of the manuscript or to comparisons of several versions of a manuscript and the type of printing. Among the many publications of this kind, only two should be mentioned. As exceptions to the rule, these publications are based on the sound scholarly work of the editor.

A critical edition of al-Fārābī's *Kitāb al-mūsīqā al-kabīr* (The Great Book of Music) was undertaken by Ghaṭṭās ʿAbdulmalik Khashabah (al-Fārābī 1967). This huge edition appeared in Cairo, presumably in the year 1967 (as in most Arabian publications, information pertaining to the year of publication is unfortunately missing). The edition consists of a detailed critical comparison between copies of the treatise that are preserved in Leiden, Istanbul, and Princeton, and the French translation of Baron d'Erlanger, who based his translation on copies preserved in Leiden, Milan, Beirut, and Madrid. The book, which contains more than twelve hundred pages, can be obtained through the Dar al-kitāb al-ʿarabī in Cairo.

A carefully annotated edition also exists of al-Kindī's *Risālah fī khubr ṣināʿat at-taʾlīf* (A Treatise on Composition). This is a treatise from the ninth century that had already been published by Lachmann and Hefni as well as by the Iraqi Zakariyā Yūsuf. The work was published in 1969 by the Egyptian Yūsuf Shawqī, who, by supplying it with a brilliant scholarly commentary, simultaneously corrected the mistakes of his predecessors in the earlier editions (Shawqī 1969). A forty-page appendix in the English language is attached. Shawqī's edition was published by the Ministry of Culture in Cairo and can be obtained there through the Maṭbaʿat dār al-kutub.

A complete French translation of the eleventh-century treatise *Kitāb kamāl adab al-ghināʾ* (Book on the Perfection of the Knowledge of Singing) by al-Ḥasan Ibn Aḥmad ʿAlī al-Kātib has been presented by Amnon Shiloah, who also commentated the work thoroughly. The translation appeared under the title

La Perfection des connaissances musicales (Shiloah 1972). A reproduction of the Arabic text is unfortunately not provided.

Publications on Music History

When one speaks of music history in connection with Arabian music, in contrast to Western-influenced concepts, the term encompasses neither the history of the development of musical genres nor the creative work of a composer in its musical historical context. What is meant here is more the musical life in general and the development of music theory, for the entire musical legacy of the Arabs consists of traditional musical forms that have been handed down orally and never written down. Hence, it has not been possible to write a music history according to the Western model. Instead, the music history research of the Arabs has been concentrated on the publication of musical treatises and critical commentaries thereof, together with sociologically oriented investigations into musical life and the personalities of individual singers and musicians throughout Arabian history. The latter were primarily artists who had already been mentioned in the *Kitāb al-aghānī* (Book of Songs) of Abū al-Faraj al-Iṣbahānī from the ninth century and in the *Tales from the 1001 Nights* from the fourteenth century. Recent publications of this kind still have a narrative character.

A fundamental study dedicated to musical life during pre-Islamic times is Naṣriddīn al-Asad's *Al-qiyān wal-ghinā' fī al-'aṣr al-jāhilī* (The Qiyān and Song in Pre-Islamic Times) (al-Asad 1960). Serving as the source for al-Asad is Arabian poetry as handed down to us from the last 150 years of the pre-Islamic epoch. In the first part of his book, the author discusses the social status of the qiyān and their song repertoire and gives—as comprehensively as possible—information on the singers mentioned in the poems. In the second part, al-Asad deals with the relationships between the songstresses and the poets of their time, and compares the text repertoire of the qiyān to the wealth of poems available to us from the Jāhiliyah. Although it is very difficult to furnish a reliable picture of the musical life of this long-past epoch, al-Asad manages to shed some light on the time from a music-sociological point of view.

The historical period that is most often dealt with in musicology literature is the one between the seventh and thirteenth centuries—from the birth of Islam to the downfall of the Arabian empire. A fundamental music-history work on this period was produced by Henry George Farmer with his book *A History of Arabian Music to the XIIIth Century* (Farmer 1967). Although published as early as 1929, this work is still considered to be the only sound and original scholarly treatise on the music history of the Arabs.

ʿAbbās al-ʿAzzāwī goes one step further, historically, with his small book *Al-mūsīqā al-ʿirāqiyah fī ʿahd al-mughūl wat-turkumān* (Iraqi Music During the Time of the Mongols and Turks). He discusses musical life, musicians, and musical instruments in Iraq from 1258 to 1534 (al-ʿAzzāwī 1951). This publication contains seventy-two pages and includes descriptions of some treatises as well as biographies of the musicians of this epoch.

Arabian musical genres and the musical practice of the nineteenth century is discussed by Habib Hassan Touma in the article "Die Musik der Araber im 19. Jahrhundert" (The Music of the Arabs During the Nineteenth Century) (Touma 1973). Touma bases his presentation on oral tradition and also on early recordings from the first two decades of this century.

Eckhard Neubauer's dissertation "Musiker am Hof der frühen Abbasiden" (Musicians at the Court of the Early Abbasids) (Neubauer 1965) complements Henry George Farmer's music history from the year 1929 with regard to the early Abbasid period (850 to 950). Neubauer reports on eighty-four musicians who were active at the Caliph court between 750 and 908 and describes the musical life of this time in general.

ʿAbdurraḥmān ʿAlī El-Ḥajjī is the author of *Tārīkh al-mūsīqā al-andalusiyah* (A History of Andalusī Music), a publication in which the author reports on the history of the al-andalus region as well as, in individual chapters, the muwashshaḥ, the muwashshaḥ poets, and the zajal (El-Ḥajjī 1970). Finally, El-Ḥajjī discusses the influence of these poetic forms on European poetry of the Middle Ages.

The same theme was the focus of Spaniard Julian Ribera's

Music in Ancient Arabia and Spain Being La Música de las Cantigas, a work that appeared in its second edition in 1970 (Ribera 1970). The author deals with the music history of Spain and musical developments during Arabian rule of the land. After an introduction on the history of music in the Mashriq, Ribera turns his attention to the Arabian music that was once cultivated in Spain and gives an account of the earliest musical notation from fifteenth and sixteenth century Spain. Also discussed are the *Cantigas de Santa Maria*, whose affinity to Arabian music is pointed out by the author, whereas theories that place the roots of the *Cantiga* in Gregorian chant are dismissed. For the research of present-day Arabian music in North Africa, Ribera's book represents an important source.

In her dissertation, *Die Theorien zum arabischen Einfluß auf die europäische Musik des Mittelalters* (The Theories of the Arabian Influence on European Music of the Middle Ages) (Perkuhn 1976), Eva Ruth Perkuhn discusses the areas of music theory, notation, and solfège; gives special attention to rhythmic modes; and deals with questions of instrument construction. Perkuhn points out the weaknesses of existing theories and advocates a more thorough methodological approach to clarifying the problems associated with this subject area.

Maḥmūd Kāmil is the author of a biography on ʿAbdū al-Ḥāmūlī, one of the great musicians of the nineteenth century (Kāmil 1971). *ʿAbdū al-Ḥāmūlī: zaʿīm aṭ-ṭarab wal-ghināʾ 1841–1901* (ʿAbdū al-Ḥāmūlī: Master of Music and Song 1841–1901) contains a selection of texts from qaṣāʾid, mawāwīl, adwār, ṭaqāṭīq, and muwashshaḥāt, which were set to music (that is, sung) by the artist. Although the musical transcription of a dūr and an analysis of the composition has been included in the book, notations of the song texts are completely lacking. Accompanying sound examples are also wanting, for without notation and sound examples, the work is of little significance for the non-Arabian.

Publications on Contemporary Arabian Art Music Practice

Simon Jargy's small book *La musique arabe* (Jargy 1971), published as part of the *Que sais-je?* series, is intended for the lay public. It fulfills its purpose as a compact introduction to Arabian music.

Also devoted to Oriental music is the *Ergänzungsband IV* of the *Handbuch der Orientalistik* (Supplementary Volume 4 of the Handbook of Oriental Studies). The volume contains an extensive article by Hans Hickmann entitled "The Music of the Arab-Islamic Sphere"—a large overview of Arabian music from the seventh century to the present (Hickmann 1970). Despite the high quality of the contribution, the choice of the term *Arab-Islamic* is unfortunate. It would have been more apt to identify the music merely as Arabian (as many others such as Farmer, d'Erlanger, and Jargy have done), for there are likewise excellent musicians among the Christian Arabs and, in a land such as Indonesia where there are more Moslems than in the entire Arabian world, the adjective *Islamic* could be applied with at least the same justification. Accordingly, the music of the Moslems in Turkey and in Persia should be understood as specifically Turkish or Persian forms of musical expression but not as typically Islamic.

In her work "The Nature of the Musical Art of Islamic Culture: a Theoretical and Empirical Study of Arabian Music," Lois Ibsen al-Faruqi describes the characteristic features of Arabian music with reference to the explanations of classical and contemporary music scholars and, with regard to content and form, draws parallels between music and other Arabian forms of artistic expression (al-Fārūqī 1974). Al-Faruqi points to similarities between music, literature, and painting, and their embedment in an environment defined by Islam.

La musique classique du Maghreb (The Classical Music of the Maghreb) is the title of a dissertation by the Tunisian Mahmoud Guettat (Guettat 1980). The work presents a comprehensive discourse on North African art music—of Morocco, Algeria, Tunisia, and Libya. The wealth of information it contains on andalusī music had, until now, been inaccessible to the reader not well-versed in Arabic. A bibliography and a discography on the art music of North Africa rounds out the publication.

Der Maqām Bayātī im arabischen Taqsīm (The Maqām Bayātī in the Arabian Taqsīm), a book now in its second edition, was originally submitted by its author, Habib Hassan Touma, as a dissertation to the Free University in Berlin (Touma 1976). On the basis of the taqsīm, the instrumental form of maqām presentation, Touma shows that a maqām is not a melodic model, that is, the melodic line is not characterized by specific motivic and measure groupings, and that the maqām performance is not bound to any definite tempo. Touma's viewpoint is musically illustrated by records such as *Arabian Music: Maqām; Taqāsīm and Layālī: Cairo Tradition* (UNESCO Collection MUSICAL SOURCES, Philips 6586006 and 6586010); and *Iraq: Ud Classique Arabe par Munir Bachir* (OCORA OCR 63). The first of the three above-mentioned records includes Touma's own recordings as well as an accompanying commentary by the author.

A comprehensive work on the maqām al-ʿirāqī was provided by the Iraqi musicologist, maqām singer, and sanṭūr player Ḥaj Hāshim ar-Rajab in his book, *Al-maqām al-ʿirāqī* (The Iraqi maqām) (ar-Rajab 1961). The book contains detailed analyses of the five main maqām cycles (fuṣūl). Lacking, however, are transcribed musical examples, for ar-Rajab wrote his work for music lovers in Iraq who are either musically active themselves, or could otherwise have become acquainted with the analyzed pieces. Records, however, are capable of musically illustrating ar-Rajab's analyses. In addition to the records produced in Iraq, one should also make reference here to the al-maqām al-ʿirāqī recording on the LP already mentioned above, *Arabian Music: Maqām.*

On the theme of al-maqām al-ʿirāqī, Shaykh Jalāl al-Ḥanafī wrote a small lexicon, *Al-mughannūn al-baghdādiyūn wal-maqām al-ʿirāqī* (The Singers of Baghdad and the Maqām al-ʿIrāqī), that lists the names of all famous maqām singers from the eighteenth century to the present (al-Ḥanafī 1964). The lexicon offers many interesting facts about the tradition of the maqām al-ʿirāqī as well as about the different schools and masters of this genre.

Jan Reichow's book *Die Entfaltung eines Melodiemodells im*

Genus Sīkāh (The Development of a Melodic Model in the Genus Sīkāh) (Reichow 1971), presents an extensive selection of folk songs, qaṣāʾid and tawshīḥ, that all rest upon the maqām rows sīkāh and huzām. Reichow investigates the development of a "melodic model" in the genus sīkāh—a model that is based upon the principal tone and certain other tones of the maqām row sīkāh.

In his book *Der Begriff des maqām in Ägypten in neuerer Zeit* (The Concept of the Maqam in Egypt in Recent Times), Jürgen Elsner investigates the problematic nature of the use of the term maqām in musical treatises of the late Middle Ages and in the European musicological literature of the present (Elsner 1973). In addition, the author concentrates on the geographic area of Egypt: he discusses and compares all important papers published after 1900 on the theme of the maqām and comprehensively explains his own position in the discussion of the maqām concept in relation to classical Arabian musical practice in Egypt. Maqām is understood by Elsner to be a tonal-melodic characteristic complex, a "tone-melos-syndrome"; the author, however, is unable to solve the problem of the definition of the maqām in this way. Nevertheless, Elsner's work represents an important contribution to the study of the maqām. Elsner also makes clear that it is not the rhythmic-temporal features that distinguish a certain maqām from other maqāmāt but the tonal-spatial characteristics.

Bruno Nettl and Ronald Riddle, in their article "Taqsim Nahawand: a Study of Sixteen Performances by Jihad Racy" (Nettl & Riddle 1973), offer an insight into Near Eastern improvisational practice based on the analysis of several taqāsīm performances. For this purpose, the maqām nahawand was performed by the Lebanese musician Jihad Racy a total of sixteen times. The different renditions are analyzed under aspects of voice-leading, modulation, sequence, scalelike melodic runs, motivic variation, ornamentation, rhythm, and tempo. As shown by this comparative examination, the musician is most flexible in treating the length of the individual segments of a taqsīm, their sequence, and the manner in which he modulates to another maqām. What prove to be the least variable are the melody typological and rhythmic features. The article contains transcriptions of two taqāsīm, whereas the analysis of the musical material is mainly represented by tables.

In the first volume of his work *Un mouvement de réhabilitation de la musique arabe et du luth oriental. L'école de Bagdad de Cherif Muhieddin à Munir Bachir*, Jean-Claude Chabrier discusses the "renaissance" of the Arabian ʿūd in connection with the Baghdad school (Chabrier 1976). This school was founded in 1936 by Sherīf Muḥiyddīn and carried on by Salmān Shukur, Jamīl Bashīr, and Munīr Bashīr. Chabrier illustrates the social background of this development with a view toward currents that were hostile to music in Islamic society, the predominance of vocal music in Arabian musical culture, and the later tendencies toward acculturation in Arabian music. Acculturation in this sense is documented through its outward manifestations, as in the piano with quarter-tone tuning, counterpoint, harmony, orchestration, and the propensity for spectacular music productions. The second volume of Chabrier's work examines the ʿūd from a historical and structural perspective. The author describes the development of the ʿūd since the seventh century and goes into detail about the performance techniques of the five- and six-string lutes. Six taqāsīm by ʿUmar Naqshbandī, a representative of the Syrian school are analyzed and compared with five taqāsīm performed by Jamīl Bashīr, a representative of the Baghdad school.

Syrian musical life is the focus of ʿAdnān bin Dhurayl in his book *Al-mūsīqā as-sūriyah* (The Music of Syria) (Dhurayl 1969). With the music historical developments in Syria during the last hundred years as a background, the Arabian tone system and the state of music research in Syria are discussed with special regard to the works of ʿAlī Darwīsh, Tawfīq Ṣabbāgh, Mīkhāʾīl Allāhwīrdī, and Majdī al-ʿAqīlī. Furthermore, in the second part of the work, the author describes some specific musical activities in contemporary Syria, such as vocal music, compositional forms, dance, and musical instruments, insofar as these relate to the Syrian domain.

The musical changes in Egyptian musical life during the first three decades of this century are investigated by Ali Jihad Racy in his work "Musical Change and Commercial Recordings in Egypt, 1904–1932" (Racy 1977). Racy deals with a period in

Egyptian music history during which an enormous upswing took place in the record industry. The author's intention is to demonstrate how commercial recordings were able to influence musical practice in Egypt. To indicate the extent of the changes that issued forth from the record, the author quotes the number of records sold per musical genre.

Changes in the urban music of Cairo are also investigated by Salwā el-Shawwān in her work "Al-mūsīkā al-ʿarabiyyah: A Category of Urban Music in Cairo, Egypt, 1927–1977" (el-Shawwān 1980).

Al-ālāt al-mūsīqiyah fī al-ʿuṣūr al-islāmiyah—dirāsah muqāranah (Musical Instruments During the Age of Islam—A Comparative Study) is the title of a publication by the Iraqi Ṣubḥī Anwar Rashīd (Rashīd 1975). The author undertakes a comparative examination of Arabian musical instruments from the seventh to the sixteenth centuries and follows the ways by which some of these musical instruments found entry into European musical life. Rashīd consults a wealth of archaeological, iconographical, and literary sources for his investigation. As a result, he has managed to produce an important work, which includes more than one hundred illustrations—without exception, indispensible pictorial documents of the musical instruments discussed.

Schéhérazade Qassim Hassan is the author of the book *Les instruments de musique en Irak et leur rôle dans la société traditionelle* (Hassan 1980). Hassan examines musical instruments in Iraq and their role in Iraqi society. In three main sections, she concerns herself with questions of instrument construction, the musician, and the social function of musical instruments. The work primarily deals with the classification of musical instruments, in which detailed descriptions of the methods of instrument construction predominate. The book, however, also represents an important ethnosociological study that is supplemented by a glossary, a bibliography, pictures, maps of distribution, and tables.

With her contribution *Die Herstellung der syrischen Rahmentrommeln. Einfluß von Material und Konstruktion auf die musikalische Qualität* (The Manufacture of the Syrian Frame Drums: Influence of Material and Construction on Musical

Quality), Heide Nixdorff presents the results of her eight-month field research in Lebanon, Syria, and Egypt (Nixdorff 1969). She supports her investigation with information from native musicians and instrument builders. With regard to the ethnic group as well as the social and religious class of the frame drum player, the author discusses the manufacturing process, the playing technique and the history and distribution of the frame drum principally in Syria. Numerous pictures and diagrams complement her descriptions.

Anthologies on Arabian Art Music

Since 1950, four important anthologies have been published in Arabic by Arabs. *Min kunūzinā* (From Our Treasures) was compiled by author and Andalus expert Fu'ād Rajā'ī and musician Nadīm ʿAlī Darwīsh (Rajā'ī & Darwīsh 1950). It is a collection of muwashshaḥāt from Aleppo. Nadīm ʿAlī Darwīsh (d. 1988) transcribed the orally transmitted melodies and notated the texts and rhythmic patterns that go with them. The collection contains a detailed introduction to andalusī poetry in general and the muwashshaḥ form in particular. There follow transcriptions of 138 muwashshaḥāt to a total of twenty-two waṣlāt; each waṣlah can include from four to eight muwashshaḥāt based on the same maqām row. Indicated here are the melody, text, names of poet and composer, the accompanying rhythmic pattern, the tempo, and the maqām row of every individual muwashshaḥ. The transcriptions have not been carried out to the last melisma. Thus, for the Oriental musician, who would never perform a composition "true to the notation," a certain freedom is granted in performing the muwashshaḥ: the fewer the ornamentations indicated in the transcription, the richer the melodic embellishments can prove to be during the course of the musician's improvisation.

A second muwashshaḥ collection was published in Beirut by the musician Salīm Ḥilū (Ḥilū 1965). *Al-muwashshaḥāt al-andalusiyah* (The Muwassaḥāt of al-Andalus) includes 116 compositions, several of which are already represented in the *Min kunūzinā*. Some twenty of the pieces in the collection were set to music by Salīm Ḥilū himself. The collection is preceded by a detailed introduction to andalusī poetry and the history of the muwashshaḥ by the writer Iḥsān ʿAbbās. A certain similarity in approach between this and the earlier collection of Rajāʾī and Darwīsh is unmistakable.

A third anthology was published in Cairo with the title *Turāthunā al-mūsīqī* (Our Musical Heritage). The publisher is the High Music Committee in collaboration with Shafīq Abū ʿŪf, the president of the committee, and Ibrāhīm Shafīq, a musician who transcribed the traditional melodies into musical notation (Abū ʿŪf & Shafīq 1963). The anthology includes 49 muwashshaḥāt and 171 *adwār* (plural of *dawr*). The latter determine the actual value of this collection, since all of the well-known adwār of the great Egyptian singers and composers of the nineteenth and early twentieth centuries are listed. Unfortunately, an essential part of the dawr form was not taken into account in the transcriptions, namely, the hank section, in which the singer, together with the group (*madhhabjiyah*), performs improvisational passages.

An anthology of the National Conservatory of Music and Dance in Tunisia was published in nine booklets by Salāḥ el-Mahdī and the Ministry of Culture (el-Mahdī 1967). The first booklet, entitled *Majmūʿah al-bashārif at-tūnisiyah* (Collected Tunisian Bashraf Pieces), contains ten *bashārif* (plural of *bashraf*). The second, *Majmūʿah al-muwashshaḥāt wal-azjāl*, includes eight complete waṣlāt. The third through ninth booklets include the following complete Tunisian nūbāt: the nūbah in the modus dhīl (third booklet); the nūbah ʿirāq (fourth booklet); the nūbāt sīkāh and ḥusayn (fifth booklet); the nūbāt rāst, ramal al-māyah, and nawā (sixth booklet); the nūbāt isbaʿayn, rāst adh-dhīl, and ramal (seventh booklet); the nūbāt of the modes iṣbahān, mazmūm, and māyah (eighth booklet); and the nūbāt nahawand, zinkūlah, ʿajam, and ʿushayrān (ninth booklet). The ninth booklet is dedicated to the work of the Tunisian musician Aḥmad al-Wāfī (1850–1921) and the seventh to that of the musician Khmayis Tirnān (1894–1964).

None of these anthologies convey a complete musical picture to the reader who is unacquainted with the material that is presented. The Western method of notation proves to be inadequate in attempting to convey a comprehensive sound picture to the reader. Whereas the European composer "prescribes" the performance of his work through musical notation, the Arab makes use of this notation only to "describe" orally transmitted compositions. Certainly, the writing down of non-European music using Western notation has meanwhile become an indispensible aid for the musicologist, who has learned to make the best out of its shortcomings. If the transcriptions were accompanied by sound examples on record or music cassette, however, these drawbacks could be corrected: through the sound example, those pitch or rhythmic arrangements recorded on paper would take on a flexibility for the reader, and the weaknesses of the notation would be exposed and made calculable.

Publications on the Folk Music of the Arabs

In his essay "Afrikansk musik ved den Persike Golf" (African Music from the Persian Gulf), Poul Rovsing Olsen investigates the African music traditions in Bahrain and Oman, which had become established in the Gulf region during the nineteenth century with the communities of African slaves (Olsen 1967). He describes individual musical instruments such as the lyre *tambūrah*, the oboe *sūrnāy*, and the drums, and he names the island of Zanzibar and the Mombasa region—both of which are also under the influence of Arabian music—as possible areas of origin.

Simon Jargy's work *La poésie populaire chantée du Proche-Orient arabe* presents a careful selection of folk song texts from Syria, Lebanon, Egypt, and Iraq (Jargy 1970). The texts are reproduced in the original Arabic as well as in French translation. Although musical transcriptions and sound examples of the song texts are lacking, Jargy's book signifies a promising beginning in the direction of a comprehensive exploration of Arabian folk music.

In his work *Studien zur ägyptischen Volksmusik* (Studies in Egyptian Folk Music), Artur Simon observes in particular the song types of collective singing, small and large forms of solo singing, and styles of instrumental music as characterized by the folk music of Egypt (Simon 1972). The transcribed pieces are painstakingly analyzed by Simon. The results should not be viewed, as the author says, "as definitive and exhaustive. They are rather to be understood as . . . a musicologically sound overview of a musical culture." This notwithstanding, Simon does manage to work out essential stylistic features and structural principles in Egyptian folk music.

An excellent record anthology has also been published on the subject of Egyptian folk music. Entitled *Al-ghinā' wal-mūsīqā ash-sha'biyah al-miṣriyah* (The Folk Music of Egypt), it came about as the result of a joint eight-month research trip by Tiberiu Alexandru, of the Institute of Ethnology and Folklore in Bucharest, and the Egyptian folk music researcher Emil Wahba (Alexandru & Wahba 1967). A detailed commentary in four languages and a map with information on the places where the recordings were made supplement both records, which are produced by Sono Cairo.

In Majdah Ṣāliḥ's "A Documentation of the Ethnic Dance Traditions of the Arab Republic of Egypt" (Ṣāliḥ 1979), the author directs her attention to folk dancing in the different cultural areas of Egypt. Dances from urban and rural environments and war dances, along with ritual and entertainment dances, are fully described and analyzed.

In a volume from the *Musikgeschichte in Bildern* (Music History in Pictures) series, the music of North Africa is presented by Paul Collaer and Jürgen Elsner with the collaboration of many other experts (Collaer & Elsner 1983). In this publication, an attempt is made "to give a glimpse into the visual aspects of . . . the musical cultures of the countries of North Africa" (Collaer & Elsner 1983; p. 5). The work includes pictorial documents of the music of Egypt, Libya, Tunisia, Algeria, Morocco, and Mauritania. Andalusī music is briefly explained under the collective term "artificial tradition" and illustrated with pictorial material. The musicological substance of the commentaries accompanying the illustrations varies from author to author: carefully formulated texts appear next to those of a more narrative character.

In Neffen Michaelides's dissertation, "Das Grundprinzip der altarabischen Qaṣīdah in der musikalischen Form syrischer Volkslieder" (Fundamental Principle of the Early Arabian Qaṣīdah in the Musical Form of Syrian Folk Songs) (Michaelides 1972), the author claims to have recognized the poetic meter of the qaṣīdah of the pre-Islamic period in Syrian folk song texts. An Arabic translation of this work was published in Damascus (Michaelides 1976).

Ḥusayn Qaddūri's anthology *Luʿab waʾaghānī al-aṭfāl ash-shaʿbiyah fī al-quṭr al-ʿirāqī* (Children's Games and Children's Songs in Iraq) includes descriptions and analyses of sixty-five games and songs collected by the author (Qaddūri 1979). Every song appears in a transcribed version and is assigned to the categories "lullaby," "party song," and "didactic song." The classification of the melodies is carried out with regard to their tonal range (major second, minor third, fourth, or fifth). A second part to this anthology appeared in 1984 with an additional sixty-two songs (Qaddūri 1984).

The music of the Berbers in Marrakesh and in other cities and villages of the Atlas mountains and the Sūs valley in southwestern Morocco is the focus of Philip Daniel Schuyler's work "A Repertory of Ideas: The Music of the 'Rwais' Berber Professional Musicians from Southwestern Morocco" (Schuyler 1979). The melodic and rhythmic organization in the music of the *Tashlḥīt*-speaking Rwais Berbers, as well as the performance practice of the professional musicians among them, is discussed in detail.

In his article "Musique et fêtes au Haut-Atlas," Bernard Lortat-Jacob deals with the Berber music of the High Atlas mountains of Morocco, primarily in their social context (Lortat-Jacob 1980). Lortat-Jacob is interested in a sociological examination of the festival traditions in a Berber village.

Aḍwāʾ ʿalā al-mūsīqā al-maghribiyah (Highlights of Moroccan Music), a richly illustrated book published in Morocco by Ṣalāḥ ash-Sharqī, comprises four chapters dealing with folk music, andalusī music, madīḥ song, and contemporary popular music (ash-Sharqī 1976). Historical pictures of musicians, musical instruments, and convention proceedings enrich the publication. An English and a French translation of the work have been available since 1981.

In Ulrich Wegner's work *Abūdhiyah und mawwāl. Untersuchungen zur sprachlich-musikalischen Gestaltung im südirak-*

ischen Volksgesang (Abūdhiyah and Mawwāl: Investigations of Linguistic-Musical Structure in Southern Iraqi Folk Singing), the abūdhiyah and the mawwāl—two poetic and song forms native to southern Iraq—are examined in minute detail (Wegner 1982). The poetry, composed in the Iraqi dialect, and the musical events appear as equally balanced components in Wegner's investigation and are accorded the same amount of attention in the analysis. In his detailed examination, the author pursues the objective of achieving a more comprehensive insight into the essence of Near Eastern folk singing, with its structural interweaving of text and music. Wegner's work represents a treatment of the theme that is, for its kind, new and original.

Arabian music in general and the Palestinian folk song in particular are the topics of a publication brought out by the Palestine Research Center in Beirut with the title *Al-funūn ash-Sha'biyah fī falasṭīn* (The Folk Arts in Palestine), with Yusrā Jawāhiriyah 'Arnīṭah listed as its author ('Arnīṭah 1968). The book contains transcriptions of folk song melodies and reproduces the song texts belonging to them. The author also discusses the festive traditions of both secular and religious character.

Publications on the Religious Music of Islam

The singing of one of the most outstanding Koran readers of Egypt is the focus of Jósef Marcin Pacholczyk's work "Regulative Principles in the Koran Chant of Shaikh 'Abd-ul-Bāsiṭ 'Abdu Ṣamad" (Pacholczyk 1970). The author undertakes scalar measurements of the musical material.

In his article "Die Koranrezitation: Eine Form der religiösen Musik der Araber" (Koran Recitation: A Form of the Religious Music of the Arabs), Habib Hassan Touma discusses the sura al-mulk (The Empire), performed by the same Egyptian Koran reciter mentioned above (Touma 1975). The analysis shows that the recitation is a representation of the maqām bayātī. The rhythmic-temporal organization of the singing is carried out subject to the speech rhythm of the Koran text, which is dependent upon the tajwīd rules.

Lura Jafran Jones follows the path of the ʿĪsāwiyah brotherhood in Tunisia in her work "The ʿĪsāwiyah of Tunisia and Their Music" (Jones 1977). Jones investigates the musical repertoire of this Islamic mystic sect, analyzes those instrumental and vocal pieces that are defined as nūbāt, and discusses in detail the relationship between text and music.

Selected Discography

Arabische Musik: Maqam
Contents: taqsīm, al-maqām al-ʿirāqī, nāyil, layālī, mawwāl, ʿatābā
Recordings and commentary: Habib Hassan Touma
UNESCO Collection MUSICAL SOURCES, Philips 6586006

Taqāsim and Layāli: Cairo Tradition
Contents: layālī, mawwāl, taqsīm, samāʿī, wazn
Commentary: Alain Daniélou
UNESCO Collection MUSICAL SOURCES, Philips 6586010

Fidjeri: Songs of the Bahrain Pearl Divers
Contents: baḥrī, khrāb, mijdāf, jīb, ʿadsānī, makhmūs, ʿashshārī, ḥissāwī
Recordings and commentary: Habib Hassan Touma
UNESCO Collection MUSICAL SOURCES, Philips 6586017

Sung Poetry of the Middle East
Contents: ʿatābā hawāwīyah
Commentary: Alain Daniélou
UNESCO Collection MUSICAL SOURCES, Philips 6586024

Zikr: Islamic Ritual, Rifaʿiyya Brotherhood of Aleppo
Contents: madīḥ, Qurʾān recitation
Recordings and commentary: Jochen Wenzel/Christian Poche
UNESCO Collection MUSICAL SOURCES, Philips 6586030

Īqāʿāt: Iraki Traditional Rhythmic Structures
Contents: al-maqām al-ʿirāqī, fann khammārī, murabbaʿ, abū-dhiyah, mawwāl, rhythmic improvisations
Recordings and commentary: Habib Hassan Touma
UNESCO Collection MUSICAL SOURCES, Philips 6586038

Zaidi und Shafiʾi: Islamic Religious Chanting from North Yemen
Contents: adhān, Qurʾān-recitation, qasīdah, tazkiyah, madīh, ḥaḍrah, mawlid
Recordings and commentary: Jochen Wenzel/Christian Poche
UNESCO Collection MUSICAL SOURCES, Philips 6586040

Tunisia
Contents: nāy, ʿūd, qānūn, rabāb, zūrnah, zajal, maʾlūf
Recordings and commentary: Alain Daniélou
UNESCO Collection A MUSICAL ANTHOLOGY OF THE ORIENT/Bärenreiter BM 30 L 2008

Morocco I
Contents: adhān, tajwīd, Qurʾān-recitation, ghnāwah, milḥūn, taqsīm, qaṣīdah
Recordings and commentary: Philip D. Schuyler
UNESCO Collection A MUSICAL ANTHOLOGY OF THE ORIENT/Bärenreiter BM 30 SL 2027

Lebanon I
Contents: dhikrayāt, munājāt, duʿāʾ, tasbīḥ, muwashshaḥ
Recordings and commentary: Jochen Wenzel/Christian Poche
UNESCO Collection A MUSICAL ANTHOLOGY OF THE ORIENT/Bärenreiter BM 30 SL 2030

Syria: Sunnite Islam
Contents: adhān, dhikr, muwashshaḥ
Recordings and commentary: Jochen Wenzel/Christian Poche
UNESCO Collection MUSICAL ATLAS EMI 3C064-17885

Algeria (Sahara)
Contents: ahillīl, tagerrabt, ḥaḍrah, amzād, qarqabou
Recordings and commentary: Pierre Augier
UNESCO Collection MUSICAL ATLAS EMI 3C064-18079

Morocco: The Arabic Tradition in Moroccan Music
Contents: Abdislām Shirqāwī, vocal and ʿūd
Recordings and commentary: Philip D. Schuyler
UNESCO Collection MUSICAL ATLAS EMI 3C064-18264

North Yemen
Contents: zaranīj, ghazal, zār, singing
Recordings and commentary: Jochen Wenzel/Christian Poche
UNESCO Collection MUSICAL ATLAS EMI 3C064-18352

Bahrain
Contents: ṣawt, ḥaflah, mkhūlfī, ʿarḍah
Recordings and commentary: Habib Hassan Touma
UNESCO Collection MUSICAL ATLAS EMI 3C064-18371

Irak
Contents: abūdhiyah, fann khammārī, sāz-Tanz
Recordings and commentary: Habib Hassan Touma
UNESCO Collection MUSICAL ATLAS EMI 3c064-18370

Luth classique, Iraq
Contents: Munīr Bashīr, ʿūd, taqsīm
Recordings and commentary: Jean-Claude Chabrier
Arabesques Anthologie EMI 2c066-95157

Cithare classique, Liban
Contents: Muḥammad Sabsabī, qānūn
Recordings and commentary: Jean-Claude Chabrier
Arabesques Anthologie EMI 2c066-95158

Flute classique, Syrie
Contents: Salīm Kusūr, nāy, taqsīm
Recordings and commentary: Jean-Claude Chabrier
Arabesques Anthologie EMI 2c066-95159

Luth traditionell, Iraq
Contents: Jamīl Bashīr, ʿūd, taqsīm
Recordings and commentary: Jean-Claude Chabrier
Arabesques Anthologie EMI 2c066-95160

Luth traditionell, Syrie
Contents:ʿUmar Naqshbandī, ʿūd, taqsīm
Recordings and commentary: Jean-Claude Chabrier
Arabesques Anthologie EMI 2c066-95161

Luth au Yemen classique
Contents: Jamīl Ghānim, ʿūd, taqsīm
Recordings and commentary: Jean-Claude Chabrier
Arabesques Anthologie EMI 2s062-53229

Cithare en Egypte
Contents: M.ʿAṭiyah ʿUmar, qānūn, taqsīm
Recordings and commentary: Jean-Claude Chabrier
Arabesques Anthologie EMI 2s062-53230

Luth au Liban traditionnel
Contents: Nāṣir Makhkhūl, buzuq, taqsīm
Recordings and commentary: Jean-Claude Chabrier
Arabesques Anthologie EMI 2s062-53231

Moroccan Music
Contents: ʿUmar Ṭinṭāwī, ʿūd, Marrākish-dance, taqsīm rasd, taqsīm kurd
Polydor 2944004

Moroccan Andalusian Music (1)
Contents: ʿAbdilkarīm ar-Rayyis and Ensemble, tawāshī ḥijāz al-mashriqī, inṣirāf ramal al-māyah
Polydor 2944002

Moroccan Andalusian Music (2)
Contents: ʿAbdilkarīm ar-Rayyis and Ensemble, inṣirāf basīṭ al-istihlāl, inṣirāf quddām al-jadīd
Polydor 2944003

Maroc: Musique classique andalou-Maghrébine
Contents: ʿAbdilkarīm ar-Rayyis und Ensemble, ḥijāz al-kabīr, al-istihlāl
Recordings and commentary: Alain Duchemin/Louis Soret
Ocora 558 588 HM 57

Taqasim: Improvisation in Arabic Music
Contents: ʿAlī Jihād Rāsī, buzuq, Simon Shahīn, ʿūd
Commentary: Philip D. Schuyler
Lyrichord LLST 7374

Munīr Bachir "récital à Genève"
Contents: Munīr Bashīr, ʿud, taqsīm nahawand, rāst, kurd, ḥijāzkār
Commentary: Simon Jargy
EMI 2C054-11803

Classical Oriental Music: Oud Solo
Contents: Munīr Bashīr, ʿūd, taqsīm ḥijāzkār, faraḥfazā
Commentary: Ramzī Rīḥānī
Philips 6353501

Meditation-Improvisation auf dem ʿūd
Contents: Munīr Bashīr, ʿūd, taqsīm maqām ḥijāzkār, maqām awj, maqām nahawand
Commentary: Jürgen Elsner
Eterna 835085

Munīr Bachir live in Paris
Contents: Munīr Bashīr, ʿūd, taqsīm maqām yakāh, nahawand, bayātī, ḥijāz
Commentary: Munīr Bashīr
Harmonia mundi MCM 20006

Egitto 1 epica
Contents: Epos Abū Zayd al-Hīlālī, rabābah, darabukkah, singing
Commentary: Giovanni Canova (co-author H. H. Touma)
Cetra/SU 5005

Andalusische Musik aus Marokko
Contents: ʿAbdilkarīm ar-Rayyis and Ensemble, nūbah rasd, nūbah māyah
Commentary: Thomas Binkley
EMI 1C 2LP 153 1695253

Syrie vol. 1—Muezzins d'alep: Chants religieux de l'Islam
Contents: adhān, qaṣīdah, muwashhsaḥ
Recordings and commentary: Gérard Deray/Christian Poche
Ocora 558513 MU 218Y

Iraq Makamat
Contents: al-maqām al-ʿirāqī, Yūsuf ʿUmar, vocal, maqām sīkāh, maqām ḥusaynī
Commentary: Schéhérazade Qassim Hassan
Ocora OCR 79

Pêcheurs de perles et musiciens du Golf Persique
Contents: fjirī, taqsīm, lyre
Recordings and commentary: Poul Rovsing Olsen
Ocora OCR 42

Musique soufi vol. 4
Contents: Ḥamīdiyah-Shādhiliyah-Brotherhood of Egypt, dhikr, inshād
Recordings and commentary: Claude Morel/Sulaymān Jamīl
Arion ARN 33658

Musique soufi vol. 5
Contents: Ḥamīdiyah-Shādhiliyah-Brotherhood of Egypt, inshād, praise songs to the Prophet Muḥammad
Recordings and commentary: Claude Morel/Sulaymān Jamīl
Arion ARN 33659

Egypt, les Musiciens du Nil
Contents: taqsīm, mawwāl, Abū Zayd al-Ḥīlālī
Commentary: Alain Weber/Pierre Sallée
Ocora OCR 558514 MU 218 Y

Anthologie al-Âla Musique Andaluci-Marocaine
Published by the Maison des Cultures du Monde, Paris, and the Ministry of Culture, Morocco, 1992: a complete documentation of the nūbah repertory in Morocco; introductory commentary in French and Arabic; complete text of the eleven nūbāt in Arabic (73 CDs)

1. Ḥāj ʿAbdilkarīm ar-Rayyis and the Orchestre al-Brīhī de Fès
   Contents: nūbah gharībat al-ḥusayn
   Collection INÉDIT W 260010 (6 CDs)

2. Ḥāj Muḥammad Ṭūd and the Orchestre Moulay Ahmed Loukili de Rabat
   Contents: nūbah ʿushshāq
   Collection INÉDIT W 260014 (6 CDs)
3. Muḥammad Larbī Temsamānī and the Orchestre du Conservatoire de Tétouan
   Contents: nūbah iṣbahān
   Collection INÉDIT W 260024 (6 CDs)
4. Aḥmad Zaytūnī Ṣaḥrāwī and the Orchestre de Tanger
   Contents: nūbah raṣd
   Collection INÉDIT W 260027 (6 CDs)
5. Ḥāj ʿAbdilkarīm ar-Rayyis and the Orchestre al-Brīhī de Fès
   Contents: nūbah istihlāl
   Collection INÉDIT W 260028 (7 CDs)
6. Ḥāj Muḥammad Ṭūd and the Orchestre Moulay Ahmed Loukili de Rabat
   Contents: nūbah raṣd adh-dhīl
   Collection INÉDIT W 260029 (6 CDs)
7. Ahmed Zaytouni Sahraoui and the Orchestre de Tanger
   Contents: nūbah ʿirāq ʿajam
   Collection INÉDIT W 260030 (7 CDs)
8. Ḥāj ʿAbdilkarīm ar-Rayyis and the Orchestre al-Brīhī de Fès
   Contents: nūbah al-ḥijāz al-kabīr
   Collection INÉDIT W 260031 (7 CDs)
9. Muḥammad Larbī Temsamānī and the Orchestre du Conservatoire de Tétouan
   Contents: nūbah ramal al-māyah
   Collection INÉDIT W 260032 (8 CDs)
10. Ḥāj ʿAbdilkarīm ar-Rayyis and the Orchestre al-Brīhī de Fès
    Contents: nūbah al-ḥijāz al-mashriqī
    Collection INÉDIT W 260033 (5 CDs)
11. Aḥmad Zaytūnī Ṣaḥrāwī and the Orchestre de Tanger
    Contents: nūbah al-māyah
    Collection INÉDIT W 260034 (7 CDs)
12. Muḥammad Brīwil and the Ensemble al-Âla du Ministère de la Culture du Maroc
    Contents: mīzān quddām bawākir al-māyah and mīzān al-quddām al-jadīd
    Collection INÉDIT W 260035 (2 CDs)

Maroc, Ustad Massano Tazi, Musique classique andalouse de Fès, 1988
Contents: nūbah ḥijāz al-kabīr and nūbah istihlāl
Recordings and commentary: Marc Loopuyt
Archives Internationales de Musique Populaire Genève
Ocora C 559035 HM 83 (CD)
Editor: Pierre Toureile

Maroc: Anthologie des Rwâyes
Published by the Maison des Cultures du Monde, Paris, and the Ministry of Culture, Morocco, 1992: introductory commentary in French, English, and Arabic (4 CDs)
Collection INÉDIT W 260023

1. a) Instrumental Music
   b) Mbarik ʿAmmūrī sings Ḥāj Bilʿīd
2. a) Ḥasan Awarūg sings Būbakr Am-Marrakshī and Mbarīk-ū-Būlaḥsin
   b) Aḥmad Amintāk sings Ḥāj Bilʿīd
3. a) Muḥammād Būnṣīr sings Būbakr Azaʿrī and Lḥusayn Jānṭī
   b) Laḥsin Idḥammū sings Būbakr Anshshād
4. a) Raqiyah Dimsiriyah sings Fṭūmah Tālgūrsht, Fāḍmah Tāgūramt, and Ṣfuyah Ūlt-tilwit
   b) Muḥammad Dāmmū sings Muḥammād Būdrāʿ

Maroc: Antholgie d'al-Melhun, Traditiones de Fes, Meknes, Sale, Marrakech
Published by the Maison des Cultures du Monde, Paris, and the Ministry of Culture, Morocco, 1990: introductory commentary in French, English and Arabic (3 CDs)
Collection INÉDIT W 260016

1. The qaṣāʾd
   a) Al-ʿarṣah sung by ʿAbdilkarīm Ginnūn of Fes
   b) Aṣ-ṣarkhah sung by Muḥammad Birraḥḥāl of Sale
   c) Al-ḥarrāz sung by Ḥāj Ḥusayn Tūlālī of Meknes
2. The qaṣāʾd
   a) Ad-damlīj sung by Ḥusayn Ghazālī of Fes
   b) Al-gnāwī sung by Saʿīd Ginnūn of Fes
   c) Laṭīfah sung by Muḥammad Dallāl of Marrakesh
3. The qaṣāʾd
   a) As-sāqī sung by Abdallāh ar-Ramḍānī of Meknes
   b) Ṭāliq al-Masrūḥ sung by Muḥammad Swīṭah of Marrakesh
   c) Kīf Ywāsī sung by ʿAbdilkarīm Ginnūn of Fes
   d) Al-yāqūtah sung by Ḥāj Muḥammad bin Saʿīd of Sale

Maroc: Musique Gharnati

Published by the Maison des Cultures du Monde, Paris, and the Ministry of Culture, Morocco, 1990: introductory commentary in French, English and Arabic

Contents: nūbah ramal performed by the Gharnāṭī Ensemble directed by Aḥmad Pīrū, Rabat

Collection INÉDIT W 260017 (1 CD)

Classical Chants from Tunisia and Middle East

Contents: Loutfi Bouchnak and the Ensemble Al Kindi, bashraf, taqsīm, qaṣīdah, muwashshaḥ, istikhbār,waṣlah

Commentary: Bernard Moussali

ALCD 113 (1 CD)

Know the Maqam, Series A

Published 1992 by Renanot, The Institute of Jewish Music, P.O. Box 7167 Jerusalem

Contents: 20 taqāsīm (also Iraqi maqāmāt) and short compositions performed by the soloist Abraham David ha-Cohen on the qānūn

Tunisie—Anthologie du Malouf: Musique Arabo-Andalouse

Published by the Maison des Cultures du Monde, Paris, and the Ministry of Culture, Tunisia, 1992/1993: introductory commentary in French, English, Spanish and Arabic (4 CDs)

1. Nūbah dhīl, performed by the Radio ensemble of Tunis with the legendary ʿūd player Khmayis Tirnān, directed by ʿAbdilḥamīd Bel ʿIljiyah, 1959
   Collection INÉDIT W 260044
2. Nūbah ramal, performed by the Radio ensemble of Tunis with the legendary ʿūd player Khmayis Tirnān, directed by ʿAbdilḥamīd Bel ʿIljiyah, 1960
   Collection INÉDIT W 260045
3. Nūbah aṣbahān, performed by the Radio ensemble of Tunis with the legendary ʿūd player Khmayis Tirnān, directed by ʿAbdilḥamīd Bel ʿIljiyah, 1962
   Collection INÉDIT W 260046
4. Nūbah al-ʿirāq, performed by the Radio ensemble of Tunis with the legendary ʿūd player Khmayis Tirnān, directed by ʿAbdilḥamīd Bel ʿIljiyah 1960
   Collection INÉDIT W 260047

Glossary

Arabic Terms Used in This Book

abyāt, 107, plural of *bayt*.

adab, 171, literature.

adhān, 157, the call to prayer from atop the minaret.

ʿadsānī, 93, one of the songs sung by the pearl divers for entertainment on the high seas. (See also *baḥrī*, *ḥaddādī*, *ḥassāwī*, and *mkhūlī*.)

adwār, 183, plural of *dawr*.

ahāzīj, 88, one of the four song forms of the *funūn al-baḥr*. (See also *fjīrī*, *ḥudwah*, and *muwwālah*.)

aḥbāb, 165, the "beloved" of the Shaykh, brothers who perform special tasks in the ceremonies of a *ṭarīqah*; also *fuqarāʾ*.

ahl al-bayt, 152, the family of the prophet Muhammad.

ahl al-ḥaḍar, 2, the sedentary population.

ʿajam, 35, a musical genre characterized by the descending sequence of seconds—minor-major-major—leading to the final tone; a major scale.

ālah, 16, one of the names used in Morocco for the *andalusī nūba*. (See *ghirnāṭī* and see also *maʾlūf* and *ṣanʿah*.)

al-andalus, 11, Islamic Spain of the Middle Ages.

andalusī, 11, belonging to Spain of the Middle Ages.

andalusī nūbah, 68, a genre of Arabian music that belongs to the Maghrib states of North Africa. (See also *nawbah*.)

aʿraj, 97, a five-line verse form, based on the *basīṭ* meter, that is used with *mawwāl* vocal form. (See also *nuʿmānī* and *rubāʿī*.)

arghūl, 129, a double clarinet with pipes of different lengths that belongs to the folk-music tradition, also known as *yarghūl*. (See also *mijwiz* or *zummārah*.)

ʿashshārī, 93, a song of the pearl divers that is sung when setting sail for a new dive location.

aṣwāt, 8, plural of *ṣawt*.

awzān, 48, plural of *wazn*.

axabeba, 129, the name used in Arab-occupied Spain for the *shabbābah*, a split-core flute.

badwah, 56, a vocal introduction to the *maqām al-ʿirāqī*, which is sometimes performed in place of the *taḥrīr*.

baḥrī, 93, one of the songs sung by the pearl divers for entertainment on the high seas. (See also *ʿadsānī*, *ḥaddādī*, *ḥassāwī*, and *mkhūlfī*.)

bam, 111, the lowest string on the *ʿūd*. (See also *mathlath*, *mathnā*, and *zīr*.)

bandīr (also *bindīr*), 136, a single-headed frame drum that, like the *mazhar*, belongs to the sphere of religious music.

barbaṭ, 111, a four-stringed Persian lute; may also be a synonym for *ʿūd*.

bashārif, 183, plural of *bashraf*.

bashraf (plural, *bashārif*), 83, an instrumental introduction to a *waṣlah*. (See also *samāʿī*.)

baṣm, 113, a technique of playing the *ʿūd*, popular in Egypt, that involves stopping a string with the index finger of the left hand while striking it with one of the other fingers of the same hand.

basseh, 88, a song of the pearl divers that is sung while striking the foresail.

bastah, 57, a song of fixed meter sung at the end of each *maqām* in a *faṣl* in Iraq.

bayātī, 30, a *maqām* row characterized by the descending sequence of seconds—major-medium-medium—leading to the final tone.

bayt (plural, *abyāt*), 107, a line of verse.

bindīr, 136, see *bandīr*.

bughyah, 70, the Moroccan name for the free-metered piece that opens a *nūbah*; also called *mishālyah*. (See also *dāʾirih*, *istiftāḥ*, and *taqʿīd aṣ-ṣanāʾiʿ*.)

būq, 129, a horn mentioned along with the *nafīr* (trumpet) in historical accounts.

al-burdah, 160, title of a *madīḥ* poem created by the ṣūfī poet al-Būṣīrī, considered to be the masterpiece of the genre.

buzuq, 114, a long-necked lute popular among the gypsies of Syria and Lebanon.

ḍābiṭ īqāʿ, 132, "he who performs the rhythm exactly," an appellation given to *riqq* players.

daff (or *duff*), 83, also called *daff zinjārī*, the Iraqi name for *riqq* (tambourine). (See also *ṭār*.)

dāʾirih, 70, the Algerian name for the free-metered piece that opens a *nūbah*; also called *taqʿīd aṣ-ṣanāʾiʿ*. (See also *bughyah*, *istiftāḥ*, and *mishālyah*.)

dāma, 127, literally "chessmen," the bridges on the Iraqi *sanṭūr*.

dār (plural, *dūr*), 90, a special house where pearl divers and seamen meet at least once a week to sing, dance, and relax.

darabukkah, 49, a goblet drum used to mark the beat of a wazn, also called durbakkih or dirbūkah. (See also dunbak and ṭablah.)

ḍarb, 48, literally "measure," the rhythmic pattern in Arabian music. (See also *mīzān*, *uṣūl*, and *wazn*.)

dawālīb, 106, plural of *dūlāb*.

dawr (plural, *adwār*), 86, see *dūr*.

dhikr, 14, "pronouncement" or "remembrance" ceremonies of religious brotherhoods, also a vocal form with religious content.

dirbūkah, 136, see *darabukkah*.

duff, 3, a hand drum played by the *qiyān*, also known as *daff*.

dūkāh, 128, the tone d.

dūlāb (plural, *dawālīb*), 106, a short instrumental piece used to introduce a vocal piece, it can also serve as a practice piece for players of melody instruments.

dum, 48, one of the two types of drumstroke used to mark the beat (*naqrah*) of a *wazn*, it is produced at the center of the drumskin. (See also *tak*.)

dunbak, 55, a goblet drum. (See also *darabukkah* and *ṭablah*.)

dūr (also *dawr*), 86, a vocal genre that developed in Egypt during the nineteenth century; also plural of *dār*.

durbakkih, 136, see *darabukkah*.

fann al-basseh, 92, the rope song performed near the beginning of the *fjīrī*.

faras, 121, the wooden bridge of a *qānūn*.

faṣl (plural, *fuṣūl*), 57, a complete *maqām* concert, comprising a fixed sequence of *maqāmāt*.

al-fātiḥah, 153, the opening sura of the Koran.

fjīrī, 88, one of the four song forms of the *funūn al-baḥr*. (See also *ahāzīj*, *ḥudwah*, and *muwwālah*.)

funūn al-baḥr, 88, music tradition of the pearl divers and seamen of the Arabian Gulf.

fuqarā', 165, the "beloved" of the Shaykh, brothers who perform special tasks in the ceremonies of a *ṭarīqah*; also *aḥbāb*.

fuṣūl, 57, plural of *faṣl*.

al-ghaydah, 129, one of the North African names for the *sūrnāy*.

al-ghayṭah, 129, one of the North African names for the *sūrnāy*.

ghinā', 13, singing.

al-ghinā' al-mutqan, 7, "the perfect singing," an artful style of singing practiced by the great singers of Mecca and Medina, who established what was later known as the Early Arabian Classical School.

ghirnāṭī, 16, one of the names used in Morocco for the *andalusī nūbah*. (See *ālah*, and see also *ma'lūf* and *ṣan'ah*.)

ghuṣn, 86, the second couplet of a *dūr*.

gnbrī, 114, a two- or three-stringed spike lute used in Morocco. (See also *gumbrī* and *jnbrī*.)

gumbrī, 114, a two- or three-stringed spike lute used in Morocco. (See also *gnbrī* and *jnbrī*.)

ḥaddādī, 93, one of the songs sung by the pearl divers for entertainment on the high seas. (See also *'adsānī*, *baḥrī*, *ḥassāwī*, and *mkhūlfī*.)

ḥadīth, 5, the handed-down body of conversations that the prophet Muhammad was said to have had with his companions during his lifetime.

ḥaḍrah, 165, God's presence among the believers, the climax of a *dhikr* ceremony.

ḥānah (plural, *ḥānāt*), 2, the premises of a *qaynah*.

ḥānāt, 2, plural of *ḥānah*.

hank, 87, the musical repetition schema within a *dūr* performance (also *tardīd*).

ḥassāwī, 93, one of the songs sung by the pearl divers for entertainment on the high seas. (See also *ʿadsānī, baḥrī, ḥaddādī*, and *mkhūlfī*.)

hazaj, 3, "simple" songs of the *qiyān*, serving as entertainment and amusement for the listener; their texts were composed in short classical metrical feet, and they were accompanied by lute, flute, or hand drum.

ḥijāz, 33, a *maqām* row characterized by the descending sequence of seconds—minor-augmented-minor—leading to the final tone.

ḥudāʾ, 2, the rousing song of the Bedouin nomad camel drivers; its rhythm corresponded to that of the camel's steps. (See also *naṣb*.)

ḥudwah, 92, one of the four song forms of the *funūn al-baḥr*. (See also *ahāzīj, fjīrī*, and *muwwālah*.)

ḥuṣūn, 8, plural of *ḥiṣn* (castle); the title of Maʿbad's songs.

ibtihāl, 162,"supplication," a religious song form belonging to the *madīḥ* repertoire. (See also *muwashshaḥ, tanzīlah, tawassul*, and *tawshīḥ*.)

ʿīd al-aḍḥā, 14, Feast of Sacrifice, a religious holiday of Islam.

ʿīd al-fiṭr, 14, the feast after Ramaḍān fasting.

istiftāḥ, 70, the Tunisian name for the free-metered piece that opens a *nūbah*. (See also *bughyah, dāʾirih, mishālyah*, and *taqʿīd aṣ-ṣanāʾiʿ*.)

jadīd, 143, the "new."

jāhiliyah, 1, "wrath," "pride," "impudence," and "fanaticism"; jāhiliyah refers to the pre-Islamic period in which these qualities characterized the life of the Arabs.

jaḥlah (plural, *jaḥlāt*), 89, a water urn used in Bahrain as a percussion instrument by beating on its mouth with a flat hand and scratching on its outer surface.

jaḥlāt, 89, plural of *jaḥlah*.

jalājil, 3, a rattle played by the *qiyān*.

jālghī baghdādī, 55, an ensemble consisting of a singer and three or four instrumentalists for performing *maqām al-ʿirāqī*.

jawāb kurdān, 112, the tone c'' (one octave above middle c) on the ʿūd.

jinn (plural *jinn*), 91, a demon or spirit.

jnbrī, 114, a two- or three-stringed spike lute used in Morocco. (See also *gnbrī* and *gumbrī*.)

jūzah, 55, a spike fiddle in Iraq. (See also *kamanjah*.)

kah, 49, an unaccented, legato drumbeat following a *tak* stroke. (See also *mah.*)

kamanjah, 83, a spike fiddle ("Arabian kamanjah"), also applied to the European violin. (See also *jūzah.*)

kāmil, 111, "complete"; the *ʿūd kāmil* (complete ʿūd) had five strings as opposed to the *ʿūd qadīm* (old ʿūd), which had only four.

khānah, (plural, *khānāt)*, 99, one of the three or four segments of a *bashraf.*

khānāt, 99, plural of *khānah.*

khatm, 108, the final *ṣawt* of a *samrah.*

khrāb, 88, a song of the pearl divers that is sung while weighing anchor.

kīrān, 3, a lutelike stringed instrument played by the *qiyān.* (See also *mizhar, muwattar, ṣanj.*)

kitāb al-mūsīqā al-kabīr, 123, the "Great Book of Music" by Abū Naṣr Muḥammad Ibn Tarkhān al-Fārābī.

kurd, 36, a *maqām* row characterized by the descending sequence of seconds—major-major-minor—leading to the final tone.

kurdān string, 112, the c' (middle c) string in a *ʿūd.*

kwītrah, 114, a short-necked lute similar to the *ʿūd*, having four pairs of strings and a body approximately the same length as its neck.

layālī, 96, a solo vocal form whose text consists of the words *yā laylī yā ʿaynī.*

laylat ʿāshūrah, 160, "ʿāshūrah night," the anniversary of Ḥusayn's death.

madā'iḥ, plural of *madīḥ.*

madhhabjiyah, 183, a singing group that performs *adwār.*

madhhab, 86, the first couplet of a *dūr.*

madīḥ (plural, *madā'iḥ*), 152, "praise," a vocal form with religious content.

madīḥ nabawī, 158, a vocal form in which the Prophet and his family are eulogized.

maghrib, 68, literally "place of the sunset" or "time of sunset"; Maghrib refers to the Arabian states of North Africa: Morocco, Algeria, Tunisia, and Libya. (See *mashriq.*)

mah, 49, an unaccented, legato drumbeat following a *dum* stroke. (See also *kah.*)

māhūrān, 112, the tone f' (f above middle c) on the *ʿūd.*

makhmūs, 93, a song of the pearl divers that is sung when the mast line is lashed.

ma'lūf, 16, the name used in Tunisia for the *andalusī nūba*. (See also *ālah*, *ghirnāṭī*, and *ṣan'ah*.)

maqām (plural, *maqāmāt*) row, 18, one of the more than seventy modes, based on heptatonic scales, that can be put together from augmented, major, medium, and minor seconds.

maqāmāt, 43, plural of *maqām*.

maqām al-'irāqī, 16, a musical genre, originating in Iraq, that is considered to be the most noble and perfect form of *maqām*.

marāwīs, 89, plural of *mirwās*.

mashriq, 68, literally "place of the sunrise" or "time of sunrise"; Mashriq refers to Syria, Lebanon, Egypt, Iraq, Jordan, and the states of the Arabian Peninsula. (See *maghrib*.)

mathlath, 111, the third highest string on the *'ūd*. (See also *bam*, *mathnā*, and *zīr*.)

mathnā, 111, the second highest string on the *'ūd*. (See also *bam*, *mathlath*, and *zīr*.)

Mawlawiyyah, 100, the "dancing dervishes" who inhabit Turkey, Egypt, Syria, Iraq, and the Maghrib states.

mawlāya ṣallī, 160, a line of text inserted after each line of the *burdah*.

mawlid, 152, "birthday," a religious festivity celebrating the Prophet's birth; also a vocal form with religious content.

mawwāl, 97, a vocal form, whose text is in colloquial Arabic, that usually follows the performance of the *layālī*.

mazhar, 135, a frame drum with iron chains rather than cymbals, which is reserved for ritual occasions because each instrument is dedicated to a saint.

mijdāf, 88, literally "oar," a song of the pearl divers that is sung while rowing.

mijwiz, 129, a double clarinet with pipes of equal length that belongs to the folk-music tradition; also known as *zummārah*. (See also *arghūl* or *yarghūl*.)

mirwās (plural, *marāwīs*), 89, a small double-headed cylindrical drum.

mishālyah, 70, the Moroccan name for the free-metered piece that opens a *nūbah*; also called *bughyah*. (See also *dā'irih*, *istiftāḥ*, and *taq'īd aṣ-ṣanā'i'*.)

mi'zafa, 7, a zither.

mīzān, 48, literally "measure," the rhythmic pattern in Arabian music. (See also ḍarb, uṣūl, and wazn.)

mizhar, 3, a lutelike stringed instrument played by the *qiyān*. (See also *kīrān*, *muwattar*, and *ṣanj*.)

mizmār, 3, a kind of clarinet played by the *qiyān*.

mkhūlfī, 93, one of the songs sung by the pearl divers for entertainment on the high seas. (See also *ʿadsānī*, *baḥrī*, *ḥaddādī*, and *ḥassāwī*.)

mrādāh "tūb tūb yā baḥr," 93, the antiphonal song of welcome sung by the wives of the seamen on their return.

mrūbaʿ, 108, literally "square," the name of a type of *ṣawt*.

mṣaddar, 70, the Tunisian name for the instrumental section that follows the opening of a *nūbah*. (See also *tūshyih*.)

muʾadhdhin (dual, *muʾadhdhinayn*; plural, *muʾadhdhinīn*), 157, the muezzin who calls the hours of daily prayers.

muʾadhdhinayn, 158, dual of *muʾadhdhin*.

muʾadhdhinīn, 158, plural of *muʾadhdhin*.

mughannī, 153, a singer.

Muḥarram, 14, the first month of the Islamic year.

mujawwid, 153, a "reader" or "reciter" who sings the Koran; also *muqriʾ*, *murattil*, or *tālī*.

mukhannath (plural, *mukhannathūn*), 5, effeminate male singers, equivalent to the female *qaynah*, who probably had homosexual tendencies.

mukhannathūn, 5, plural of *mukhannath*.

mulaḥḥin, 86, a composer.

muqriʾ, 153, a "reader" or "reciter" who sings the Koran; also *mujawwid*, *murattil*, or *tālī*.

muraddidūn, 87, plural of murāddid, a chorus that performs alternately with the solo singer.

murattil, 153, a "reader" or "reciter" who sings the Koran; also *mujawwid*, *muqriʾ*, or *tālī*.

mūsīqā, 13, a term that applies to theoretical treatises on music, tone systems, musical instruments, music aesthetics, etc.; music.

muṭrib, 86, the singer of a *dūr* or of a *ṣawt*, often also its composer (*mulaḥḥin*).

muwālī, 6, converts to Islam who were disciples of a free-born Arab.

muwashshaḥ (plural, *muwashshaḥāt*), 70, a poem written in classical Arabic used as text for the *andalusī nūbah*; also a religious song form belonging to the *madīḥ* repertoire. (See also *ibtihāl*, *tanzīlah*, *tawassul*, and *tawshīḥ*.)

muwashshaḥāt, 16, plural of *muwashshaḥ*.

muwattar, 3, a lutelike stringed instrument played by the *qiyān*. (See also *kīrān*, *mizhar*, and *ṣanj*.)

muwwālah, 92, one of the four song forms of the *funūn al-baḥr*. (See also *ahāzīj*, *fjīrī*, and *ḥudwah*.)

nafīr, 129, a trumpet, mentioned along with the *būq* (horn) in historical accounts, that is still occasionally played in North Africa during Ramaḍān.

nagham, 10, musical tone.

nahhām, 88, the solo singer in the *fjīrī* music of the Arabian Gulf.

nahawand, 32, a *maqām* row characterized by the descending sequence of seconds—major-minor-major—leading to the final tone.

nakrīz, 34, a *maqām* row characterized by the descending sequence of seconds—minor-augmented-minor-major—leading to the final tone.

naqarāt, 48, plural of *naqrah*.

naqāryah, 139, large-sized *naqqārāt* mounted on either side of a camel, played by a musician while riding the camel.

naqqārāt, 49, a pair of kettle drums used to mark the beat of a *wazn*.

naqrah (plural, *naqarāt*), 48, the beat or unit of time of a *wazn*.

naqrazān, 139, medium-sized *naqqārāt*, carried by a donkey.

naṣb, 2, a "simple and naive" genre of singing practiced by Bedouin youths; refers also to the dirges sung by women. (See also *ḥudāʾ*.)

nashʾatkār, 114, a short-necked lute, played in Syria, having five pairs of wire strings.

nawbah, 68, literally "turn," as in what artists had to wait for when performing for the caliph; *nawbah* also referred to the piece performed, eventually replacing the word *ṣawt*.

nawā, 18, the tone g. (See also *yakāh* and *ramal tūtī*.)

nawbah, 68, classical Arabic for *andalusī nūbah*.

nāy (plural, *nāyāt*), 70, an end-blown flute.

nāyāt, 129, plural of *nāy*.

nīm, 27, a slightly lowered pitch.

nūbah (plural, *nūbāt*), 68, see *andalusī nūbah.*

nūbāt, 70, plural of *nūbah.*

nuzhah, 123, the name used by Ṣafī ad-Dīn al-Urmawī for the *qānūn.*

pakhawaj, 90, an Indian drum related to the *ṭabl.*

peshrev, 15, a Turkish compositional form popular among the Arabs. (See also *semai.*)

qadīm, 84, a designation meaning "old" that is used when the poet and composer of a *muwashshaḥ* are not known.

Qādiriyah, 135, a sūfī sect. (See also *Rifāʿiyah.*)

qānūn, 70, a box zither.

qarār, 27, the lower octave.

qarār jahārkāh, 112, the tone F on the *ʿūd.*

qarār sīkāh, 112, the tone E𝄳 on the *ʿūd.*

qāriʾ, 55, singer (also *qāriʾ al-maqām*).

qaṣāʾid, 149, plural of *qaṣīdah.*

qaṣīdah, 96, a poem set to music in which all lines are based on the same classical meter of Arabian poetry; also a vocal form with religious content.

qaylamī, 88, a song of the pearl divers that is sung while striking the mainsail.

qaynah (plural, *qiyān*), 2, a singer and servant in one, whose duties included not only singing and performing but also pouring wine and providing other sensual pleasures.

qirbah, 129, a bagpipe; also known as *ruwāqah.*

qiyān, 2, plural of *qaynah.*

quṣṣāb, 3, a kind of flute played by the *qiyān.*

rabāb, 70, a bow-necked lute. (See also *rebec.*)

rabāb ash-shāʿir, 117, "the rabāb of the poet," a single-stringed instrument, played primarily by impoverished musicians to accompany epic songs.

Ramaḍān, 14, Islam's month of fasting.

ramal tūtī, 18, the third octave, starting two octaves above the lowest tone in the singer's register. (See also *yakāh* and *nawā.*)

raqīq, 5, prisoners and slaves who introduced new manners and customs, including new cultural forms of expression, in Medina during the seventh century.

rāst, 29, a *maqām* row characterized by the descending sequence of seconds—medium-medium-major—leading to the final tone.

rebec, 70, a bow-necked lute. (See also *rabāb*.)

ribāṭ, 49, the musical notation for a tie, indicating that there are two beats for one unit of time.

Rifāʿiyah, 135, a sūfī sect. (See also *Qādiriyah*.)

riqq, 49, a frame drum used to mark the beat of a *wazn*. (See also *ṭār*.)

rīshah, 112, the plectrum, made from the quill of an eagle feather, that is used to pluck the strings of a *ʿūd*.

rubāʿī, 97, a four-line verse form, based on the *basīṭ* meter, that is used with *mawwāl* vocal form. (See also *aʿraj* and *nuʿmānī*.)

ruwāqah, 129, a bagpipe, also known as *qirbah*.

ṣabā, 44, a *maqām* row characterized by the descending sequence of seconds—minor-medium-medium—leading to the final tone.

ṣafqah, 107, hand-clapping used as a rhythmic accompaniment to a song.

ṣaḥābah, 154, a follower of the prophet Muhammad.

ṣājāt, 139, copper castanets played by both male and female dancers in public performances.

samāʿ, 162, spiritual concert.

samāʿī, 83, an instrumental introduction to a *waṣlah*. (See also *bashraf*.)

samrah, 107, a cyclic form within which several *aṣwāt* are performed, typically at weddings and other festivities.

ṣanʿah (plural, *ṣanʿāt*), 16, the name used in Algeria for the *andalusī nūba*. (See also *ālah*, *ghirnāṭī*, and *maʾlūf*.) Also the poem that is sung during a *nūbah* performance.

ṣanʿāt, 76, plural of *ṣanʿah*.

ṣanj, 3, a lutelike stringed instrument played by the *qiyān*. (See also *mizhar*, *kīrān*, and *muwattar*.)

sanṭūr, 15, a hammer dulcimer.

sattār, 68, the "curtain man" who signaled to artists waiting to appear before the caliph when it was their turn to perform.

ṣawt, 8, a song. (See *nawbah*.)

sayyid, 2, master.

semai, 15, a Turkish compositional form popular among the Arabs. (See also *peshrev*.)

shabbābah, 129, a split-core flute belonging to the folk tradition of Syria, Lebanon, and North Africa; also known as *axabeba* in Arab-occupied Spain.

sīkāh, 31, a musical genre characterized by the descending sequence of seconds—major-major-medium—leading to the final tone.

sinād, 3, one of the extraordinary virtuosic singing styles of the *qiyān*; its texts deal with themes of seriousness, dignity, fame, pride, and arrogance; composed in the long classical metrical feet of Arabian poetry. (See also *hazaj*.)

ṣūfī, 96, a fraternity of Islamic mystics.

ṣunūj, 139, cymbals that are played during religious musical exercises.

sūrnāy, 129, a double-reed wind instrument, or oboe, that belongs to the folk-music tradition. Used to play African music in Bahrain and Oman, the *sūrnāy* is known in North Africa as *zukrah*, *al-ghayṭah*, or *al-ghaydah*.

sūryah, 93, the song sung by the pearl divers when setting the sail against the wind.

ṭabʿ, 68, the basis for the *andalusī nūba*, similar to the *maqām*.

ṭabl (plural, *ṭubūl*), 89, a double-headed cylindrical drum used primarily in Arabian folk music.

ṭablah, 55, the goblet drum in Iraq. (See also *dunbak* and *darabukkah*.)

taghbīr, 155, a reading of the Koran; also *tajwīd* or *tartīl*.

taḥmīlah, 105, a genre of instrumental music native to Egypt in which each player of a melody instrument has a solo opportunity to improvise on the same simple theme.

taḥrīr, 55, a vocal passage that generally begins a *maqām al-ʿirāqī* performance.

tajwīd, 155, a reading of the Koran; also *taghbīr* or *tartīl*.

tak, 48, one of the two types of drumstroke used to mark the beat (*naqrah*) of a *wazn*, it is produced at the edge of the drumskin. (See also *dum*.)

takht, 86, literally "bed," "seat," or "podium," an instrumental ensemble of from three to six musicians.

tālī, 153, a "reader" or "reciter" who sings the Koran; also *mujawwid*, *muqri'*, or *murattil*.

tambūrah, 184, a lyre used to play African music in Bahrain and Oman.

ṭanbūr, 15, a long-necked lute of Persian or Turkish origin.

tanzīlah, 162,"revelation," a religious song form belonging to the *madīḥ* repertoire. (See also *ibtihāl*, *muwashshaḥ*, *tawassul*, and *tawshīḥ*.)

taqāsīm, 98, plural of *taqsīm*.

taq'īd aṣ-ṣanā'i', 70, the Algerian name for the free-metered piece that opens a *nūbah*; also called *dā'irih*. (See also *bughyah*, *istiftāḥ*, and *mishālyah*.)

taqsīm (plural, *taqāsīm*), 97, the instrumental presentation of the tonal-spatial model of a *maqām*.

ṭār (plural *ṭīrān*), 49, the name used in North African for a *riqq* (tambourine). (See also *daff*.)

ṭarab, 13, the joy that one feels when listening to music.

tardīd, 87, the musical repetition schema in Arabian music; also *hank*.

ṭarīqah (plural, *ṭuruq*), 164, "way" or "path," the mystical doctrine of the Sufis.

tartīl, 155, a reading of the Koran; also *taghbīr* or *tajwīd*.

ṭāsah (plural, *ṭūs*), 89, a small metal cymbal.

Tashlḥīt, 186, a Berber language in Morocco.

taslīm, 99, an unchanging intermezzo or ritornello played between *khānāt* in a *bashraf*.

taslūm, 56, a descending melodic passage in a *maqām al-'irāqī* performance that leads immediately back from the musical climax to the *finalis* of the *maqām* row.

tawassul, 162, "beseechment," a religious song form belonging to the *madīḥ* repertoire. (See also *ibtihāl*, *muwashshaḥ*, *tanzīlah*, and *tawshīḥ*.)

tawshīḥ, 162, a religious song form belonging to the *madīḥ* repertoire. (See also *ibtihāl*, *muwashshaḥ*, *tanzīlah*, and *tawassul*.)

tawshīḥah, 107, the final part of a *ṣawt*.

tawsīd, 74, a technique for learning the rhythmic patterns of the *andalusī nūbah* by striking the thigh with an open hand on the dark strokes and with a fist on the light strokes, while reciting in a loud and clear voice.

tīk, 27, a slightly raised pitch.

ṭīrān, 89, plural of *ṭār*.

ṭubūl, 89, plural of *ṭabl*.

tūf miryam, 135, "Miriam's drum," the Jewish name for the *daff* tambourine.

ṭuruq, 164, plural of *ṭarīqah*; also the generic term for religious orders that established themselves during the twelfth and thirteenth centuries.

ṭūs, 89, plural of *ṭāsah*.

tūshyih, 70, the Moroccan and Algerian name for the instrumental section that follows the opening of a *nūbah*. (See also *mṣaddar*.)

ʿūd, 3, literally "wood," a present-day short-necked lute.

ughniyah, 144, a contemporary Arabian "pop" song, which embodies the *jadīd* in Arabian music.

ʿurab, 121, detachable metal bridges placed beneath the strings of a *qānūn* to alter their tuning.

ʿushshāq turkī, 43, a *maqām* row characterized by a descending sequence of seconds—major-medium-medium—leading to the final tone.

uṣūl, 48, literally "measure," the rhythmic pattern in Arabian music. (See also *ḍarb*, *mīzān*, and *wazn*.)

waṣlah (plural *waṣlāt*), 83, a cycle consisting of an instrumental introduction followed by up to eight *muwashshaḥāt* performed in succession.

waṣlāt, 84, plural of *waṣlah*.

wazn (plural, *awzān*), 48, literally "measure," the rhythmic pattern in Arabian music. (See also *ḍarb*, *mīzān*, and *uṣūl*.)

wusṭā-zalzal tone, 22, a third that is larger than a tempered minor third and smaller than a tempered major third, whose ratio is 27/22.

yakāh, 18, the lowest tone of the scale, which corresponds to the lowest tone in the singer's register. (See also nawā and ramal tūtī.)

yamānī, 108, the (8/8) wazn of a ṣawt.

yarghūl, 129, a double clarinet with pipes of different lengths that belongs to the folk-music tradition; also known as *arghūl*. (See also *mijwiz* or *zummārah*.)

zajal, 71, another name for the poetic form called muwashshaḥ.

zāwiyah, 165, "corner," a place outside the mosque where *dhikr* ceremonies are held.

zīr, 111, the highest string on the *ʿūd*. (See also *bam*, *mathlath*, and *mathnā*.)

zuhayrī, 61, a colloquial poem used as text in *al-maqām al-ʿirāqī*.

zukrah, 129, one of the North African names for the *sūrnāy*.

zummārah, 129, a double clarinet with pipes of equal length that belongs to the folk-music tradition; also known as *mijwiz*. (See also *arghūl* or *yarghūl*.)

Musicians of the ʿĪsāwiyah Brotherhood during a dhikr in Fez, Morocco. Photo: H. H. Touma.

Bibliography

ʿAbd al-Jalīl, ʿAbd al-ʿAzīz bin

1983 *Madkhal ilā tārīkh al-mūsīqā al-maghribiyah.* Kuwait: ʿĀlam al-maʿrifah.

1988 *Al-mūsīqā al-andalusiyah (funūn al-adāʾ).* Kuwait: ʿĀlam al-maʿrifah.

Abū ʿŪf, Shafīq, and Ibrāhīm Shafīq

1963 *Turāthunā al-mūsīqī.* Four volumes. Cairo: Maṭbaʿat al-amīn.

Alexandru, Tiberiu and Emil Wahba

1967 Al-ghināʾ wal-mūsīqā ash-shaʿbiyah al-miṣriyah. Cairo.

ʿAlī, Aḥmad

1980 *Al-mūsīqā wal-ghināʾ fī al-kuwait.* Kuwait: Sharikat ar-rabīʿān.

Allāhwīrdī, Mīkhāʾīl

1949 *Falsafat al-mūsīqā ash-sharqiyah.* Damascus: Ibn Zaydūn.

al-ʿAlwajī, ʿAbd al-Ḥamīd

1964 *Rāʾid al-mūsīqā al-ʿarabiyah.* Baghdad: Al-jumhūriyah Press.

1975 *Al-murshid ilā an-nitāj al-mūsīqī.* Baghdad: Al-lujnah al-waṭaniyah al-ʿirāqiyah lil-mūsīqā.

ʿArnīṭah, Yusrā Jawāhiriyah

1968 *Al-funūn ash-shaʿbiyah fī falasṭīn.* Beirut: Munaẓẓamat at-taḥrīr al-filisṭīniyah, markaz al-abḥāth.

al-Asad, Naṣr ad-Dīn
1968 *Al-qiyān wal-ghinā' fī al-'aṣr al-jāhilī*. Cairo: Dār al-ma'ārif bimiṣr.

'Azzām, Nabīl Salīm
1990 "Muḥammad 'Abd al-Wahhāb in Modern Egyptian Music." Ph.D. diss., University of California, Los Angeles.

al-'Azzāwī, 'Abbās
1951 *Al-mūsīqā al-'irāqiyah fī 'ahd al-mughūl wat-turkumān*. Baghdad: Sharikat at-tijārah waṭ-ṭibā'ah al-maḥdūdah.

Binjallūn, Idrīs
1980 *At-turāth al-'arabī al-maghribī fī al-mūsīqā*. Casablanca: Maṭba'at ar-ra'īs

Braune, Gabriele
1987 *Die Qaṣīdah im Gesang von Umm Kulthūm. Die arabische Poesie im Repertoire der größten ägyptischen Sängerin unserer Zeit*. Hamburg: Karl Dieter Wagner.

Briyūl, Muḥammad
1985 *Nūbah gharībat al-ḥusayn*. Fez: Maṭ-ba'at an-najāḥ.

Chabrier, Jean-Claude
1976 *Un mouvement de réhabilitation de la musique arabe et du luth orientale. L'école de Bagdad de Cherif Muhieddin à Munir Bachir*. Paris: Sorbonne.

Collaer, Paul, and Jürgen Elsner
1983 "Nordafrika." Pt. 8 of *Musikethnologie*. Vol. 1 of *Musikgeschichte in Bildern*. Leipzig: Deutscher Verlag für Musik.

Dhurayl, 'Adnān bin
1969 *Al-mūsīqā as-sūriyah*. Damascus: Maṭba'at alif bā'

Elsner, Jürgen
1973 *Der Begriff des maqām in Ägypten in neuerer Zeit*. Leipzig: Deutscher Verlag für Musik.

d'Erlanger, Baron Rodolphe
1949 *La musique arabe*, vol. 5. Paris: Librairie Orientaliste Paul Geuthner.
1959 *La musique arabe*, vol. 6. Paris: Librairie Orientaliste Paul Geuthner.

al-Fārābī, Abū Naṣr Muḥammad Ibn Tarkhān

1967 *Kitāb al-mūsīqā al-kabīr*. Edited by Ghaṭṭās ʿAbd al-Malik Khashabah. Cairo: Dār al-kitāb al-ʿarabī.

Farmer, Henry George

1925 *The Arabic Manuscripts in the Bodleian Library*. London: William Reeves.

1926 *The Influence of Music from Arabic Sources*. London: William Reeves.

1929 *Historical Facts for the Arabian Musical Influence*. London: William Reeves.

1933 *An Old Moorish Lute Tutor: Being Four Arabic Texts from Unique Manuscripts*. Glasgow.

1945 *The Minstrels of the "Arabian Nights."* Bearsdon: Hinricksten Edition.

1957 "The Music of Islam." In *New Oxford History of Music*, vol. 1: *Ancient and Oriental Music*. Edited by Egon Wellesz. London: Oxford University Press, 421.

1965 *The Sources of Arabian Music*. Leiden: E. J. Brill.

1967 *A History of Arabian Music to the XIIIth Century*. London: Luzac and Co. (first edition: 1929).

al-Fārūqī, Lois Ibsen

1974 "The Nature of the Musical Art of Islamic Culture: A Theoretical and Empirical Study of Arabian Music." Ph.D. diss., University of Syracuse.

1981 *An Annotated Glossary of Arabic Musical Terms*. Westport, Connecticut: Green Press.

Guettat, Mahmoud

1980 *La musique classique du Maghreb*. Paris: La bibliothèque arabe Sindbad.

al-Ḥajjī, ʿAbd ar-Raḥmān

1969 *Tārīkh al-mūsīqā al-andalusiyah*. Beirut: Dār al-irshād.

al-Ḥanafī, Jalāl

1964 *Al-mughannūn al-baghdādiyūn wal-maqām al-ʿirāqī*. Baghdad.

Hassan, Schéhérazade Qassim

1980 *Les instruments de musique en Irak, et leur rôle dans la société traditionelle*. Cahiers de l' homme, Nouvelle Série 21. Paris: Mouton.

al-Hefnī, Maḥmūd

1931 *Ibn Sīnās Lehre.* Berlin: Otto Hellwig.

Hickmann, Hans

1949–51 "Ägyptische Musik." In *Die Musik in Geschichte und Gegenwart.* Vol. 1. Edited by F. Blume. Kassel: Bärenreiter, 92–105.

1970 "Die Musik des arabisch-islamischen Bereiches." In *Handbuch der Orientalistik*, erste Abteilung, Ergänzungsband IV, *Orientalische Musik.* Leiden: E. J. Brill, 1–135.

Ḥilū, Salīm

Al-muwashshaḥāt al-andalusiyah. Beirut: Dār maktabat al-ḥayāt.

al-Jabaqjī, ʿAbd ar-Raḥmān

1972 *Al-fulklūr al-ʿarabī wal-qudūd al-ḥalabiyah.* Aleppo: published by the author.

Jarārī, ʿAbbās

1978 *Muʿjam muṣṭalaḥāt al-malḥūn al-faniyah.* Morocco: maṭbaʿat faḍḍālah.

Jargy, Simon

1970 *La poésie populaire traditionelle chantée du Proche-Orient arabe. I. Les textes.* Le Monde d'outre-mer passé et present. Deuxième série, documents XIV. Paris: Mouton.

1971 *La musique arabe.* No. 1436 of *Que sais-je?* Paris: Presses Universitaires de France.

Jones, Lura Jafran

1977 "The ʿĪsāwiyah of Tunesia and Their Music." Ph.D. diss., University of Washington, Seattle.

Kāmil, Maḥmūd

1971 *ʿAbdū al-Ḥāmūlī: zaʿīm aṭ-ṭarab wal-ghināʾ, 1841–1901.* Cairo: Muḥammad al-amīn.

Kāẓim, A.

1964 *Al-iṣṭilāḥāt al-mūsiqiyah.* Baghdad: Maṭbaʿat dār al-jumhūriyah.

Krüger-Wust, Wilhelm J.

1983 *Arabische Musik in europäischen Sprachen.* Wiesbaden: Otto Harrasowitz.

Lortat-Jacob, Bernard

1980 *Musique et fêtes au Haut-Atlas. Publications de la société française de musicologie*, 3rd series, vol. 4. Paris: Société française de musicologie.

el-Mahdī, Salāḥ

1972 *La musique arabe*. Paris: Alphonse Leduc.

1967–75 *Ensemble des "Bashrafs" Tunisiens*. Tunis: Republic of Tunisia, Ministry of Cultural Affairs.

1967–75 *Patrimonie Musical Tunesien, 2e Fascicule. Ensemble de Tawchihc et Zajals Tunisiens*. Tunis: Republic of Tunisia, Ministry of Cultural Affairs.

1967–75 *Patrimonie Musical Tunesien, 3e Fascicule.*
La nawbah dans le maghreb arabe.
Nawbet edhil Tunisienne. Tunis: Republic of Tunisia, Ministry of Cultural Affairs.

1967–75 *Patrimonie Musical Tunesien, 4e Fascicule.*
La Nawbah à travers l'Histoire Islamique.
Nawbet el Irak. Tunis: Republic of Tunisia, Ministry of Cultural Affairs.

1967–75 *Patrimonie Musical Tunesien, 5e Fascicule.*
Ahmed al Wafi (1850–1921).
Nawbet Es-Sica et Nawbet El-Houcine. Tunis: Republic of Tunisia, Ministry of Cultural Affairs.

1967–75 *Patrimonie Musical Tunesien, 6e Fascicule.*
La Musique Tunesienne au XXe Siécle.
Nawbets Rasd, Ramel El Maya et Nawa. Tunis: Republic of Tunisia, Ministry of Cultural Affairs.

1967–75 *Patrimonie Musical Tunesien, 7ème Fascicule.*
Khmaïs Ternane (1894-1964).
Nawbats: Asbïen—Rast Dhil-Raml. Tunis: Republic of Tunisia, Ministry of Cultural Affairs.

1967–75 *Patrimonie Musical Tunesien, 8me Fascicule.*
Étude Comparative des Modes Tunesiens.
Nawbets Asbahane, Mazmoume et Maya. Tunis: Republic of Tunisia, Ministry of Cultural Affairs.

1967–75 *Patrimonie Musical Tunesien, 9me Fascicule.*
Les Rhythmes dans la Musique Arabe.
Nawbets Nahawand, Zingoulah et Ajam Ouchairane. Tunis: Republic of Tunisia, Ministry of Cultural Affairs.

Manik, Liberty

1969 *Das arabische Tonsystem im Mittelalter.* Leiden: E. J. Brill.

Michaelides, Neffen

1972 "Das Grundprinzip der altarabischen Qaṣidah in der musikalischen Form syrischer Volkslieder." Ph.D. ḍiss., Universität Halle.

Mīshāqā, Mīkhā'īl

1899 "Ar-risālah ash-shihābiyah." In *Al-muqtaṭaf,* 146–151, 218–224, 296–302, 408–415, 561–566, 629–632, 726–731, 883–890, 928–934, 1018–1026, 1073–1082. Beirut: Maṭba'at al-muqtaṭaf.

Nettl, Bruno and Roland Riddle

1973 "Taqsīm Nahawand: A Study of Sixteen Performances by Jihad Racy." In *Yearbook of the International Folk Music Council* 5: 11–50.

Neubauer, Eckhard

1965 *Musik am Hof der frühen Abbasiden.* Phil. diss., J. W. v. Goethe-Universität Frankfurt.

1971 "Neuere Bücher zur arabischen Musik." In *Der Islam* 48(1): 1–27.

Nixdorff, Heide

1969 "Die Herstellung der syrischen Rahmentrommeln. Einfluß von Material und Konstruktion auf die musikalische Qualität." In *Baessler-Archiv* 18: 101–31.

Ogger, Thomas

1987 *Maqām Segāh/Sīkāh. Vergleich der Kunstmusik des Iran und des Irak anhand eines maq?m-Modells.* Hamburg: Karl Dieter Wagner.

Olsen, Poul Rovsing

1967 "Afrikansk musik ved den Persike Golf." In *Dansk Musiktidschrift* 42 (4): 73–79.

1974 "Six Versions de Taqsim en Maqam Rast." In *Studia instrumentorum musicae popularis III. Festschrift to Ernst Emsheimer on the occasion of his 70th birthday, January 15th 1974.* 197–202.

Pacholczyk, Jósef Marcin

1970 "Regulative Principles in the Koran Chant of Shaikh 'Abd'l-

Bāsiṭ ʿAbd'ṣ-Ṣamad." Ph.D. diss., University of California, Los Angeles.

Perkuhn, Eva Ruth

1976 *Die Theorien zum arabischen Einfluß auf die europäische Musik des Mittelalters.* Walldorf-Hessen: Verlag für Orientkunde Dr. H. Vorndran.

Qaddūrī, Ḥusayn

1979 *Luʿab wa aghānī al-aṭfāl ash-shaʿbiyah fī al quṭr al-ʿirāqī.* Pt. 1. Baghdad: Dār ar-rashīd lin-nashr.

1984 *Luʿab wa aghānī al-aṭfāl ash-shaʿbiyah fī al quṭr al-ʿirāqī.* Pt. 2. Baghdad: Dār al-ḥurriyah liṭ-ṭibāʿah.

Racy, ʿAlī Jihād

1977 "Musical Change and Commercial Recordings in Egypt, 1904–1932." Ph.D. diss., University of Urbana, Illinois.

Rajā'ī, Fu'ād, and Nadīm Darwīsh

1950 *Min kunūzinā.* Aleppo.

ar-Rajab, Hāshim

1961 *Al-maqām al-ʿirāqī.* Baghdad: Dār al-ḥurriyah liṭ-ṭibāʿah.

Rashīd, Bahījah Ṣidqī

1968 *Aṭ-ṭaqṭūqah ash-shaʿbiyah.* Cairo: Maṭbaʿat al-madanī.

Rashīd, Ṣubḥī Anwar

1975 *Al-ālāt al-mūsīqiyah fī al-ʿuṣūr al-islāmiyah—dirāsah muqāranah.* Baghdad: Dār al-ḥurriyah liṭ-ṭibāʿah.

1984 "Mesopotamien." In *Musik des Altertums.* Vol. 2 of *Musikgeschichte in Bildern.* Leipzig: VEB Deutscher Verlag für Musik.

Reichow, Jan

1971 *Die Entfaltung eines Melodiemodells im Genus Sīkāh.* Regensburg: Gustav Bosse.

Ribera, Julian

1970 *Music in Ancient Arabia and Spain.* New York: Da Capo Press (First Edition: 1929).

Righini, Pietro

1983 *La Musica Araba Nell'Ambiente nella storia.* Padova: G. Zanibon.

ar-Rizqī, Ṣādiq

1967 *Al-aghānī at-tūnisiyah*. Tunis: Ad-dār at-tūnisiya lin-nashr.

Ṣāliḥ, Mājdah

1979 "A Documention of the Ethnic Dance Traditions of the Arab Republic of Egypt." Ph.D. diss., New York University.

as-Sāmirrā'ī, ʿĀmir Rashīd

1974 *Mawwālāt baghdādiyah*. Baghdad: Dār al-ḥurriyah liṭ-ṭibāʿah.

Schuyler, Philip Daniel.

1979 "A Repertory of Ideas: The Music of the 'Rwais' Berber Professional Musicians from Southwestern Morocco." Ph.D. diss., University of Washington.

Shāmī, Yūnis

1979 *Nūbah ramal al-māyah*. Casablanca.

1980 *Nūbah raṣd adh-dhīl*. Casablanca.

1984 *Nūbah ramal al-māyah*. Casablanca: Benimid.

1986 *Nūbah ʿushshāq*. Casablanca: Benimid.

ash-Sharqī, Ṣalāḥ

1981 *Moroccan Music. Musique Marocaine*. Mohammedia, Imprimerie de Fedala.

1976 *Aḍwā' ʿalā al-mūsīqā al-maghribiyah*. Muḥammadiyah: Maṭbaʿat faḍlallah.

Shawqī, Yūsuf

1969 *Qiyās as-sullam al-mūsīqī al-ʿarabī*. Cairo: Maṭ- baʿat dār al-kutub.

el-Shawwān, Salwā

1980 "Al-mūsīqā al-ʿarabiyyah: A Category of Urban Music in Cairo, Egypt 1927–1977." Ph.D. diss., Columbia University.

Shiloah, Amnon

1972 *Al-Hasan Ibn Ahmad Ibn ʿAli al-Katib. La perfection des connaissances musicales*. Translation and commentary by Amnon Shiloah. Vol. 5 of *Bibliothèque d'études islamiques*. Paris: Paul Geuthner.

1979 *The Theory of Music in Arabic Writings (900–1900). Descriptive Catalogue of Manuscripts in Libraries of Europe and the USA*. München: F. Heinle.

Simon, Artur

1972 *Studien zur ägyptischen Volksmusik*. Hamburg: Karl Dieter Wagner.

Touma, Habib Hassan

1973 "Die Musik der Araber im 19. Jahrhundert." In *Musikkulturen Asiens, Afrikas und Ozeaniens im 19. Jahrhundert.* Edited by Robert Günther. Regensburg: Gustav Bosse, 49–71.

1975 "Die Koranrezitation: Eine Form der religiösen Musik der Araber." In *Beiträge zur Musik des Vorderen Orients und seinen Einflußbereichen. Baessler-Archiv* 23 (1): 87–120.

1976 *Der Maqām Bayātī im arabischen Taqsīm.* Hamburg: Karl Dieter Wagner.

Wegner, Ulrich

1982 *Abūdhiyah und mawwāl. Untersuchung zum sprachlichen Volksgesang.* Hamburg: Karl Dieter Wagner.

Wright, Owen

1978 *The Modal System of Arab and Persian Music* A.D. *1250–1300.* Oxford: Oxford University Press.

Yelles, Jellūl and Amqrān al-Ḥifnāwī

1972 *Al-muwashshaḥāt waz-zajal.* 2 vols. Algier: Maṭbaʿat ash-sharikah al-waṭaniyah.

Index

A

B

N

U